Oxford Bibliographical Society
Publications

NEW SERIES VOLUME XVI

The Old Library, All Souls College
now used as a lecture-room

RECORDS OF
ALL SOULS COLLEGE
LIBRARY
1437–1600

N. R. KER

Published for

THE OXFORD BIBLIOGRAPHICAL SOCIETY

by the OXFORD UNIVERSITY PRESS

1971

Inquiries about the Society and its publications
should be addressed to the Hon. Secretary, Oxford Bibliographical Society
c/o Bodleian Library, Oxford

The Society is grateful to the Warden and Fellows of All Souls College
for a generous subvention towards the cost of this book

Standard Book No. 901420 04 2

CONTENTS

INTRODUCTION

THE collection of books at All Souls College, Oxford, in the fifteenth century and the sixteenth was not particularly important, but it has a special claim on our attention because we know more about its history than about the history of any other English collection in the years of transition from medieval to modern times. Only here can we see in some detail how a 'libraria' of manuscripts turned into a 'bibliotheca' of mainly printed books.[1] The beginnings of this process are in Lists XIII (theology) and XIX (law). Its end came when the old desks were done away with in favour of horizontal shelving: after 1597–8 lack of space was not a motive for removing books. How many printed books were on the desks in the 1490s and how many in 1548 and in 1575? A fairly exact answer to these questions could have been given once from evidence in the Vellum Inventory, but only an approximate answer now, because about one-third of each leaf of the Inventory has perished. What remains is enough to show that the great majority of the books were manuscripts in the nineties. List XIII, compiled then, records certainly four printed books, Alexander Carpenter's *Destructorium Viciorum* (**560**), the Oxford Lathbury (**565**), Duns Scotus on the fourth book of the Sentences (**567**), and Duns on the four books of the Sentences (**1007**), and perhaps a few more that I have failed to identify as printed. Reliance on gifts meant that printed books reached college collections slowly and that those that came were not printed books of the newest sort. All Souls had its first large gift of printed books from James Goldwell in 1499: most of the thirty-nine survivors were printed before 1475 and all before 1484.

A gift the size of Goldwell's—we know it only from what survives—posed a problem familiar to librarians today. How can we fit in all these new books? It was not an insoluble problem, because new acquisitions did not have to be put as a rule in the room where the books lay in chains on desks, the room about which we know comparatively so much. Unless the wishes of a donor that his books should be chained were respected, the college authorities had a choice. They could chain a book or they could make it one of the 'libri distribuendi' or 'concurrentes

---

[1] The new word 'bibliotheca' is first used in the account for 1504–5.

inter socios'.[1] If they chose to chain, then, probably, some book had to be taken off a chain to make room for it. The discard might be added to the circulating collection or, as often happened, it seems, removed from college as useless. We know about the circulating collection at two moments, *c.* 1440 and in the early sixteenth century. The earlier list is complete, the later incomplete. There is a striking difference between them. Out of 255 books in the earlier list[2] only two are now at All Souls, and both of them were transferred to the chained collection before the end of the fifteenth century. Out of 100 books in the later list,[3] thirteen—all printed books—are still at All Souls. This contrast between the fate of the earlier and later 'concurrentes' is shown also in two other lists which are not solely concerned with chained books.[4] All Souls has managed to keep many books which were not put in chains in 1532 (Warham's gift) and in 1575 (Pole's gift). In fact, chaining has been a *sine qua non* for the survival at All Souls of books which were there already before 1499, but not for books which first came there in 1499 (Goldwell's gift) or in the sixteenth century.

I have avoided the word 'library' in the preceding paragraphs and feel some misgivings about using it in my title because the word suggests to us a room full of books and from which books are borrowed, and this is fundamentally different from what we find in a medieval college, where the borrowable and non-borrowable books form two separate collections. But 'library' does at least convey, as 'books' and 'collections' do not, that chapel-books are not in question. Lists of books in the chapel at All Souls in the fifteenth and sixteenth centuries are to be found in Misc. 209 and 210 and in the Vellum Inventory and there are many references to them and to their binding and chaining in the college accounts under the heading 'Capella'. This book is not concerned with them: their place is with the other furniture of the chapel. But in the interpretation of entries in the accounts, especially the early accounts, their existence must not be forgotten. Some of the forty-nine books which came to All Souls in 1437 were probably for the chapel, not the library.

Powicke's *Medieval Books of Merton College*[5] is a model for work of this kind. His method was to print the medieval book-

---

[1] These are the terms used in Lists II and XXIV. 'In electione sociorum' occurs in List XVIII. 66.   [2] List II, nos. 85–107, 139–80, 269–369, 395–483.
[3] List XXIV.   [4] Lists VII and IX.
[5] F. M. Powicke, *The Medieval Books of Merton College* (Oxford, 1931).

lists first and then a list of his own making in which acquisitions are arranged in chronological order and are assigned running numbers in bold type. It would have been possible to make a similarly arranged 'Medieval and sixteenth-century books of All Souls College' and perhaps I ought to have done so. My running numbers in bold, **1-1543,** covering Lists I–XXIV, were assigned, however, a long time ago. To have altered them would have been unwise, I think, and a considerable effort.[1] My chief departure from chronology is to put the desk lists of the Vellum Inventory together and to group the five lists of the theology side (XIII–XVII) before the six lists of the law side (XVIII–XXIII). Lists XXVIII and XXIX have been compiled to help those who would like to study the collection in as nearly as may be the order in which it came to All Souls. Of my other lists, XXV covers the period 1577–1600 in this order and XXVI picks up what is not in the inventories. XXVII includes all the relevant material I could find in the college accounts.

An advantage of the present arrangement is to bring together the records of what is essentially the same collection of books at different stages of its history. We might have expected that once a desk-list had been established in the Vellum Inventory cataloguers would have been content to add to it and emend it. This expresses fairly well the relation between List XIII and List XIV and between List XIX and List XX, but the later cataloguers seem to have paid no attention to what their predecessors had done. List XV is striking in this respect. Books which had been given proper titles a decade earlier are now described so as to convey little or nothing.[2] The secundo folios chosen in 1575–6 consistently differ from and are less useful than those chosen *c.* 1548.[3] Most of the lists contain additions by later hands, but only the list made *c.* 1548 shows signs of having been examined for losses.[4]

I spent many happy hours exploring the All Souls library in the late 1940s, and, if I remember rightly, it was the sight there of leaves of a beautiful twelfth-century English missal inside the covers of Albericus de Rosate and other books and leaves of an

---

[1] To avoid alteration I intercalated numbers when examination of the Vellum Inventory under ultra-violet light revealed entries I had not seen before, e.g. list XIII. 38a–f. See also the introduction to List XVI, p. 55 n. 1.

[2] Compare, for example, the listing of six volumes of Lyra on the Bible, List XIV, nos. 4, 5, 7–10, and List XV, nos. 8, 9, 12–15.   [3] Cf. Appendix IV.

[4] Cf. List XVI, nos. 85, 87, 124, 146; List XXII, nos. 40–2, 71, 89, 90, 97, 125–7; additions to List XXII, nos. 79, 80.

eleventh-century English manuscript of the sermons of Gauden-
tius inside the covers of Hector Pinto[1] that made me think that
a *Pastedowns in Oxford Bindings* would be worth compiling. Sir
Edmund Craster was librarian. I owed much then to his advice
and encouragement, and now his *History of All Souls College
Library*[2] relieves me from the necessity of writing a longer
introduction.

The writer of a book about a college library makes many de-
mands on the time and patience of its custodians. I am most
grateful for the kindness shown to me on many occasions by Dr.
E. F. Jacob and Mr. G. Webb. As for Dr. Emden, I was asking
him questions about fellows of All Souls College long before
BRUO was published: they were always fully and promptly
answered. My references in List XXVIII to books in P.C.C.
wills are mostly taken from photographs in the Emden collection
in the Bodleian Library. My latest debt is to Mr. Malcolm
Underwood who found two stray leaves of the Vellum Inventory
in December 1970 tucked inside the book which once stood next
to the Inventory in the archives of All Souls. I heard of this
discovery in time to print the original form of List III and a new
desk list, XIIA, among Addenda, pp. 215 sqq.

The Vellum Inventory is a difficult manuscript, because of the
damage it has suffered. I should like to thank the people who
have got it from typescript into print for their vigilance and care.

---

[1] Ker, *Pastedowns*, nos. 309, 1209.

[2] At press. In the *History*, which Professor Jacob kindly allowed me to read in
typescript, the last five of the six pairs of catalogues in the Vellum Inventory are
called A, B, C, D, E, following my usage when I was working on the Inventory
twenty years ago. Lists XIII and XIX are Craster's A, Lists XIV and XX his B,
Lists XV and XXI his C, Lists XVI and XXII his D, and Lists XVII and XXIII
his E.

SOURCES

THE sources I have used for the early history of the library are: (1) inscriptions in extant books; (2) the wills referred to in Lists XXVIA and XXVIII; (3) the Vellum Inventory; (4) the Benefactors' Register; (5) the college accounts excerpted in List XXVII; (6) for List I, P.R.O., Privy Seal Office, Warrants P.S.O. 1/8/404; (7) for List II, All Souls College, Archives, Misc. 209 and 210; (8) for List IX, All Souls College, Ledger A; (9) for Lists XVI and XXII, All Souls College, Archives, Misc. 230; (10) for List XXVIc, J. Bale, *Index Britanniae Scriptorum*; (11) for List XXVID, T. James, *Ecloga Oxonio-Cantabrigiensis*. (5–11) are noticed in the appropriate places, (3) and (4) here.

The Vellum Inventory

The Vellum Inventory,[1] from which Lists IV–XXIV are taken, is a book of fifty-three leaves in which the goods of the college in chapel and library and gifts of money were recorded for more than a hundred years. It was once a stately volume measuring perhaps some 500 mm. in height. The full width, *c.* 275 mm., remains, but the lower part of each leaf has gone and no leaf is now more than 280 mm. high. The damage has been caused by damp.[2] The book was repaired at the Public Record Office in 1933 and again in 1948. No evidence of the original quiring remains. One can only set out the contents in the order in which they occur and deduce what one can from internal evidence, headings, and handwriting.

1. f. 1. List V.
2. ff. 1ᵛ–2ᵛ. List XIII.
3. ff. 3–4ᵛ. List XIX.
4. (i) f. 5. 'Inuentorium rerum capelle collegii'. (ii) ff. 5ᵛ–8. Chapel inventory, including on ff. 6ᵛ–7 a list of service-books. The heading on f. 5ᵛ is 'Tempore Thome Hobbys 6ⁱ Custodis'. (iii) ff. 8ᵛ–9. Chapel inventory, s. xvi. f. 9ᵛ is blank.
5. ff. 10–11. List XVIII. f. 11ᵛ is blank and f. 11ʳ nearly blank.
6. f. 12ᵛ. List IV. f. 12ʳ is blank.
7. ff. 13–14ᵛ. Chapel inventories, 1554–6. No books.

---

[1] LR 5. b. 2. MS. 399. See Addenda.

[2] Or so I think. But Trice Martin writing in 1877 (*Archives of All Souls' College*, p. 416) calls it 'a vellum book, of which the lower half has been burnt away'.

8. f. 15^{rv}. Chapel inventory, s. xv. No books.

9. f. 16^{rv}. Memoranda of gifts of vestments, etc., by (i) Joan Croxford in 1455, (ii) Richard Andrew, first warden, (iii) Mr. Wraby, (iv) the executors 'domini Walteri Hol[. . .]', (v) Roger Keys, 'nuper Custodis', (vi) the executors 'domine Wyche', (vii) the executors of (Robert) Clopton, (viii) Mr. Pikenham, (ix) Seymour, (x) Thomas 'Bowgier alias Boweier nuper Cant' archiepiscopi (†1486)', (xi) Thomas Kemp, bishop of London. f. 16 is headed ∴IHC ∴maria∴.

10. f. 17. Further notes of gifts to the chapel headed (i) 'Tempore T. Hobbys', (ii) 'Tempore Willelmi Broke'.

11. f. 17^v. Chapel inventory 'tempore magistri Roberti Wodwarde custodis decretorum doctoris'.

12. f. 18. List of service-books in the chapel, s. xv.

13. f. 18^v. 'Indentura Iocalium', 4 Nov., 31 Henry VI (1452).

14. f. 19. List of plate, etc. 'in cista superiori' (in the tower). f. 19^v is blank.

15. ff. 20–21^v. 'Registrum quorundam iocalium. vestimentorum. librorum. aliorumque bonorum huic Collegio perquisitorum et Collatorum tempore M. Iohannis Stokes . . .', including List VI.

16. f. 22. 'Registrum certarum summarum pecunie Collegio perquisitarum et Collatarum tempore M. Iohannis Stokes . . .' f. 22^v is blank.

17. f. 23. List of vestments dated 26 April 1550.

18. ff. 23^v–24. List XIV.

19. ff. 24^v–25. List XX.

20. ff. 25^v–26^v. List XXIV. f. 26^r is blank.

21. ff. 27–8. List XV.

22. ff. 28^v–29. List XXI. f. 29^v is blank.

23. f. 30. 'Registrum eorum que tempore Magistri Roberti Woodwarde Custodis huic Collegio dono dabantur.' Includes List VIII.

24. ff. 30^v–31. List VII. f. 31^v is blank.

25. ff. 32^v–34^v. List XVI. f. 32^r is blank.

26. ff. 35–37. List XXII.

27. f. 37^v. 'A note out of certene Bursars rowles circa annum 1540'.

28. ff. 38^v–39^v. Lists of gifts to the chapel, money, etc., 12 May 1556, and of purchases for the chapel when Seth Holland was warden. f. 38^r is blank.

29. ff. 40–1. Chapel inventory, 1 November 1556. Includes List XXVIA, Goldwell 4.

30. f. 41^v. Record of the distribution of £13 received from the executors of Dr. Bull in October 1556 and of a gift by Dr. (Richard) Bartlatt, 7 May 1556.

31. f. 42. Gifts to the chapel and gifts of money in 1557.

32. ff. 42^v–43. 'Ornamentes of the churche procured' in 1557.

33. f. 43^v. Gifts in the time of Warden Hovenden 1576 and 1584–8, including Lists X and XII.

34. Gifts of money for 'Silver Cuppes', 1571–84 (f. 44^{rv}) and 1588–99 (f. 45^{rv}). f. 46^{rv} is blank.

35. f. 47^{rv}. List IX, dated in 1575.

PLATE I. Vellum Inventory, f. 24^{v}. The beginning of List XX

See pp. 76–9

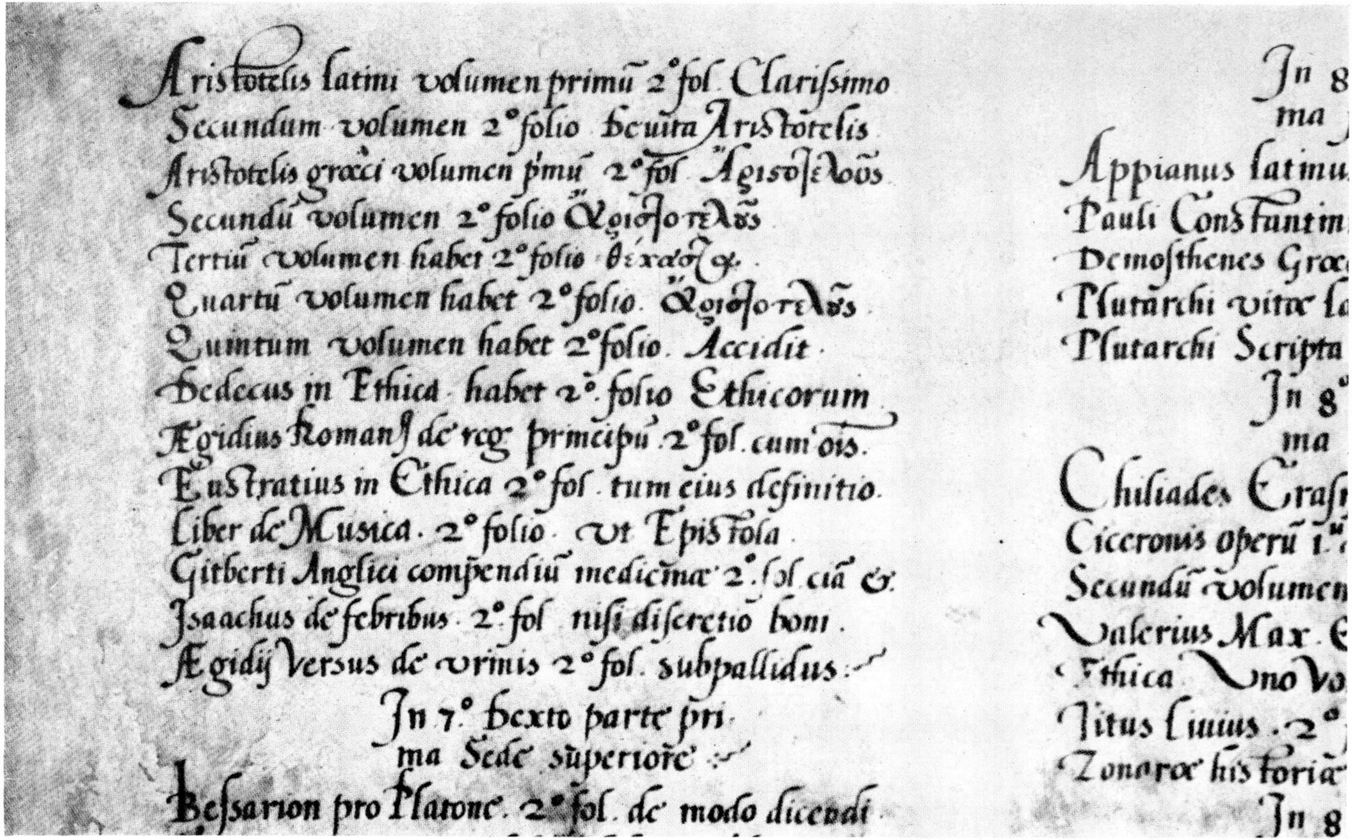

Plate II. Vellum Inventory, f. 51. Part of List XVII in the hand of Warden Hovenden

See pp. 64–6

36. f. 48. List of books without heading. All the titles but one are titles of books in List IX. The exception is 'Iason super tt de actionibus Inst' vno vol' '.

37. ff. 48ᵛ–49ᵛ. List XXIII, dated in 1575.

38. ff. 50–1. List XVII, dated in 1576.

39. f. 51ᵛ. Lists X (dated in 1576) and XI and a note of a gift of money in 1588 and of £10 given by Mr. Roger James to be bestowed in books or otherwise at the discretion of the warden. ff. 52–53ᵛ are blank.

Chronologically the entries in the Vellum Inventory may be divided into seven groups.

(*a*) *c*. 1460. Nos. 5, 8, 9 (i), 12, 13, all in similar script and perhaps by one hand. 9 (i) is in or after 1455. 13 is in or after 1452. For the date of 5 see before List XVIII.

(*b*) In the time of Warden Stokes, 1466–94. Nos. 1–3, 4 (i), 6, 9 (ii–xi), 14–16. For the date of 1–3, 4 (i), which are in one hand, see below, (*c*), and Lists V, XIII, XIX. 9 (ii–xi), and 14 are in one hand. 15 and 16 are in one hand.

(*c*) In the time of Warden Hobbys, 1494–1503. Nos. 4 (ii), 10 (i). 4 (ii) may be in the same hand as 4 (i). The heading of 4 (ii) suggests that 4 (i) belongs to the time of Warden Stokes.

(*d*) In the time of Warden Broke, 1503–25. Nos. 10 (ii), 18–22. For the date of 18–22 see before Lists XIV, XV, XX, XXI, XXIV. 18 and 19 are in one hand.

(*e*) In the time of Warden Woodward, 1528–33. Nos. 11, 23, 24.

(*f*) In the time of Wardens Warner, 1536–55, and Holland, 1555–9. Nos. 4 (iii), 7, 17, 25, 26, 28–32. 28–32 are in one hand. For the date of 25, 26 see Lists XVI, XXII.

(*g*) In the time of Warden Hovenden, 1571–1614. Nos. 33–9. These are dated.

The Benefactors' Register

The Benefactors' Register[1] dates from 1605. Expenses incurred in its preparation are in the accounts for five years: 1601–2, £1. 18*s*. 4*d*. 'for 33 skins for a Register booke';[2] 1602–3, 10*s*. for binding 'a Register booke for the Liberary';[3] 1603–4, 3*s*. for a pair of clasps for it;[3] 1604–5, 3*s*. to 'Myles for rulinge the Colledge register booke' and £1 'for writing the names of the librarie bookes and the givers etc. in the register booke'; 1605–6, 6*d*. 'for settinge vp a deske in the library where the regester booke stand*es*' and 1*s*. 8*d*. 'for a cover for the Register booke in the library'. Though it is now called the Benefactors' Register, the title on the leaf before p. 1, 'Catalogus librorum ad Bibliothecam Collegii Animarum omnium Fidelium defunct: de Oxon: spectantium et donatorum eorundem', and the words of the

---

[1] LR 5.l.10.

[2] There are ninety leaves (forty-five bifolia) paginated (i, ii), 1–178.

[3] Gilt centre-piece of the college arms, with large gilt angle-pieces and cornerpieces like ornament 52 in Ker, *Pastedowns*. The two clasps are missing.

1604–5 entry show that it was intended to be like the contemporary book at Hereford Cathedral, a complete list of books in the library. Two bifolia at the beginning (pp. 1–8) were reserved for the titles of books already in the library before 1605, in so far as they could be listed under the names of donors. New acquisitions begin on p. 9 with 'Compendium Medecinæ Gilberti Anglici'[1] and two other books given by William Osbern. After the Register had been in use for a dozen years an attempt was made to collect together under one heading the 'Libri empti a Colleg:'. The 133 titles here (pp. 11–13) are partly made up of books bought between 1605 and 1618,[2] and partly of manuscripts— fourteen items are marked 'MS'—and early printed books in which no donor's name is to be found.

The compilation of pp. 1–8 listing donors from Henry VI (the three existing books) to John Parker (1602) involved search on the shelves and the copying of inscriptions of gift—and led to the creation of a few ghosts, Thomas Agors instead of Thomas Mors (p. 3), Lyngton instead of Darlyngton, and Richard Gwent instead of Richard Gaunt. The record needs to be accepted cautiously, but it is a valuable one, not least for the assurance it gives us that there was not much in the library in 1605 that is not there now.[3] It has value also because of the use made of the Vellum Inventory before it was damaged.[4]

[1] SR 58. g. 2. Lyons, 1510.

[2] For example, i. 11. 11, Cureus, bought in 1616 and SR 75. c. 4, Photius, bought in 1618.

[3] The compiler listed three titles of now apparently missing books under the names Mason and Topclyffe (see List XXVIA) and appears to have had access to now missing records for the benefactions of Norfolk (see List III), Harlow, and Wyche (see List XXVIA).

[4] See below, **522, 525, 544, 587–92, 636–44, 675–680, 771–86, 841–61, 904– 22**. Unfortunately 'secundo folios' were not copied.

ABBREVIATIONS AND CONVENTIONAL SIGNS

Bale, *Index*: J. Bale, *Index Britanniae Scriptorum*, ed. R. L. Poole and M. Bateson. Anecdota Oxoniensia, Mediaeval and modern series, 9 (Oxford, 1902)

Ben. Reg.: the Benefactors' Register of All Souls College.

Biblia Sacra: *Biblia sacra iuxta Latinam vulgatam versionem, ad codicum fidem* (Rome, 1926– , in progress).

BLR: *Bodleian Library Record*.

BQR: *Bodleian Quarterly Record*.

BRUO: A. B. Emden, *A Bibliographical Register of the University of Oxford to A.D. 1500*. 3 vols. (Oxford, 1957–9).

CMA: (E. Bernard) *Catalogi Manuscriptorum Angliae et Hiberniae* (Oxford, 1697).

DNB: *Dictionary of National Biography*.

Gibson: S. Gibson, *Early Oxford Bindings* (Oxford, 1903).

GKW: *Gesamt-Katalog der Wiegendrucke* (1925– , in progress).

Gray: G. J. Gray, *The Earlier Cambridge Stationers and Bookbinders* (Oxford, 1904).

Hain: L. Hain, *Repertorium bibliographicum*. 2 vols. (1826–31).

Hain–Copinger: W. A. Copinger, *Supplement to Hain's Repertorium*, part 2, 2 vols. (1898–1902).

Ker (or Ker, *Pastedowns*): N. R. Ker, *Pastedowns in Oxford Bindings*. Oxford Bibliographical Society, New Series, v (Oxford, 1954).

McCusker: H. McCusker, 'Books and Manuscripts formerly in the Possession of John Bale', *Transactions of the Bibliographical Society*, new series, xvi (1935), 144–65.

MLGB: N. R. Ker, *Medieval Libraries of Great Britain*, Royal Historical Society, Guides and Handbooks, No. 3. 2nd ed. (1964).

Oldham: J. B. Oldham, *English Blind-Stamped Bindings* (Cambridge, 1952).

Oldham, *Panels*: J. B. Oldham, *Blind Panels of English Binders* (Cambridge, 1958).

Pellechet: M. Pellechet, *Catalogue général des incunables des bibliothèques publiques de France*. 3 vols. 1897–1909.

PL: *Patrologia Latina*, ed. J. Migne.

Registrum Chichele: *The Register of Archbishop Henry Chichele*, ed. E. F. Jacob. Canterbury and York Society. 3 vols. (1943–7).

Reichling: D. Reichling, *Appendices ad Hainii-Copingeri Repertorium bibliographicum* (Munich, 1905–14).

SC: *A Summary Catalogue of Western Manuscripts in the Bodleian Library*. 7 vols. (Oxford, 1895–1953).

Savigny: F. C. von Savigny, *Geschichte des römischen Rechts im Mittelalter*, 2nd ed. (Heidelberg, 1834–51).

Schulte: J. F. von Schulte, *Die Geschichte der Quellen und Literatur des canonischen Rechts.* 3 vols. (Stuttgart, 1875–80).

Stegmüller: F. Stegmüller, *Repertorium biblicum Medii Aevi* (Madrid, 1950– , in progress).

Syon: *Catalogue of Syon Monastery, Isleworth,* ed. Mary Bateson (Cambridge, 1898).

Thorndike and Kibre. L. Thorndike and P. Kibre, *A Catalogue of Incipits of Mediaeval Scientific Writings in Latin.* 2nd ed. (1963).

Square brackets enclose words and parts of words illegible as a result of damage. If the end of an entry is illegible, the opening bracket is followed by three points and there is no closing bracket.

Carets, ` ´, show additions in the manuscripts.

A point below a letter, as in List XIII. 59, 60, 113, shows that it has been expunged in the manuscript.

A row of points shows where each volume of the Vellum Inventory comes to an abrupt end, for example in List XIII, after 21d, 38f, 62, 90a, 117.

Words enclosed in round brackets and serial numbers are editorial additions.

An asterisk against a number shows that the book in question is still in existence.

In references in the notes and in Appendix III to the position of the chainmark on bindings, F1, F2, H1, H2 denote the foot/head of the upper/lower cover and FS1, FS2, HS1, HS2, the side of the upper/lower cover near foot/head.

'secundo folio' is written by the scribes in various ways, but usually as '2° fo'. I have generalized '2 fo'.

Symbols for pounds, shillings, and pence are normalized as £, *s.*, *d.*

The first number against each entry in Lists I–XXIV, the running number which covers all these lists, is in bold type on its first occurrence and when referred to in the introductions to lists and in the notes.

RECORDS OF ALL SOULS COLLEGE LIBRARY 1437–1600

LIST I. KING HENRY VI'S GIFT[1]

1–27 from Public Record Office, Privy Seal Office, Warrants P.S.O. 1/8/404. This is the schedule attached to a letter, 1/8/405:

By the King.

Right trusty and welbeloued. We late yow wite howe that of oure Habundant grace we have graunted vnto the Werdeyn and scoliers of oure Collage of al Sowlen within oure vniuersite of Oxenford. the bokes and volumes. the names of whiche been writen and described in a Cedule here enclosed. for to haue thayme of oure yifte and to remayne perpetuelly to the vse prouffit and encrece of lerning of the Wardeyn and scoliers in the saide Collage for the tyme being. Werfore we wol and charge yow that vndre oure priue seel being in your warde. ye make lettres of warant in deue fourme. directed vnto the Tresorier and Chambreleyns of oure Eschequier. and to othir yf nede be. or yf the cas require hit. to make deliuerance of the forsaide bokes and volumes vnto the wardeyn aboue saide. And thees oure lettres shal be your warant. yeuen vndre oure signet at oure Manoir of Kenyngton. the x day of Iuyn. The yere of oure Regne xviii. W. Crosby.

On the back are the words 'To oure Right trusty and welbeloued Clerc maister William Lyndewode keper of oure priue seel. Canterbury'.

Only the three surviving books of this gift, **14**, **19**, **20**, are listed in the Benefactors' Register, p. 1.

(Public Record Office, P.S.O., Warrants 1/8/404)

Libri Iuris Ciuilis

1	1	Paruum volumen 2 fo in textu elam in quibus
2	2	Iacobus de bello visu doctor iuris ciuilis 2 fo hic loquitur
3	3	Petrus in Repeticionibus super ff veteri 2 fo dico tamen
4	4	Iacobus de Rauenna super ff nouum 2 fo Rethia sua

Libri Iuris Canonici

5	5	Prima pars hostiensis in lectura 2 fo alia aleganda
6	6	Hostiensis in lectura abbreuiat' 2 fo religiosi
7	7	Willelmus Durant' abbreuiat' super decr' 2 fo ciones
8	8	Iohannes super vi[tum] compostolanus et dignus 2 fo vnum
9	9	Secunda pars hostiensis in lectura 2 fo debet recipere

[1] Cf. R. Weiss in *English Historical Review*, lvii (1942), 102–5.

Libri Theologie

10	10	Augustinus de Trinitate 2 fo in processu libri encie abscondit'
11	11	Thomas de cristiana religione 2 fo musicus accipit
12	12	Liber de quadriplici sensu sacre scripture compilatus per M. E. Lacy 2 fo Ebreis in flumine
13	13	Comentum super primo et quarto sentenciarum 2 fo enim est precipuus
*****14**	14	Liber Iob glosatus cum aliis tractatibus 2 fo omni genere
15	15	Comentum super ysaiam et alios libros biblie 2 fo generale quod numquam
16	16	Lincoln' de decem preceptis 2 fo liberius et melius
17	17	Boecius de Trinitate 2 fo mirati sunt
18	18	Diuersa opera beati Anselmi 2 fo cum igitur
*****19**	19	Liber Ysodori de ecclesiasticis officiis 2 fo carmine
*****20**	20	Liber Rufini presbiteri in lib' ecclesiastic' histor' 2 fo de cruciatibus
21	21	Innocencius de Pontificali et sacerdotali officio cum diuersis tractatibus beati Augustini 2 fo domini leuite
22	22	Stephanus Archiepiscopus Cant' super libr' Regum 2 fo Ebrei
23	23	Glosa beati Ieronimi super genesim 2 fo que nostra
24	24	Hugo de sancto victore in angelica Ierarchia 3 fo legie mundi
25	25	Augustinus in suo Encheridion' et interp' nominum Hebreorum 2 fo imus colend'
26	26	Casterdon' Barenguidum Costesay super apocalips' 2 fo vero quod accidit

Libri Philosophie

27	27	Burley super libris Ethicorum et politicorum 2 fo idio sub doctrina

W Crosby

LIST II. INVENTORY MADE IN THE LIFETIME OF THE FOUNDER

28–471 from All Souls College, Archives, Misc. 209, 210, two inventories of vestments, books, and other goods belonging to All Souls College soon after its foundation. They include twenty-two of the twenty-seven books listed in I.

Misc. 209 is a paper book of seven leaves headed on f. 1 'Inuentorium bonorum collegii omnium animarum in Vniuersitate Oxon''. The books are listed on ff. 4–7 after vestments, chapel-books, and plate, and number 369.

Misc. 210 is a parchment roll of two membranes, with a covering membrane bearing the title 'Communis Indentura omnium bonorum collegii'. The heading of the first membrane is 'Hec sunt bona data Collegio animarum omnium fidelium defunctorum in Oxon' per Reuerendissimum in cristo patrem et dominum Dominum Henricum Chichele permissione diuina Cantuarien' Archiepiscopum fundatorem Collegii predicti. Qui vero aliqua eorundem a predicto Collegio contra statuta dicti fundatoris alienauerit Anathema sit amen.' The books, except two, are listed on the front of membrane 2 and on the dorse of membranes 1 and 2, after vestments, chapel books, and plate. At first they were exactly the same 369 books as are listed in Misc. 209, apart from four omitted by accident.[1] Later, 97 additional books were entered: 87 at the end, in the main hand (**12, 376–461**); 8 intercalated into the original list by another hand (**462–9**); 2 on the covering membrane, both of them books missed at the time of the original inventory, because they were out to a fellow of the college (**470, 471**).

In Misc. 209 the order is by subjects, first the books which were chained and then the books which were not chained, subject by subject. In Misc. 210 the subject order is preserved, but all the chained books are listed first and then all the unchained books. The only other difference is that a biblical concordance (**96**) is entered immediately after a Bible (**28**). The changes in order suggest that Misc. 210 is a revision of Misc. 209. Its secondary character is evident from its mistakes: **183** left out, because its title was the same as the title of **184**; **177** and **178** left out by homoioteleuton, the secundo folio of **176** being quibus and the

---

[1] **177, 178, 183, 186.** For **177, 178, 183** see below.

secundo folio of **178** de quibus; **231** given the same secundo folio as **237**, probably because the scribe was copying Misc. 209 or a similarly arranged list in which **223–31** and **232–7** form blocks of equal size, separated by a space from what goes before and after.

Misc. 210 was revised fairly soon after it was written. The reviser: (1) entered eight new titles, four in the section of chained books (**462–5**) and four in the section of unchained books (**466–9**); (2) recorded the promotion to chaining of twelve books, **163, 171, 175, 375, 379, 380, 384, 400, 414, 432, 438, 444,** by entering them a second time in the appropriate sections; (3) re-entered nine other books, **27, 121, 123–6, 149, 231, 408,** the first seven probably because it was felt that they had been listed before in the wrong places, **231** to correct the error in the original entry, and **408** perhaps by inadvertence.[1] As a result of these additions and changes the total number of entries in the main list in Misc. 210 was increased from 365 to 394.

Misc. 210 was printed as an appendix to Professor E. F. Jacob's 'Two Lives of Archbishop Chichele'.[2] I have not collated it, except where its titles appear to be deliberate changes of titles in Misc. 209. The changes suggest that there was a now missing copy of the inventory in which corrections had been made and that the writer of Misc. 210 was following this copy and not Misc. 209.[3]

[1] It seems likely also that **393** is a second listing of **147**.
[2] *Bull. of the John Rylands Library*, vol. xvi (Manchester, 1932), 428–81.
[3] Order of Misc. 210 (nos. 1–394) as compared with Misc. 209.

Misc. 210	Misc. 209	Misc. 210	Misc. 209
1	1	158 = 451 (**432**)	
2	82	159–82	237–60
3–82	2–81	183 = 294 (**375**)	
83–4	83–4	184 = 457 (**438**)	
85 = 296 (**27**)		185 = 463 (**444**)	
86 = 300 (**123**)		186–93	261–8
87 = 301 (**124**)		194–294	269–369
88 = 298 (**121**)		295 New entry (**466**)	
89 = 374 (**171**)		296–316	108–28
90 New entry (**462**)		317 = 398 (**379**)	
91 = 303 (**126**)		318 = 366 (**163**)	
92 = 302 (**125**)		319 = 329 (**149**)	
93 New entry (**463**)		320–9	129–38
94 New entry (**464**)		330–52	85–107
95 = 378 (**175**)		353–79	139–65
96 = 403 (**384**)		380–3	168–71
97 = 419 (**400**)		384–5	173–4
98 = 399 (**380**)		386–90	176–80
99 New entry (**465**)		391 New entry (**467**)	
100–48	181–229	392 New entry (**468**)	
149 = 142 (**231**)		393 = 427 (**408**)	
150 = 433 (**414**)		394 New entry (**469**)	
151–7	230–6		

Thirty-six books, or perhaps thirty-eight, survive out of the 466 books recorded in Misc. 209 and 210. All but two of them were either chained books from the first or (**182** and **308**) were chained before the end of the fifteenth century. The three which were not chained are all now at Antwerp (**109, 411, 415**). The donors of surviving books were Richard Andrew (**43, 54, 80**?), Thomas Gascoigne (**59**), Henry Penwortham (**75, 77, 182**), John Southam (**245**) and, presumably, Chichele (**415**): cf. also **121**. Chaining was usually from a staple attached to the lower cover by six nails (four nails, **142, 245**; two nails, **147**), but **182, 197,** and **242** were not chained in this way.

(Misc. 209, f. 4)

Libri theologie cathenati

28	1	Biblia 2 fo ba d(e)i
29	2	Magister historiarum 2 fo quia tenent
30	3	Magister historiarum 2 fo festinans ad
31	4	Prima pars Lire 2 fo liber et
32	5	2ª pars eiusdem 2 fo pronunciatum est
33	6	Lira super nouum testamentum 2 fo facierumque
34	7	3ª pars Lire 2 fo non est in eo
*35	8	Ysiderus super Pent*ateuchum* 2 fo videt hic
36	9	Goram super iiii^or euang*elia* 2 fo Cristi per adopcionem
37	10	Liber de figuris Biblie 2 fo et finaliter
*38	11	Thomas super lucam et Iohannem 2 fo esse nemo
39	12	Boneuentura super lucam et Iohannem 2 fo non aliorum
40	13	Liber xii prophetarum postill' 2 fo annis xvi
41	14	Glosa ordinaria super ysayam 2 fo ergo prudens
23	15	Glosa super Genesim 2 fo que nostra est
42	16	Exposicio super apo*calypsim* 2 fo in prima
*43	17	Radulphus super apo*calypsim* (*sic*) 2 fo loquente
44	18	Psalterium glosatum glo' communi 2 fo tulus non
45	19	Psalterium glosatum glo' communi 2 fo Itaque
*14	20	Liber Iob glosatus 2 fo omni genere
46	21	Flores psalterii 2 fo in hebreo
47	22	Postilla super Iohannem 2 fo 2^m cum
48	23	Augustinus super psalmo lxxx 2 fo si vixit
49	24	Milleloquium Augustini 2 fo de trinitate

18 Misc. 210 Glosa communis super psalterium   19 Misc. 210 Glosa communis super psalterium   20 Misc. 210 Iob glosatus   24 Misc. 210 Augustinus in melleloquio

50	25	Augustinus de ciuitate 2 fo de pudore
51	26	Augustinus de verbis domini 2 fo sermo eiusdem
25	27	Augustinus in suo encheridion 2 fo imus colendum
52	28	Augustinus de quantitate 2 fo lium voluntaria
10	29	Augustinus de trinitate 2 fo enscie absconditos
53	30	Augustinus de trinitate 2 fo scriptura diuina
*54	31	Bernardus super cantica 2 fo differenter
55	32	Bernardus super missus est 2 fo congruum
56	33	Diuerse epistole Ieronomi 2 fo vincit pudor
57	34	Ieronomus contra Rufinum 2 fo impietatis
58	35	Omelia Gregorii 2 fo Iacobus alter
*59	36	Gregorius in registro 2 fo patimur
60	37	Gregorius super cantica 2 fo vocat
61	38	Prima pars Gregorii in moralibus 2 fo exquirentes
62	39	2ª pars eiusdem 2 fo mescit qui
63	40	3ª pars eiusdem 2 fo illius in desperacione
64	41	Prima pars moralium cum tabula 2 fo in textu coniunccione
65	42	Parisiensis super dominicalia 2 fo aduentum
66	43	Distincciones Holcote 2 fo sapiens uero
16	44	Dicta Lincolniensis 2 fo liberius et melius
26	45	Casterton' super apo*calypsim* 2 fo vero quod accidit
*19	46	Epistole ysidori 2 fo carmine
67	47	Dieta salutis 2 fo in libro tamquam
68	48	Ysidorus de summo bono 2 fo inest ei
69	49	Prima pars Walden' 2 fo nostre patrone
70	50	2ª pars eiusdem (2 fo) in textu per aduentum
71	51	Reuelaciones Brigitte 2 fo O vere stupenda
21	52	Innocencius de pont' et sac' officio 2 fo domine leuite
72	53	Parisiensis de virtutibus 2 fo sobrietatis
22	54	Stephanus Cantuariensis 2 fo Hebrei non
*73	55	Beda de gestis anglorum 2 fo quibusdam
(*)74	56	Malmesburi de gestis anglorum 2 fo solent
*75	57	Omelia Eusebii 2 fo et amicus carus
*20	58	Eusebius in ecclesiastica historia (2 fo) in tabula in cruciatibus
18	59	Monologium Anselmi 2 fo cum igitur
76	60	Rabanus de mistica significacione rerum 2 fo arcium
*77	61	Flores historiarum cum speculo stultorum 2 fo quasi abrahi
78	62	Rosarium theologie 2 fo sionis culpe
79	63	Petrus in aurora 2 fo nam quasi
(*)80	64	Caton' glosatus 2 fo insuper vero
81	65	Liber florum 2 fo quid tres
82	66	Liber de emendacione vite 2 fo cuncta que
83	67	Ianuensis in opere quadragesimali 2 fo filia populi
84	68	Magister sentenciarum 2 fo in tabula an posse
85	69	Magister sentenciarum 2 fo ata

*86	70	Thomas in 2ª parte summe 2 fo mathamatice
87	71	Thomas (in) 2ª secunde 2 fo signorum
88	72	Thomas de cristo 2 fo necessarii
11	73	Thomas in prima parte summe 2 fo musicus accipit
89	74	Thomas in 2ª parte summe 2 fo cui attribuuntur
13	75	Boneuentura super primum et 4ᵐ 2 fo enim est
90	76	Thomas de veritatibus theologie 2 fo Greg'
91	77	Petrus de Candia super libro sentenciarum 2 fo causabunt
92	78	Bradwardinus de causa dei 2 fo bonum et malum
93	79	2ª pars eiusdem 2 fo sit racione
94	80	Ianuensis 2 fo numquam
95	81	Ianuensis 2 fo Scribantur
		Summa cathen' iiiiˣˣ volumina
96	82	Vna concordancia 2 fo sicut vestimentum
		Vnum pontificale in 2ᵇᵘˢ voluminibus
97	83	2 fo prime partis ea recompensare
98	84	2 fo 2ᵉ partis ordo ad seruicium

Libri theologie distribuendi

99	85	Magister sentenciarum 2 fo ipsum reseratur
100	86	Magister historiarum 2 fo quidem celum
101	87	Lincolniensis 2 fo lingua hominis
102	88	Exposicio Gilberti super epistolas Pauli 2 fo intelligenciam
103	89	Reductorium morale 2 fo inde tacere
104	90	Franciscus Detrarcha (sic) 2 fo que videatur
105	91	Euangelia 2 fo hominibus
106	92	Moralitates super Iob 2 fo sed uti
107	93	Vita Sancti Iohannis Heremite 2 fo annis
108	94	Epistole Pauli glosate 2 fo stulti facti
17	95	Boicius de Trinitate 2 fo mirati sunt
*109	96	Augustinus de ciuitate 2 fo curaui
15	97	Lectura super Ysayam 2 fo generale quod numquam
110	98	Horologium sapiencie 2 fo libet predictis
111	99	Stimulus diuini amoris 2 fo id est in propria
112	100	Psalterium glosatum 2 fo propheᵃ de cristo
113	101	Vita sancti Malachie 2 fo malachiam
114	102	Speculum humane salutis 2 fo siba filius
115	103	Tractatus de dictamine 2 fo regraciando
116	104	Elucidarium 2 fo sicud nec infers
117	105	Fasciculus morum 2 fo epistola
118	106	Liber de Sacramentis ecclesie 2 fo pater omnia
119	107	Liber cum sermonibus 2 fo neque tunc dormitant
		Summa xxiii

91 Misc. 210 Euangelium   96 Misc. 210 Augustinus de ciuitate (*altered to* trinitate)   98 Misc. 210 Horologium diuine sapiencie   107 Misc. 210 Quaternus cum diuersis sermonibus

Philosophia moralis et naturalis cathenand'

27	108	Burlay super libros ethicorum 2 fo Ideo sub
120	109	Liber Ethicorum 2 fo igitur eruditus
*121	110	Burlay 2 fo philosophus
122	111	Textus philosophie 2 fo neque iam
123	112	Exposicio super libros de generacione 2 fo carnem et os
*124	113	Scharpe super viii lib' phisicorum cum aliis contentis 2 fo sine illis
		Summa vi

Logica Cathen'

| **125** | 114 | Vnus textus logic' 2 fo in particularibus |
| **126** | 115 | Alius textus log' 2 fo sunt circa |

Astronomia Cath'

127	116	Iohannes de Lyneriis 2 fo et tunc
*128	117	Liber nouus iudic' 2 fo mutacionem
129	118	Liber heremetis de xii signis 2 fo les vt ostenderet
130	119	Tractatus spere 2 fo quatuor cecli
131	120	Commendacio antiquorum sapientum 2 fo et scientes
132	121	Quadripartitum Tholomei 2 fo et potest
133	122	Astronomia Alsham 2 fo et si
134	123	Summa Iudicialis de accidentibus mundi 2 fo iungatur
*135	124	Tholomeus in almagesti 2 fo tatim genus
136	125	Liber astronomie 2 fo tabula
137	126	Liber astronomie 2 fo eciam diuinitas
138	127	Canones Azar 2 fo additis
139	128	Liber astronomie 2 fo me^{ta} habetur
		Summa xiii

(f. 5)

Libri Medicine Cath'

*140	129	Nicholaus in antidorio 2 fo .q.s.
141	130	Med' Almazorii 2 fo receptacula
*142	131	Liber morborum 2 fo ciam et accencionem
143	132	Auicenna de Med' 2 fo capitulum
144	133	Dieta vniuersalis 2 fo quosdam
*145	134	Rosa Medicine 2 fo isto sanguine
*146	135	Tegni Galieni 2 fo recedit
*147	136	Medicine Ysaac 2 fo nisi discrecio
148	137	Constantinus viaticus 2 fo in textu igneis
149	138	Geometria euclidis cum commento 2 fo latera
		Summa x

Libri diuersarum facultatum distribuendi

| **150** | 139 | Medicin' 2 fo in modum |
| **151** | 140 | Medicin' 2 fo de hiis qui |

122 Misc. 210 Astronomia Hals'   130 Misc. 210 Almazorius   132 Misc. 210 Avicenna

152	141	Medicin' 2 fo corrumpat
153	142	Medicin' 2 fo venas
154	143	Medicin' 2 fo pill'
155	144	Medicin' 2 fo calidum
156	145	Medicin' 2 fo hoc esse potest
157	146	Medicin' 2 fo et facta
158	147	Medicin' 2 fo attrahendo
159	148	Medicin' 2 fo et est calidior
160	149	Medicin' 2 fo submergitur
161	150	Medicin' 2 fo dantur
162	151	Ypocras 2 fo vtitur
163	152	Astronomia 2 fo sequitur
164	153	Astronomia 2 fo bus planetarum
165	154	Astronomia 2 fo et tenebrosos
166	155	Astronomia 2 fo potest homo
167	156	Astronomia 2 fo terrea
168	157	Methephisica 2 fo inter duo
169	158	Questiones philosophie 2 fo tradit scienciam
170	159	Liber philosophie 2 fo finitam
171	160	Egidius de celo et mundo 2 fo seu dimencio
172	161	Libellus de ortu scienciarum 2 fo istam russus
173	162	Questiones super libros methaphisice 2 fo Item populo di- uiditur
174	163	Liber Philosophie 2 fo trice est
175	164	Tabula Philosophie moralis 2 fo quomodo erit
176	165	Logica Dulmelton' 2 fo quibus
177	166	Textus logice 2 fo philosophos
178	167	Textus logice 2 fo de quibus
179	168	Predicamenta Alyngton' 2 fo idem nouum
180	169	Ouidius in methamorphos' 2 fo pena metus
181	170	Lucanus de bell' punic' 2 fo senciet
*182	171	Virgilius 2 fo assidue (*altered from* senciet)
183	172	Arsmetrica 2 fo que quia
184	173	Arsmetrica 2 fo de clauibus
185	174	Geomancia 2 fo globo constitutum
186	175	Liber Gall' 2 fo inest
		Summa xxxvii

187	176	Summa logice 2 fo proprium vt vsibile	
188	177	Liber de substancia logice 2 fo circa dif- finicionem	dat' per
189	178	Aristoteles de animalibus 2 fo separatur ex aliis	Petrum Partrigge
190	179	Textus philosophie 2 fo infinit'	
191	180	Expositorium super eodem 2 fo perfectum	

(f. 5ᵛ)

Libri iuris Canonici Cath'

192	181	Liber decretorum 2 fo di facultas
193	182	Liber decretorum 2 fo pontificum
194	183	Archidiaconus in Rosario 2 fo ex eodem
195	184	Archidiaconus in Rosario 2 fo iustius
196	185	Tabula super decret' 2 fo cautela
*197	186	Lectura Iohannis de Fanntis 2 fo 2 3 5
198	187	2ª pars eiusdem 2 fo cedat limitato
199	188	Petrus de Salinis 2 fo fendendo
200	189	Petrus de Salinis 2 fo de crimine
201	190	Liber decretalium 2 fo natissimam
202	191	Liber decretalium 2 fo dampnamus
203	192	Summa Goffredi 2 fo quod non
204	193	Summa Roffredi 2 fo decreto
205	194	Innocencius 2 fo Di. C.
206	195	Innocencius 2 fo et infra
207	196	Hostiensis in Summa 2 fo qualit'
208	197	Hostiensis in 2ª parte 2 fo naturalis
209	198	Hostiensis in lectura 2 fo fatuum est
210	199	Hostiensis in 2ª parte 2 fo visitat
5	200	Hostiensis in lectura 2 fo alia alliganda
9	201	Hostiensis in 2ª parte 2 fo debet recipere
211	202	Iohannes in nouella 2 fo vltra id
212	203	Iohannes in nouella in 2ª parte 2 fo scilicet recipiunt
213	204	Iohannes in nouella 2 fo quod est
214	205	Iohannes in Coll' 2 fo prime partis vel vi
215	206	2ª pars eiusdem 2 fo cum eo
216	207	Iohannes de Lyniano 2 fo attendi
217	208	2ª pars eiusdem 2 fo tendit ad
218	209	Lectura Karoli de Zambucariis 2 fo Iohannes an
219	210	Antonius de butrio super 2° decretalium 2 fo se presentant
220	211	Sabrellus super iiii decretalium 2 fo dicto c
221	212	Iohannes in nouell' super speculum 2 fo vt ibi scripsi
222	213	Tabula super decret' 2 fo monasterii
223	213	Distincciones Iohannis Caldrini 2 fo diffendere
224	215	Speculum 2 fo id est multi
225	216	Speculum 2 fo docuerunt
6	217	Hostiensis abreuiatus 2 fo religiosi
226	218	Sextus cum Io card' Ar et Dino 2 fo id est confessione
227	219	Sextus cum eisdem 2 fo huius

190 Misc. 210 Decretal'   191 Misc. 210 Decretal'   209 Misc. 210
Karolus de Zambucariis   211 Misc. 210 Sabrellus super iiii libro

228	220	Iohannes in mercurialibus super quibusdam regulis iuris 2 fo habetur
229	221	Petrus de Anchorano 2 fo querit circa
230	222	Idem in alio volumine super Clem' 2 fo dicit sponsalia
231	223	Petrus de Anchorano 2 fo de prelacione
232	224	Clement' cum Io W G et pau 2 fo ipse tamen
233	225	Clement' cum eisdem doctoribus 2 fo suum motum
234	226	Lectura Sabrelli 2 fo doctoribus
235	227	Constituciones Io xxii glosate per Gess' 2 fo a canonibus
236	228	Summa Raymundi de casibus 2 fo est annexum
237	229	Willelmus in sacrament' 2 fo tario regis
		Summa xlix

(f. 6)

Libri iuris ciuilis Cath'

238	230	Paruum volumen 2 fo rerum cotidianarum
239	231	Paruum volumen 2 fo tum ab inicio
*240	232	Iohannes Fabri 2 fo dicit azo
241	233	Iohannes Fabri 2 fo cristi qui
*242	234	Iohannes de Platea 2 fo hoc nota
243	235	2ª pars eiusdem 2 fo in glosa
2	236	Iacobus de bello visu 2 fo sic loquitur
244	237	Codex 2 fo composicionem
*245	238	Codex 2 fo mare prospeximus
246	239	Odefredus 2 fo libri .l.
247	240	2ª pars eiusdem 2 fo et retineo
248	241	Cinus 2 fo de decur'
249	242	Cinus 2 fo et ideo
250	243	Prima pars Baldi 2 fo non criminis
251	244	2ª pars eiusdem 2 fo quia potest
*252	245	ff vetus 2 fo uirium
253	246	ff vetus 2 fo bet admergi
254	247	Odefredus 2 fo intellegenti
255	248	Prima pars Odefredi 2 fo de vsu ca
256	249	2ª pars eiusdem 2 fo in iure
257	250	Iacobus de Botr' 2 fo consuetudo
258	251	Petrus in repeticionibus 2 fo consuetudinario
*259	252	ff inforciatum 2 fo ro eius
260	253	ff inforciatum 2 fo ex die
261	254	Reynerius 2 fo soluto
262	255	Addiciones Cini 2 fo de her' Inst'
263	256	Iacobus de Rauen' 2 fo et hoc dicit

226 Misc. 210 Lectura Zabrelli   250 Misc. 210 Iacobus de botzing'

*264	257	ff nouum 2 fo predii
265	258	ff nouum 2 fo opida
*266	259	Azo cum Rofredo 2 fo de hereticis
*267	260	Iudicialis iuris 2 fo superiorem
268	261	Barth' super C 2 fo nec dicitur
269	262	Prima pars Barth' super prima parte ff inforciati cum diuersis tractatibus 2 fo sed quid
270	263	Prima pars eiusdem super ff inforc' 2 fo supra de iure do
271	264	Barth' super ff nouum 2 fo si placuerit
272	265	Barth' super ff inf' 2 fo priuilegium
273	266	Barth' super ff veteri 2 fo hic lex
274	267	Consilia Frederici 2 fo de hiis
275	268	Beliall' 2 fo quis ibit

(f. 6ᵛ)

Libri iuris canonici distribuendi

276	269	Liber decretorum 2 fo adiciant
277	270	Archidiaconus in rosario 2 fo omnis
278	271	Iohannes de deo 2 fo et dicitur quod
279	272	Textus decretalium 2 fo habent substanciam
280	273	Decretal' 2 fo sacro
281	274	Decretal' 2 fo in vnum
282	275	Decretal' 2 fo et filius
283	276	Decretal' 2 fo illud potissimum
284	277	Decretal' 2 fo ecclesie
285	278	Decretal' 2 fo nolo inquiens
286	279	Decretal' 2 fo singulis
287	280	Innocencius 2 fo sicud tres
288	281	Innocencius 2 fo faciend'
289	282	Innocencius 2 fo scripta est
290	283	Innocencius 2 fo tero fierent
291	284	Goffridus 2 fo de Symon'
292	285	Compostol' cum reportorio W Durant 2 fo tenere
293	286	Hostiensis in lectura 2 fo sumpsit
294	287	Hostiensis in Summa 2 fo huius glose
295	288	Tabula super decretal' 2 fo verbis contine
296	289	2ª pars eiusdem 2 fo malicia
297	290	Chilyngden' super decret' 2 fo et sic
298	291	Sextus 2 fo declaracione
299	292	Sextus 2 fo rentem
300	293	Sextus cum doctoribus 2 fo in quo istud
301	294	Iohannes An super vi 2 fo vocat
302	295	Iohannes super vi 2 fo xxix di

269 Misc. 210 Decreta   272 Misc. 210 Decretal'   290 Misc. 210 Chelyngton super decret'

303	296	Quidam Rubeus liber 2 fo penitenciali
304	297	Archidiaconus super vi 2 fo pape
305	298	Clem' 2 fo Clemens episcopus
306	299	Clem' 2 fo spiritu perforare
307	300	Clem' 2 fo inmaculata
*308	301	Chelyngden' 2 fo et alia conclusio
309	302	Summa Goffridi 2 fo quasi
310	303	Summa eiusdem 2 fo prioris
311	304	Goffridus cum casuario bernardi 2 fo rescripta
312	305	Reportorium Baldi super Innoc' 2 fo abbas
313	306	Speculum 2 fo compluit
314	307	Speculum 2 fo ordo
7	308	Reportorium W Durant 2 fo siones
315	309	Reportorium 2 fo per archidiaconum

Libri iuris ciuilis distribuendi

316	310	Institut' 2 fo seruientes
317	311	Instit' 2 fo in generis
318	312	Instit' 2 fo scriptum
319	313	Instit' 2 fo collectum
320	314	Instit' 2 fo sed et quod principi
321	315	Instit' 2 fo per firma
322	316	Instit' 2 fo constituebat
323	317	Paruum volumen 2 fo et elimenta
324	318	Paruum volumen 2 fo sipientibus
325	319	Paruum volumen 2 fo scriptum ius
326	320	Paruum volumen 2 fo libet preceptis
327	321	Paruum volumen 2 fo commissarie
328	322	Paruum volumen 2 fo sponsa prudentem
329	323	Paruum volumen 2 fo perpetua voluntas
330	324	Paruum volumen 2 fo Iuris precepta
331	325	Paruum volumen 2 fo situm est
332	326	Codex 2 fo ris veterum
333	327	Codex 2 fo iuris doctor
334	328	Codex 2 fo Sanctitatem
335	329	Codex 2 fo atores
336	330	Codex 2 fo optulerunt
337	331	Codex 2 fo huic igitur
338	332	Codex 2 fo nem iuris
339	333	Codex 2 fo atque patricius
340	334	Codex 2 fo ex qua diuidendo
341	355	Codex 2 fo Composite
342	336	ff vetus 2 fo dinem
343	337	ff vetus 2 fo doctrinam
344	338	ff vetus 2 fo de testis

345	339	ff vetus 2 fo alterum
346	340	ff vetus 2 fo dulcerit
347	341	ff vetus 2 fo lumine
348	342	ff vetus 2 fo dicitur
349	343	ff vetus 2 fo facundissimos
350	344	ff vetus 2 fo promittentibus
351	345	ff inforciatum 2 fo que marite
352	346	ff inforciatum 2 fo diuorcio facto
353	347	ff inforciatum 2 fo pedicinos
354	348	ff inforciatum 2 fo vtique
355	349	ff inforciatum 2 fo Iulianus
356	350	ff inforciatum 2 fo ebantur
357	351	ff inforciatum 2 fo si fundus
358	352	ff inforciatum 2 fo mus diuertit
359	353	ff inforciatum 2 fo erit non
360	354	ff inforciatum 2 fo maritus

(f. 7)

361	355	ff nouum 2 fo tur opus
362	356	ff nouum 2 fo postea
363	357	ff nouum 2 fo ceterum
364	358	ff nouum 2 fo aut iuris
365	359	ff nouum 2 fo mum est
366	360	ff nouum 2 fo nisi ad ipsius
367	361	ff nouum 2 fo ter plures
368	362	ff nouum 2 fo omnes ciues
369	363	Reportorium 2 fo et ita
370	364	2ª pars eiusdem 2 fo que sic
371	365	Summa alberti super ff no 2 fo ad 1 ro
372	366	Iohannes de Blanasco 2 fo primo
373	367	De ordine Iudiciali 2 fo eaque
374	368	Casuarius super C 2 fo iubent
375	369	Barth' super ff no 2 fo vt restituas
		Summa (blank)

(Misc. 210)

376	395	Passionarium sanctorum 2 fo quam racionabile
377	396	ff inforciatum 2 fo viro fundum
378	397	ff vetus 2 fo fere (?) populus
379	398	Allocen' artis perspectiue 2 fo libet
380	399	Psalterium glosatum cum aliis contentis 2 fo ad literam
381	400	Paruum volumen 2 fo generaliter
382	401	Augustinus in diuersis tractatibus 2 fo quoniam cecidit

367 Misc. 210 Liber de ordine iudiciali 399 re-entered as 98 and called there 'Hodilstone super psalterium': Professor Jacob suggests Richard Ullerston

383	402	Biblia vsque ieremiam 2 fo est (?) p^i i^i c^2
384	403	Bromyard 2 fo dicitur esse
385	404	Porphirius 2 fo cum species
386	405	Liber artis perspectiue 2 fo cum ille
387	406	Sextus 2 fo domini alletura
388	407	Geomancia Gerardi 2 fo nexit qui inter
389	408	Summa azonis 2 fo incipit
390	409	Sextus 2 fo sunt viciose
391	410	Psalterium Gallicum etc' 2 fo tunc reges
392	411	Summa iuris canonici 2 fo dominum nostrum
393	412	Liber medicine 2 fo nisi discrecio
394	413	Liber philosophie 2 fo vel commento
395	414	Casuarius super decret' 2 fo capituli sunt
396	415	Liber geomancie 2 fo puella
397	416	Albertus (*altered to* Rasis) 2 fo petigine
398	417	Liber iudicum 2 fo ad honorem 'alias illicita'
399	418	Perspectiua Baconis 2 fo cum prima vel 4^a
400	419	Grysostomus 2 fo eius ostenderetur
401	420	Goff*ridus* 2 fo eius (*canc.*) deuocione
402	421	De lxx verbis aristotelis 2 fo dix^i in alio
403	422	Capud diaboli 2 fo annexa
404	423	Geomancia 2 fo negocio
405	424	Forma literarum papalium 2 fo indubitatam
406	425	Geometria 2 fo fiunt lius
407	426	Alkemia 2 fo hactenus
408	427	Geometria 2 fo sectorem sicut
409	428	Allocen' artis perspectiue 2 fo in loco
410	429	Tractatus de conuersione sancti Pauli cum aliis contentis secundum Petrum blesenc' 2 fo agala

Libri diuersarum facultatum

*411	430	Decret' 2 fo Iulie Cornelie
412	431	Liber cum diuersis contentis 2 fo comprehendere
413	432	Rydevaus 2 fo ascensus
414	433	Iohannes in addic' 2 fo incipit
*415	434	Innoc' 2 fo poterant
416	435	Septuplum 2 fo fecit ibidem
417	436	Psalterium glosatum 2 fo ac noua
418	437	Lactencius 2 fo celeste pabulum
419	438	Antiquus liber 2 fo q: u*er*a
420	439	Decretal' 2 fo na que natura
421	440	Sextus 2 'fo' ante quorum
422	441	Abbas 2 fo constitucio
423	442	Hostiensis in prima parte lecture 2 fo septima

424	443	Decretal' 2 fo ne ascendet
425	444	Doctor ignotus 2 fo creta sunt
426	445	Clem' 2 fo et essencialiter
427	446	Glosa super ff veteri 2 fo sub condicione
428	447	Barnardus 2 fo auctoritas
429	448	Instit' 2 fo valere
430	449	Sextus cum doctoribus 2 fo salubri
431	450	Paruum volumen 2 fo bantur
432	451	Tabula super utroque iure 2 fo baal xxii
433	452	Palladius 2 fo postea
434	453	Quidam doctor super decretal' 2 fo inter cetera
435	454	Innoc' 2 fo vel ex relacionibus
436	455	Codex 2 fo istorum etenim
437	456	Archidiaconus super vi 2 fo in suis principiis
438	457	Iacobus de Rauenna 2 fo in Anglia
439	458	ff inforciatum 2 fo quasi dotis
*440	459	Paruum volumen 2 fo ex vnaquaque
441	460	ff nouum 2 fo Opus
442	461	Codex 2 fo dicens
443	462	Decretal' 2 fo consenciatur
444	463	Conclus' Bal' super innoc' 2 fo nota de deo
445	464	Augustinus de verbis domini 2 fo sermo eiusdem
446	465	Codex 2 fo nobis optulerunt
447	466	Paruum volumen 2 fo quasi quo iure
448	467	Innoc' 2 fo citare (?) beneficiorum
449	468	ff inforciatum 2 fo Res sit
450	469	ff inforciatum 2 fo statum
451	470	ff nouum 2 fo tutore
452	471	Codex 2 fo Re pe
453	472	Paruum volumen 2 fo bulis
454	473	Codex 2 fo Ratum
12	474	Edmundus Lacy 2 fo Hebreis
455	475	Hugo de sancto Victore 2 fo et in
456	476	Tabula aurea 2 fo de hoc vltimo
457	477	Casuar' super decretal' 2 fo epistolam
458	478	Antonius de bu(trio) super iiii° decret' 2 fo et in causis (?) c[. .]
459	479	Reportorium iuris 2 fo iuxta illud
460	480	Magister sentenciarum 2 fo gignitur
461	481	Mesue 2 fo omnium memoria
462	90	Textus philosophie 2 fo sem et statu
463	93	Gregorius in Registro 2 fo omnium atque
464	94	Augustinus 2 fo insultare
465	99	Holcote super sap' (2 fo) in tabula consciencia

457 re-entered as 184 and called 'Iacobus de Rauenna super C'

466	295	Barth' Brixen' 2 fo de censibus (?)
467	391	Bibliam 2 fo nec scire dignantur
468	392	Bibliam 2 fo edisserunt pro aula
469	394	Astronomie librum 2 fo coquitur

(on the membrane forming the cover of Misc. 210)

| 470 | 482 | Item Bartholomeus de proprietatibus rerum 2 fo nes quia | } In manibus M. Dryell' |
| 471 | 483 | Item Ianuensis 2 fo quosdam | |

LIST III. GIFT OF JOHN NORFOLK

472–496 from the *Benefactors' Register*, p. 1. The compiler of the Register appears to have had access to a now lost document recording Norfolk's gift.[1]

Ex dono M^{ri} Iohannis Norfolke primi vicecustodis.

472	1	Aquinas super 3^{ium} sententiarum
473	2	Landulphus super primum et 4^{tum} sententiarum
474	3	Pastoralia Gregorii
475, 476	4, 5	Doctor subtilis super 1um et 4^{tum} sententiarum 2^{obus} vol.
477	6	Cowton super 4^{or} libros sententiarum
478	7	Ægidius super 1 sententiarum
479	8	August: de verbis D^{ni} et Apostoli
480	9	Quodlibeta Hen: de Gandavo
481	10	Questiones super 3^{es} libros Ioannis Duns
482	11	Questiones super 3^{es} libros de animalibus
483	12	Magister sententiarum
484	13	Apparatus super Raimundum
485	14	Postillator super Genes: Exod: et Levit:
486	15	Holcot in 12 Prophetas
487	16	Aquinas de potestate Papali
488	17	Rhetorica M. Tho: de Capua
489	18	Homiliæ Chrysostomi
490	19	Quæstiones Scoti in Metaphys:
491	20	Franciscus de virtutibus moralibus
492	21	Sermones per annum
493	22	Quæstiones Theologicæ
494	23	Liber Medicinæ
495	24	Liber logicalis cum aliis
496	25	Burleus super Ethic. MS.

[1] This list in its original form is printed in the Addenda.

LISTS IV–XXIV. LISTS IN THE VELLUM INVENTORY

LIST IV

497–529 from the Vellum Inventory, f. 12ᵛ. Thirty-three books given by Richard Andrew on 26 October 1471. **505, 508, 510, 512–21, 524, 525** are listed under Andrews's name in the Bene-factors' Register, p. 1, in that order.

The list is in a skilled and ornate hand.

522 and **525** are the only survivors.

(f. 12ᵛ)

Isti sunt libri 'iuris canonici et ciuilis' ex dono Magistri Ricardi Andrew anno domini millesimo cccclxxi° xxvi die mensis octobris.

497	1	In primis vnum par decretalium et incipit in 2° fo proprietates
498	2	Item vnum sextum 2 fo currere
499	3	Item alium sextum 2 fo de sine (?) t'
500	4	Item alium sextum 2 fo quia consuetudo
501	5	Item alium sextum 2 fo funtos libros
502	6	Item sextum cum clementinis in vno volumine 2 fo in textu superflue videretur
503	7	Item librum clementinarum cum doctoribus Willelmo et Gosselino 2 fo do die in diem
504	8	Item librum clementinarum cum Willelmo de monte an(duno) et tabula iuris canonici 2 fo in textu obicionibus
505	9	Item 1 ff vetus 2 fo in textu Edilium
506	10	Item inforciatum 2 fo in textu Maritus
507	11	Item alium inforciatum 2 fo in textu tuociorem
508	12	Item ff nouum 2 fo in textu Prouinciale
509	13	Item Willelmum in spe(culo) 2 fo deriuando
510	14	Item Innoc' 2 fo quod omnes
511	15	Item Guidonem 2 fo Merorum
512	16	Item Innoc' 2 fo vel nigrum
513	17	Item casu' Barnardinum 2 fo cur'. Vnde mala
514	18	Item alium casu' Barnardinum 2 fo futura tantum
515	19	Item Bartholomeum Brixensem super decreta 2 fo canon
516	20	Item Goffridum in summa 2 fo virtutes
517	21	Item tabulam iuris canonici cum aliis diuersis tractatibus 2 fo quid si a summa (?)
518	22	Item aliam tabulam iuris canonici 2 fo deferre

519	23	Item conclusiones rotales 2 fo Rerum permut'
520	24	Item conclusiones rotales cum aliis diuersis tractatibus 2 fo li. vi^{to} et claudere
521	25	Item tabulam Martini 2 fo in tabula valet homicidio
*522	26	Item Cynum 2 fo istius ciuitatis
523	27	Item Willelmum de cunio 2 fo glo quia
524	28	Item decretales Nicholai 2 fo luculentissimus
*525	29	Item [canones] generales consiliorum 2 fo Comitatum

[. .] dono (?) predict' M' Ric' Andrew die et anno supradictis.

526	30	[. . . . .] 2 fo tercius est
527	31	[. . . . .] 2 fo [. . .
528	32	[. . . . .] 2 fo [. . .]a Collectio
529	33	[. . . . .] 2 fo [. . . . .]alibus

LIST V

530–52 from the Vellum Inventory, f. 1. Eleven books given by William Goldwyn (†1482), eleven books given by William [Denis] in the time of Warden Stokes, and a book (552) or books given by [Richard Salter]. 552 is the last legible title. Four or five others follow it, but cannot be read. The lower part of the leaf was probably blank. The Benefactors' Register lists 530, 532, 534–5, 537–8, 540, in that order, under Goldwyn's name, 541, 544, and 551, in that order, under Denis's name, and 552 under Salter's name (p. 2).

530, 531, 535, 537, 538 survive. 538, a circulating book, was alienated and returned to All Souls only in 1938.

(f. 1)[1]

(a) Ex dono Magistri Willelmi [Gold]wyn

*530	1	Consilia montagnana 2 fo [. . . .] et in [. . .
*531	2	Item alius liber cum diuersis [. . . . .] 2 fo visus addatur
532	3	Item Avicenna 2 fo que proueniunt
533	4	Item textus de medicinis 2 fo in textu frigidat
534	5	Item breuiarium Constantini 2 fo admiscamus
*535	6	Item anothomia abbreuiata cum aliis [tract]atibus 2 fo ossa plurima
536	7	Item Gatesden in rosa medicine 2 fo bitur in quantitate
*537	8	Item textus amphorismorum ypocratis (?) cum aliis 2 fo in commento de natura morbi

541–52 are included in a bracket against which is 'Tempor[e] M Iohannis [Stokes] quinti Cus[todis]'.

*538	9	Item amforismi ypocratis cum exposicione cardinalis 2 fo oribasius
539	10	Item myluerley super uniuersal' 2 fo [. . .]duatur
540	11	Item Gilbertus anglicus 2 fo fe non est (?) natis (?)

(b) Ex dono Magistri Willelmi [Denis]

541	1	Mesue de simplicibus medicinis 2 fo [. . .
542	2	Item alius liber practice medicine 2 fo [. . .] paruus (?)
543	3	Item alius liber gallicanus 2 fo [. . .
544	4	Item alius liber [spec]uli humane [con]sciencie 2 fo [. . .
545	5	Item alius liber in quo continentur sermones (?) 2 fo [. . .
546	6	Item alius liber in quo continetur [. . .
547	7	Item alius liber in quo continetur op[. . .
548	8	Item alius liber medici[ne] in quo continetur [. . . .]do[. . .
549	9	Item alius liber paruus in quo ph[. . .
550	10	Item alius liber sermonum 2 fo [. . . .]d[. . .
551	11	Item Gatesden in rosa medicine 2 fo [. . .

(c) [Ex dono Magistri Richardi Salter]

552	1	Antonius de butrio super [. .] decretal' 2 fo [. . .

.   .   .   .   .

LIST VI

553-608 from the Vellum Inventory, f. 21^{rv}, and the Benefactors' Register, pp. 1, 2. According to the heading this is a list of books acquired in the time of Warden Stokes (1466–94). More probably it is a list of books put into the chained library in his time, since it includes **104, 183, 308,** and **418,** all books listed in II among circulating books and known to have been transferred to chains later, and **572** and **574,** which were given to the college before Stokes became warden. The order is nearly that in which the books occur in Lists XIII, XIV, XVIII, and XIX. The Benefactors' Register has a long list of gifts under the name of Warden Stokes: they are nos. 2–6, 8–12, 16–20, 22–7, 31, 28–30, 32–4, 37, 45, 47, 50–6, 58, and one of 59–62 of the present list, in that order, together with six volumes after no. 37, which were no doubt on the now missing part of f. 21 (**587–92**).

Of the eight surviving manuscripts and one surviving printed book which first appear in this list, **571** was bought at an unspecified date, **572** was given by John Dryell in 1457, **574** was bequeathed by Walter Hopton (†1459), **585** was bequeathed by John Racour (†1487), and **594** was given by William Elyot in 1483. Of now missing books **584** is listed in Racour's will, **558** and **598** were the gift of John Stokes (†1466), and **607** and **608** may be the copies of Antonius de Butrio mentioned in Stokes's will (*BRUO*, p. 1782).

(f. 21)

Adhuc de eodem registro pro tempore M. Iohannis Stokes. Custodis quinti etc'.

553	1	In primis Biblia in anglico 2 fo Cay[.] and [. . .
554	2	Item alia Biblia 2 fo Iesrael
*555	3	Item biblia 2 fo prime partis scientie dei
*556	4	Item 2 fo partis secunde vir ille
*557	5	Item hugo de vienna super lucam et Iohannem 2 fo ad eam
558	6	Item Rippynton super dominicalia ex dono Magistri Iohannis Stokes nuper officialis de arcubus 2 fo colligatio impietatis
559	7	Item Bachonthorpe super libros augustini de ciuitate dei 2 fo time vt dicit
560	8	Item destructorium viciorum 2 fo Arrogantia
561	9	Item Augustinus de caritate 2 fo pergebat
562	10	Item Augustinus de spiritu et anima 2 fo quibus omnia
563	11	Item Augustinus de Correptione et gratia 2 fo dicere quid
564	12	Item Augustinus in epistolis suis 2 fo (*blank*)
565	13	Item lathbury super trenis 2 fo (*blank*)
566	14	Item Sanctus Thomas de aquino super 4^m sentenciarum 2 fo oris curacionis
*567	15	Item doctor subtilis super 4^m sentenciarum impressionis paris' 2 fo et spes
568	16	Item haymo super epistolas pauli 2 fo esse humanitatis
569	17	Item Sermones Parisien' 2 fo in operando
570	18	Item tabula diuersorum operum 2 fo Ascensus
418	19	Item lactancius de institucionibus diuinis 2 fo celeste pabulum
104	20	Item franciscus petrarcha de remediis vtriusque fortune 2 fo que videatur
*571	21	Item Eustrachius super libros ethicorum emptus per Collegium 2 fo tum eius
*572	22	Item Expositor super Musicam boecii 2 fo vt in epistola
573	23	Item Iohannes Canonicus 2 fo communia (?) tenet
*574	24	Item questionista super libros ethicorum 2 fo tristiciam cum includit
575	25	Item Coment' Aueroys super libros phisicorum 2 fo diffinicio vero eius
576	26	Item Albertus de origine anime 2 fo tatem eo
577	27	Item Egidius de anima 2 fo illam rursus
578	28	Item Comment' Boetii super Porphirium 2 fo res subiectas
579	29	Item Topica Boetii 2 fo esse volubile
580	30	Item quodlibeta Henrici 2 fo cum falso

553 Title and secundo folio erased

183	31	Item liber arsmetrice boecii 2 fo [. . .] quia
581	32	Item Almagest' Tholomei 2 fo signorum
582	33	Item Duns super predicamenta 2 fo rationis
583	34	Item Cardinalis Cameracensis 2 fo vero numero
584	35	Item Ysagoge 'Iohannicii' 2 fo hii.vel quia
*585	36	Item versus Egidii 2 fo subpall[idus]
586	37	Item [. . . . . .] Gerardi Cremonensis 2 fo [. . .

. . . . .

(Benefactors' Register, p. 2)

587	38	De conservanda sanitate tractatus aureus
588	39	Margarita Poetica
589-92	40-3	Doctor de Lyra cum additionibus et replicis in 4 vol:

(Vellum Inventory, f. 21^v)

Adhuc continuatur Registrum pro tempore M' Io. Stokes Custodis quinti etc'.

593	44	Item Antonius de butrio in 2^a parte 2 fo 2^e partis Ventione partium
*594	45	Item libellus componendi instrumentorum 2 fo pater pie
595	46	Item Petrus de Ancharano super vi^{to} 2 fo stipendium
596	47	Item Prothodosinus de ordine Iudiciario 2 fo lent.co.de Iudi.
597	48	Item Antonius de butrio super 4to 2 fo vt dato
598	49	Item Iohannes in nouella super vi^{to} 2 fo id est diserte alias discrete 'gestum' Ex dono M' Iohannis Stokes nuper officialis Curie de Arcubus
518	50	Item Tabula vtriusque Iuris 2 fo differre
520	51	Item Conclusiones rotales 2 fo li. vi
*308	52	Item Reportorium Thome Chiselden 2 fo alia conclusio
599	53	Item Abbas super primo libro decretalium et prima parte 2 fo iusti qui
600	54	Item Abbas super 2° decretalium in 2^a parte 2 fo nota ibi
601	55	Item Abbas super eodem libro et 2^a parte 2 fo ac si clerici
602	56	Item Abbas super 3° decretalium 2 fo nobiliori
603	57	Item Abbas super 4° decretalium 2 fo ecclesia
604	58	Item lynwode ex dono doctoris Pykenham 2 fo condentis
605	59	Item secunda pars Antonii de butrio super primo decretalium 2 fo tollitur contrarium
606	60	Item Antonius de butrio super primo decretalium 2 fo fal. quam
607	61	Item Antonius super 3° 2 fo deponuntur
608	62	Item Antonius super 5° 2 fo antequam denuncietur

LIST VII

609–99 from the Vellum Inventory, ff. 30ᵛ–31, and the Benefactors' Register, pp. 6–7. The list of books given by Archbishop
Warham (†1532) contained originally, no doubt, ninety-one
titles, but only seventy-seven now remain (**609–36, 645–74, 681–
99**). The others, entered on the now missing lower part of each
leaf, are known from the Benefactors' Register. The entries
common to both lists are in the same order in both. Probably
only **631, 679, 681–2, 693** were manuscripts. Only **651, 677,** and
698 were put into the chained library. Two of these three and
seventeen other books survive.

(f. 30ᵛ, col. 1)

Hii libri sequentes sunt ex dono Reuerendissimi in cristo patris ac domini
domini Willelmi Warham nuper cantuariensis archiepiscopi

609	1	Vita cristi in magn' 2 fo tumeliarum
610	2	Sermones bernardi super cantica 2 fo eo quod ad singulos
611	3	Epistole bernardi 2 fo vndique alios
612	4	Tractatus de passione cum aliis 2 fo obsequio
*613	5	Summa antonini in 4ᵒʳ partibus 2 fo prime acquisitum
614	6	2 fo 2ᵉ cientibus tantum est
615	7	2 fo 3ᵉ noticiam parentum
*616	8	2 fo 4ᵉ gentiles
617	9	Tres partes anthonini et deest quarta pars 2 fo prime quam esse liber
*618	10	2 fo 2ᵉ rum eas custodit
619	11	2 fo 3ᵉ do quia facit
*620	12	Opera gersonis in tribus voluminibus 2 fo primi affectus proprietas
*621	13	2 fo 2ⁱ aliter non oportet
622	14	2 fo 3ⁱ tabula quarti libri
623	15	Concordantie biblie 2 fo abluendus
624	16	Concordantie biblie 2 fo sunamite
625	17	Due partes glose ordinarie 2 fo primi nantur nec aucupantur
626	18	2 fo alterius Augustinus cristus
627	19	Prima pars lyre 2 fo nondum ea
628	20	2ᵃ pars lyre 2 fo in textu 'pto' vocaui
629	21	3ᵃ pars lyre 2 fo in texti nec habens quicquam
630	22	4ᵃ pars lyre 2 fo hominis generatio
*631	23	Gesta passionis cristi liber scriptus 2 fo Respondentes
632	24	Quadragesimale Roberti de licio 2 fo philosophus
*633	25	Speculum morale vincentii 2 fo quia sicut
634	26	Speculum exemplorum 2 fo vir sanctus

*635   27   Speculum exemplorum 2 fo paruit quod
*636   28   [. . . . .] 2 fo petra scandali

· · · · ·

(Benefactors' Register, p. 6)
*637   29   Ambrosii epistolæ
638   30   Aquinas in epistolas Pauli
*639   31   Theologia naturalis
*640   32   Quæstiones evangeliorum Iohannis de Turrecremata
641   33   Florarium Bartholomæi MS
642   34   Lactantii opera
643   35   Pantheologia
644   36   Destructorium vitiorum

(Vellum Inventory, f. 30ᵛ, col. 2)
645   37   Crisostomus in geneseos 2 fo disputaturus
646   38   prima pars crisostomi 2 fo quintus (?) et reliqui
647   39   2ᵃ pars crisostomi 2 fo quod ne accidat
*648   40   Summa summarum siluestrini 2 fo eligi debet
649   41   Opuscula anselmi 2 fo hominem aliquem
*650   42   Margarita poetica 2 fo quod fit
*651   43   Biblia pangnini 2 fo quot annis vixerit
652   44   Bruno super epistolas pauli 2 fo per humilitatem
653   45   Postilla super evangelia 2 fo titiones
654   46   Racionale diuinorum 2 fo translato
655   47   Racionale diuinorum 2 fo translato
656   48   Sermones biga salutis 2 fo aliquid adhuc
657   49   Sermones biga salutis 2 fo bonitatem
658   50   Psalterium glosatum in pergameno 2 fo hoc modo tractat
659   51   Sermones Pauli Wan' de sanctis 2 fo audierunt
660   52   Lima viciorum 2 fo primo lege
661   53   Oraciones francisci philelphi 2 fo bus et excelsis
662   54   Sermones pomerii de sanctis pars estiualis 2 fo nitatis notan-
              dum
663   55   Sermones pomerii 2 fo tua sunt precipua
664   56   Quadragesimale pomerii 2 fo Ecclesia die dominico
665   57   Quadragesimale Iohannis raulini in duobus 2 fo primi
              secunda veritas
666   58   2 fo 2ⁱ pedibus cristi
667   59   Opus aureum de veritate contricionis 2 fo Vita anime
668   60   Gregorius super nouum testamentum 2 fo quem reproba-
              uerunt
669   61   Historia scolastica 2 fo ta qua paulatim

636 Ben. Reg. 'Holcot in lib. sapientiæ'

670	62	Preceptorium nider' 2 fo sed quid facit
671	63	Marcus marulus de modo bene viuendi 2 fo dentes afferebant
*672	64	Biblia aurea de contemptu mundi 2 fo runt et victoriam
673	65	De origine bonorum regum 2 fo quia tamen
674	66	[Opera] hieronimi 2 fo scriptura

. . . . .

(Benefactors' Register, p. 6)

675	67	De puritate conceptionis beatæ Mariæ
676	68	Scotus super 4: lib: sententiarum
*677	69	Psalterium Philini
*678	70	Stimulus divini amoris
679	71	Gregorii Dialogus MS
680	72	Compendium Theologiæ

(Vellum Inventory, f. 31)

Ex dono predicti domini domini Willelmi Warham Cant' archiepiscopi

681	73	Augustinus de Anchona de potestate ecclesie liber scriptus in pergameno 2 fo sanctissimo et reuerendissimo
682	74	Meditacio scripturarum liber scriptus in pergameno 2 fo Inquirebat
683	75	Opuscula Richardi de sancto Victore 2 fo tus est in terra
684	76	Summa viciorum et virtutum 2 fo notandum ergo
685	77	Sermones michaelis de Vngaria 2 fo omnium bonorum
686	78	Defensorium reucline (?) 2 fo cui benefacitis
687	79	Gregorius super ezechielem 2 fo quia de preterito
688	80	Recuperaciones fesulane 2 fo mathei bossi
689	81	Omeliarum 40 Gregorii 2 fo gimus quod terre motus
*690	82	Sermones de Voragine in duobus voluminibus 2 fo primi ce quia sibi
691	83	2 fo 2^i philippus non
692	84	Sermones Pomerii de beata virgine 2 fo catur in esse
693	85	Omelia Originis liber scriptus 2 fo pacabatur
694	86	Opuscula hugonis de sancto victore 2 fo itur ad bonitatem
695	87	Sermones Gabrielis 2 fo legitur de noviciis
696	88	Horalogium diuine sapientie 2 fo perfecte nunc
697	89	De vita et beneficiis saluatorum 2 fo inmensurabilis
698	90	Sexta pars augustini 2 fo quapropter
699	91	Lathburie super libris trenorum 2 fo signum exterminatum

LIST VIII

700–14 from the Vellum Inventory, f. 30. The same fifteen titles are in the Benefactors' Register, p. 3, in a different order. Like

Warham's, John Moore's books seem to have been printed books not of the newest sort. None of them went into the chained library. **706** and **711** survive.

Item idem Magister Iohannes more dedit hos libros subscriptos numero sedecim.

700	1	In primis destructorium vitiorum
701	2	Omelie Iheronimi aug' ambrosii aliorumque doctorum super euangelia dominicalia de tempore et de sanctis per totius anni circulum
702	3	Item figure biblie fratris antonii
703	4	Item opuscula beati anselmi
704	5	Item ovidius in metamorphoseos
705	6	Item Summa magistri Iohannis de sancto Geminiano
*****706**	7	Item liber moralitatum lumen anime dictus
707	8	Item augustinus de ciuitate dei cum commento
708	9	Item Concordantie biblie
709	10	Item liber aurore
710	11	Item registrum in sermones Iacobi de voragine
*****711**	12	Item moralia diui Gregorii
712	13	Item sermones thesauri noui de tempore
713	14	Item augustinus in epistolas pauli
714	15	Item integra biblia

LIST IX

715–964, **964a** from the Vellum Inventory, f. 47^{rv}, the Benefactors' Register, pp. 4–5, and Ledger A. The list of books received by All Souls College in 1575 under the will of David Pole, bishop of Peterborough, †1568, extends over four columns of the Vellum Inventory. The loss of the lower part of each column has taken away the titles of **773–86, 841–61, 907–22**. They are known from the Benefactors' Register, which takes the theological books before the law books, but is otherwise in the same order. A third list, Ledger A, pp. 42–4, is perhaps the rough list made when the books were unpacked at All Souls, since it is in no order and enters volumes of sets in different places. **964a** occurs only in Ledger A. The titles in Ledger A are sometimes fuller than those in the Vellum Inventory.[1]

The list in Ledger A is headed 'Be it knowen vnto all men by these presentę that we Robert Houendon warden and the colleadge of the sowlę of all faythfull people deceassed of Oxon' haue receyued and had in the daye of the date of these presentę

[1] Cf. **797, 801, 862, 890, 893, 909, 915, 916, 921, 949.**

of Thomas Fitzherbert knight executor of the last will and
testament of the Reuerend D. Poole somtyme bisshope of
Peterborough by the hande of Mr Thurstan Morrey, one of the
prebendaris of Peterborough aforseide all such bookes of lawe and
diuinitie as are heare vnder specified due vnto ou^r said colleadge
by the last will and testament of the said late bisshope. In witnes
wherof we haue vnto these presente put ou^r common seale the
(*no date*).' One of the fellows, Robert Mowsherst, fetched the
books from Peterborough. The expenses he incurred, totalling
£6. 2s. 2d., are entered in the college accounts. 'Anno 1575°
Mensis Aug. 2° repositus in communi libraria' is written inside
751.
    All Pole's books were printed. Thirty-two volumes of law and
eleven volumes of theology were put into the chained library. All
but one of them survive. The total number of books surviving
from this bequest is 132. **716, 738, 748, 755, 757, 760** were
rebound soon after they were received (cf. Appendix II).

(f. 47, col. 1)

Hii libri sequentes sunt ex legato Venerabilis Viri Dauidis Poli Legum Doctoris nuper Episcopi Peterburgensis ac quondam huius Collegii Socii 1575 'R.
Houenden Custode 15°'.

*715–19	1–5	Corpus ciuile cum glossis quinque voluminibus
*720–4	6–10	Iasonis opera quinque voluminibus
*725–6	11–12	Salycetus super C duobus voluminibus
*727	13	Cynus super C vno volumine
728–9	14–15	Consilia Alexandri duobus voluminibus
*730–2	16–18	Bauldus super C et ff infort. et no. tribus vol.
*733–4	19–20	Speculator duobus voluminibus
*735–6	21–2	Petrus Ancoranus duobus voluminibus
*737	23	Prepositus super quarto decretal. vno vol.
*738	24	Innocentius vno volumine
*739	25	Collectarius vno volumine
740–1	26–7	Felinus duobus voluminibus
*742	28	Baldus super 1, 2, et 3 decretal. cum novella I. Andr. super sexto vno volumine
*743–5	29–31	Immola super decretal. tribus vol.
*746–7	32–3	Hostiensis duobus vol.
*748	34	Provinciales constitutiones vno vol.
*749–52	35–8	Panormitanus quatuor vol.
*753	39	Distinctiones Bowicki vno vol.
*754	40	Barbatius de præstantia Cardinalium vno vol.
*755	41	Philippus francus super sexto vno vol.

*756	42	Archidiaconus super sexto vno vol.
*757	43	Bonifacius super Clement. vno vol.
*758	44	Prepositus super distinct. vno vol.
*759	45	Archidiaconus super decret. vno vol.
*760	46	Prepositus super causis vno vol.
*761	47	Summa Angelica vno vol.
*762	48	Singularia Romani cum aliis vno vol.
763	49	Philippus decius de constitut' vno vol.
764	50	Mandagotus de elect' vno vol.
765	51	Prepositus super causis vno vol.
766	52	Philippus decius super except. vno vol.
767	53	Contrarietates inter ius ciuile et canonicum
*768	54	Tabula prepositi vno vol.
769	55	Iohanes de turræcremata super decret' vno vol.
770	56	Practica Lanfranci
771	57	[Prouin]tiales cons[titutiones . . . . .] vno vol.
772	58	[Decre]ta cum glos[sa . . .

. . . . .

(Benefactors' Register, p. 5)

773	59	Sextus in Decreta
774	60	Practica Iohannis de Ferrariis
775	61	Goffredus super decret:
*776	62	Iason super tit: de actis institut:
777	63	Dinus de reg: iur:
778	64	Institutiones cum glossa
779	65	Alcieti paradoxa: disput: et lect: in 3 lib: cod:
780	66	Sepulveda de ritu nuptiarum
781–4	67–70	Bartolus super vet: infort: nov: et cod: 4^{or} vol:
785	71	Angelus in Institut:
786	72	Practica Mansurii

(Vellum Inventory, f. 47, col. 2)

*787	73	Epiphanius cum Damasceno
*788	74	Bernardus
*789	75	Gregorius
*790	76	Annotationes Erasmi
*791	77	Novum Testamentum Erasmi
*792	78	Brensius in Lucam
*793	79	Concordant' Bibliae
794	80	Veterum theologorum elenchus
*795	81	Quatuor concilia generalia
*796	82	Ciprianus et Cirillus
797	83	Alphonsus de Castro cum aliis
*798–9	84–5	Theophilact' duobus vol.

*800	86	Lactantius firmianus
801	87	Theodoreti dialogi
*802–4	88–90	Waldensis tribus vol.
805	91	Paraphrasis Erasmi in Iohan.
*806	92	Idem in Evangelia et Acta
*807	93	Eiusdem Paraph. in Epist. Pauli
*808	94	Idem in quatuor ewangelia et Acta
809	95	Idem in Lucam
*810–12	96–8	Dionysius Carthusian' tribus vol.
813–19	99–105	Lyra septem vol.
*820	106	Ludolphus de vita Christi
*821	107	Bernardus
*822	108	Hylarius
*823	109	Cyrillus
*824	110	Basilius
825	111	Tertulianus
*826–30	112–16	Hieronimus quinque vol.
*831–2	117–18	Origenis opera duobus vol.
*833–4	119–20	Origenis opera duobus vol.
*835–6	121–2	Chrisostomus duobus vol.
*837	123	Hieronimus in quatuor evangelistas
*838–9	124–5	Augustini comment' in vetus et nouum testamentum collect' per Brisacenst' duobus vol.
*840	126	Sermones Augustini collect'

. . . . .

(Benefactors' Register, p. 4)

*841	127	Idem de ciuitate dei cum comment:
*842	128	Piggii Hierarchia
843	129	Idem de controversiis
*844–5	130–1	Operum Gersonis pars 3 et 4 2^{obus} vol:
*846	132	Simon de Cassia in Evangelia
847	133	Iohannes de Lateburio in Lament: Ieremiæ
*848	134	Iacobus de Valentia in vetus et novum testament:
*849	135	Remigius in Psalterium
*850	136	Catena aurea super psal:
851	137	Problema Indulgentiarum
852	138	Pe: Sutor de translatione Biblii
*853	139	Hosiandri Harmo: Evangelica
*854–6	140–2	Barkarii Dictionarium 3 vol:
*857	143	Magister sententiarum
*858	144	Destructorium vitiorum
*859	145	Anselmi opera
*860	146	Bartholomæus Anglicus
*861	147	Haymo in epist: Pauli

(Vellum Inventory, f. 47ᵛ, col. 1)

862	148	Speculum moralium
*863	149	Catalogus sanctorum Petri de natalibus
*864–72	150–8	Pipinus novem vol.
*873	159	Antididagma
874	160	Antididagma
875	161	Gagnei in Epist. Pauli expositio
*876	162	Declaratio articulorum per Ruardum Tappaert
877	163	Historia scholastica
878	164	Loci communes hoffmesterii
*879	165	Ecclesia per Michaelem busingerum
880	166	Melancthonis comment' in Epist' Pauli
*881	167	Iohanis valensis de regimine vitæ humanæ
882	168	Opus nicolai deonisii super sentent'
*883	169	Nicolaus de Orbellis in quatuor sentent' libros
*884	170	Fundamentum aureum Nicolai de gorrha
*885	171	Guilielmus Parisiensis et hugo de sancto victore
*886	172	Wesselus
887	173	Bernardus Franciscanus de sacrament' com'
888	174	Anima fidelis
889	175	Dionisii Ariopagitæ opera
890	176	Brevitolii compendium
891	177	Manipulus curatorum
892	178	Isiodorus de summo bono
893	179	Confessio fidei exhibita Charalo quinto
894	180	Ioh. Tavernerius de veritat' corporis christi
895	181	Dechacordum christianum Vigerii
896	182	Vetustus codex incerti autoris
897	183	Compendium dissidii bunderii
898	184	Stephani Paris expositio verbum caro factum est
899	185	Enchiridion Bibliæ per Io. fabr'
900	186	Elucidarius in Epist. canonicas
*901	187	Wicelius de eucharistia
902	188	Summa virtutum Peraldi
903	189	Wicelius de eucaristia
904	190	[Hipodi]digmata Wiselii
905	191	[Collectari]um Ioh. de Peccano
*906	192	[Trittenhem de scriptori]bus ecclesiast'

· · · · ·

(Benefactors' Register, pp. 4–5)

907	193	Consolatorium theologicum
*908	194	Algerius de veritate corporis
909	195	Lutherus in psal: 13 et 51

910	196	De verit: corp: Christi in sacram: adversus Lutherum
911	197	Marci Antonii Constitut:
912	198	Decreta Concil: Provincialis
913	199	Tonstall de veritate corporis in sacramento
914	200	Io: Genesio de ritu Nuptiarum
915	201	Examen ordinandorum
916	202	Confirmatio præsentiæ corporis per Olivarium
917	203	Vincent: Lyrinensis de fidei authoritate
918	204	Consilium vtile super Eucharistia
919	205	Smith de coelibatu
920	206	Dionysius Rickell in epistolas Canon: et Apocal:
921	207	Pandectæ scripturarum Bruselsii
***922**	208	Peresius de ecclesiasticis traditionibus

(Vellum Inventory, f. 47^{v}, col. 2)

923	209	Dictionarius Pauperum
924	210	Expositio missæ per Titelmannum
925	211	Hoffmesterius de autoritate ecclesię
926	212	Repertorium lyræ
***927**	213	Lamprigii sermones
***928**	214	Lectiones ex Epist' et euangel'
***929**	215	Homiliæ Io.Fabri
***930**	216	Homiliarius doctorum
***931**	217	Postillæ maiores
***932**	218	Sermones quadragesimales
933	219	Sermones discipuli de tempore
934–6	220–2	Homiliæ Clichtovii tribus vol.
***937**	223	Homiliæ hoffmesterii per totum annum
938	224	Homiliæ aliæ eiusdem
939–43	225–9	Homiliæ Royardi quinque vol.
944–7	230–3	Ecchii quatuor volumina
948	234	Enarrationes evangeliorum Schofori
949	235	Homiliæ Bedæ
950	236	Sampsonis Expositio in Epist' ad Rom.et primam ad Cor.
951	237	Postillæ frederici
952	238	Sermones 13 Michaelis de hungaria
953	239	Postillæ epistolarum et euangeliorum
954	240	Petri Anlopæi Sermones
***955**	241	Sermones Dorbelli
956–7	243–3	Sermones Io. (*sic*) de voragine duobus vol.
***958**	244	Sermones Gabrielis Barelety
959	245	Sermones Maillardi
960	246	Fundamentum aureum Nicolai de Gorrha
961	247	Sermones quintini
962	248	Sermones ad omnes status

| *963 | 249 | Sermones nicolai deniise |
| *964 | 250 | Gemma predicantium eiusdem |

(Ledger A)

| *964a | 251 | Petri Berthorii morale reductorium vno vol. |

(Vellum Inventory, f. 47ᵛ, col. 2)

Qui quidem libri traditi sunt Magistro Roberto Hovenden custodi ʻ[. . . .] colle-gioʼ per Robertum Mousherste socium eiusdem collegii, in præsentiis Magistri Wagstaffe, Magistri Dunne et Magistri Smythis secundo [die mensis augu]sti [anno domini MDLXXV].[1]

LIST X

965–74 from the Vellum Inventory, f. 51ᵛ. This bequest is entered twice in the Inventory, first on f. 43ᵛ and then on f. 51ᵛ, where it follows List XVII in the same hand. The entry on f. 51ᵛ is the better of the two.

Mᵣ Andrew Kingsmillʼ late fellowe dying in Fraunce bequeathed to the col-ledge five poundes, to be bestowed on Calvin and Martyrs workes in Allsoln col-ledg librarye which was performed Anno 1576 on theise bookes following

*965	1	Caluini opuscula	xviii*s*.
*966	2	Caluinus in Moysen	xv*s*.
*967	3	Idem in Evangelia et acta	x*s*.
*968	4	Idem in Paulum et canonicas epistolas	x*s*.
*969	5	Idem in Esaiam et Ieremiam	xvi*s*.
*970	6	Idem in Danielem et duodecim prophetas	xiiii*s*. iiii*d*.
*971	7	Petrus Martyr in lib. Iudicum et Samuelem	xiiii*s*. iiii*d*.
*972	8	Idem in librum Regum	x*s*.
*973	9	Idem ad Rom. Corinthios	xiiii*s*. iiii*d*.
*974	10	Idem contra Marcum Constantium	viii*s*.
		Summa vi^{li'} vii^s	
		ʻThe overplus of v^{l'} the collegd payedʼ	

LIST XI

975–9 from the Vellum Inventory, f. 51ᵛ. Books bought with £3 given by (William) Jones, canon of Wells (†1589), and £2 bequeathed by (Thomas) Bastard, canon of Worcester (†1584). Jones's gift is noted also on f. 43ᵛ, but not how it was used, only that it was ʻto be imployed as the warden should thinke goodʼ:

---

[1] For the date see **751**.

the date is given as 10 December 1584 and it is said that Jones had his beginning at All Souls. Cf. List XXVII, at 1586–7.

*975–9   1–5   Doctor J[ones] civili[an] cannon resident of Welles sent vnto the colledge to be imployed at their pleasure iii^li Item Mr Bastard cannon resident of Worcester 'and sometyme fellowe' gave by his will and testament to the colledge in like manner xl^s with two which summes of 3 and 2 were bought the generall councells imprinted at Venise in [5] volumes, price in quiers vnbound v^li. for the bindinge the colledge did paye.

LIST XII

980–987 from the Vellum Inventory, f. 43^v. It follows immediately the note of Jones's gift (List XI).

*980–7   1–8   i^a die aprilis 1585[1] Mr Francis Milles 'm^r of arts and' late fellow of the colledg did give to the common vse of the colledg to be laide in the librarie Bibliam Sacram Hebraicè, Caldaice, Græce, Latinè, sett out by [. . . . . .] phillip in viii volumes. pro ligatura soluit collegium.

LIST XIII

988–1047 from the Vellum Inventory, ff. 1^v–2^v (six columns). The second list of books on the theology side[2] is written in a clear hand of medium size: 9 lines take up 50 mm. The same hand wrote List V (f. 1^r) and List XIX. One hundred and thirty-four original entries remain, some of them hardly legible, out of perhaps about 180.

The books in this list not already recorded in List II are 54 or 55: seventeen of them are in List VI. The number suggests that the total accession of chained theology since the drawing up of List II is likely to have been about eighty volumes. Surviving books among the newcomers are **996** given in 1483, **1007** given in 1490, and **1016** bequeathed in 1485.

The additions, **1026–47**, probably consisted largely of books given by James Goldwell, †1499. Four out of the six survivors are his.

---

[1] The last figure of the year is hard to read. It could be 5 or 1, but not 4. '1584' is written in the books themselves and their bindings were paid for in 1583–4. 1581, the date given in my *Pastedowns*, pp. xi, 93, is wrong.

[2] For the earliest list, XIIA, see Addenda.

(f. 1ᵛ, col. 1)

Hii libri subscripti continentur in bibliotheca collegii animarum Oxonii. In theologia et artibus.

In primis in superiori parte primi dextus.

| 554 | 1 | Biblia 2 fo iesrael |
| **988** | 2 | Item glosa super prologos beati Ieronimi in bibliam 2 fo numero sub |

Inferius in eodem dextu

96	3	Concordancie 2 fo sicut vestimentum
31	4	Item primum volumen lire 2 fo liber
989	5	Item 2ᵐ volumen eiusdem 2 fo dati cum dicitur
32	6	Item 3ᵐ volumen eiusdem 2 fo pronunciata
34	7	4ᵐ 2 fo non est in eo
990	8	5ᵐ 2 fo ficaciter
991	9	6ᵐ 2 fo secundum carnem
992	10	Item Gorram super epistolas pauli 2 fo vsque

Item subtus eodem dextu

553	11	Biblia anglicana 2 fo the begynnyng
994	12	Lira super Iohannem 2 fo autem
42	13	Hugo de Vienna super apocalipsim 2 fo [. . .

In secundo dextu in media parte

995	14	Holcot super sapien' 2 fo tare [. . .
*996	15	Hugo de sancto victore super ecclesias[ten] 2 fo rum
*555	16	Prima pars biblie 2 fo scientie dei
*557	17	Hugo de vienna super [. . .
*556	18	2ª pars biblie 2 fo vir i[lle] simplex

Inferius

12	19	Liber de quadriplici sensu [. . .
997	20	Prosper de vita contempla[tiua . . .
37	21	Liber de figuris bibl[ie . . .
39	21a	Bonauent[ura . . .
	21b	Sermones[. . .
	21c	Item S[. . .
	21d	Augus[. . .

·   ·   ·   ·   ·

(col. 2)

Inferius in eodem dextu

| 563 | 22 | Augustinus de correpcione ac gracia 2 fo dicere |
| 51 | 23 | Augustinus de verbis domini 2 fo sermo eiusdem |

| 562 | 24 | Augustinus de spiritu et anima 2 fo quibus omnia |
| 49 | 25 | Milleloquium augustini 2 fo de trinitate |

In 3° dextu

Superius

*59	26	Registrum sancti gregorii 2 fo patimur longius
998	27	Statuta gregorii 2 fo leoni episcopo in tabula
60	28	Gregorius super Cantica 2 fo vocat

In media parte eiusdem dextus

999	30	Moralia gregorii 2 fo nam si illatas in tabula
1000	31	Moralia gregorii 2 fo daniel vir in tabula
400	32	Crisostomus in opere imperfecto (2 fo) eius ostenderetur
560	33	Destructorium viciorum 2 fo arrogancia in tabula

Inferius

| 63 | 34 | Moralia Gregorii a xxi° libro 2 fo illius |
| 565 | 35 | Exposicio ac moralizacio trenorum 2 fo Signum exterminatiuum |

Ex altera parte eiusdem dextus

[S]uperius

1001	36	[. . . . .] 2 fo Ieronimus in tabula
58	37	Exposicio [super] marcum euangelistam 2 [fo] Iacobus [. . .
1002	38	[Com]mentariolus b[. . . . . . Ps]alterium [2 fo] que sit via

In media p[arte]

55	38a	[Sanctus] Bernardus 2 [fo congru]um videatur
57	38b	Epistola beati Ieronimi contra Rufinum here[ticum] 2 fo impietatis
*54	38c	Bernardus in cantic' canticorum [2 fo . . . .]
30	38d	Historia scolastica 2 fo fe[. . .
47	38e	Postilla super Iohannem 2 fo cum

In inferiori parte eiusdem

| *80 | 38f | Commentum [ca]tonis moralizat[. . .
Th[. . . |

．　．　．　．　．

(f. 2, col. 1)

Inferius

| 40 | 39 | Glosa super oseam 2 fo annis xvi |
| 41 | 40 | Glosa super ysayam 2 fo ergo prudens |

Subtus eodem dextu

70	41	Magister thomas Walden in 5^m librum doctrinalis antiquita-tum 2 fo prologus
23	42	Glosa Ieronimi super genesim 2 fo que nostra est
46	43	Lethbertus abbas de titulis superscripcionum in libro psalmorum 2 fo in hebreo dicitur
69	44	Primus prologus in doctrinale antiquitatum ecclesie cristi et contra blasphemias Wyclyf' 2 fo certare exopto
*75	45	Liber omeliarum Eusebii emiseni 2 fo et amicus

Ex altera parte eiusdem dextus

Superius

1003	46	Liber fratris Rogeri Bakon de retardacione senectutis et senii 2 fo agala in tabula
92	47	Liber Thome de bredwardina contra pelagium de virtute causarum 2 fo bonum

In media parte

1004	48	Liber Rabani de deo 2 fo Incipit
*19	49	Ysydorus de ecclesiasticis officiis 2 fo carmine
1005	50	'Isidorus de summo bono 2 fo [c]ut et reliqua'

Inferius

67	51	Dieta salutis 2 fo tam[quam] infideles
82	52	Libellus de emendacione vite 2 fo cuncta que
93	53	Bredewardyn 2 fo sit racio[ne]

In 5° dextu

Superius

1006	54	Doctor subtilis super 4^m sentenciarum 2 fo consequentis
*1007	55	Idem super 3^es primos libros sentenciarum 2 fo rales

In media parte

13	56	Commentum super primum et 4^m sentenciarum 2 fo enim est
1008	57	Liber questionum de fyssakre 2 fo quia ista
91	58	Petrus de Candia 2 fo causabunt
1009	59	Hugo de Vienna super magistrum sentenciarum 2 fo est de

Inferius

11	60	Thomas de cristiana religione 2 fo musicus
*86	61	Thomas [in secunda] parte summe de theologia 2 fo math' quantitatis

Subtus

84	62	[. . . . . . .] 2 fo an posse in tabula

. . . . .

(f. 2, col. 2)

*1010	63	Iulius Solinus 2 fo vrbe roma
*74	64	Malmesbery de gestis anglorum 2 fo solent

Ex altera parte

Superius

*567	65	Doctor subtilis super 4^m sentenciarum 2 fo et spes

In media parte

81	66	Quidam fidelis in librum florum 2 fo quia tres
79	67	Aurora versificata 2 fo nam quasi
*73	68	Beda de gestis anglorum 2 fo quibusdam

In sexto dextu

Superius

83	69	Iacobus Ianuensis in opere 40^{li} (2 fo) filia populi
569	70	Item liber sermonum notabilium 2 fo in operando
570	71	Liber tabularum complurium operum diuersorum 2 fo ascens[us] in tabula

In media parte

1011	72	Dicta lincoln' 2 fo cuteret nullum
66	73	Distincciones holcot 2 fo sapiens
90	74	Liber veritatis theologie 2 fo greg' omnia
384	75	Tractatus iuris ciuilis et canonici fratris Iohannis de bromyard 2 fo dicitur esse in tabula

Inferius

78	76	Floretum theologie 2 fo sionis culpe
1012	77	Parisiensis in sermones de euangeliis dominicalibus secundum usum sar' 2 fo caritas signatur in tabula
568	78	Tractatus hamonis super epistolas pauli 2 fo esse humanitatis in opere
72	79	Parisiensis de virtutibus 2 fo sobrietatis

Subtus eodem dextu

*1013	80	[Egi]di[us] de regimine principum 2 fo cum omnis

Ex altera parte in media parte

*574	81	Questionista super ethica aristotelis 2 fo tristiciam
*571	82	Commentum Eustracii super librum etichorum 2 fo [tu]m eius
1014	83	[. . . . . .] ethicorum 2 fo quidem et th[. . .
418	84	Lactantius 2 fo celeste pabulum
*572	85	Expositor super musicam boecii 2 fo vt in epistola

Inferius

27	86	Burleus super ethica 2 fo ideo
120	87	Sanctus thomas super ethica aristotelis 2 fo igitur
104	88	Liber de remediis vtriusque fortune 2 fo que [. . .
470	89	Bartholomeus de proprietatibus rerum 2 fo [. . .
*1015	90	Iohannes Gower 2 fo hic corripit

In septimo dextu

In media [parte]

| | 90a | Sanctus [. . . |

. . . . .

(f. 2ᵛ, col. 1)

Ex altera parte superius

*1016	91	Questiones de sompno et vigilia cum aliis contentis 2 fo eleuantur quidem
1017	92	Item duns super libros metheorum cum aliis 2 fo aret
1018	93	Item questiones iohannis canonici in physica aristotelis 2 fo vtrum in quolibet

In medio eiusdem partis

123	94	Albertus super diuersa opera 2 fo carnem et os
1019	95	Item questionista bonus 2 fo eo quod quid
1020	96	Item liber Ruralium commodorum 2 fo de lenticula in tabula
*135	98	Item liber almagesti tholomei 2 fo tatur genus

Inferius

| 1021 | 101 | Exposicio alberti 2 fo et nigram et albam in opere |
| 379 | 102 | Item Alacens' in perspectiuis 2 fo libet et quod |

In superiori parte primi lateris octaui dextus

132	103	In primis quadripartitum tholomei 2 fo et potest
139	104	Item liber almagesti tholomei 2 fo metᵃ habetur corda
163	105	Item theorica planetarum cum aliis 2 fo sequitur de
185	106	Item Aggregatorium tocius artis geomancie 2 fo globo con- stitutum

In medio

*128	107	Liber noue(m) iudicum 2 fo mutacione[m] ab al[. . .] in opere
583	108	Item Cardinalis cameracens' de concordia theologie et astro- nomie 2 fo v[ero numer]o
130	109	Item liber calendarum [. . .] cum aliis contentis 2 fo quattuor cicli

Inferius

| 1022 | 110 | Liber domini Iohannis de spira 2 fo et tunc nichil f[. . . |

| 133 | 111 | Item Abraham Auenesre de natiuitatibus 2 fo Et [. . . |
| 581 | 112 | Item almagesti tholomei 2 fo signorum |

Subtus

579	113	Liber logice boecii 2 fo [esse] volubi[le]
131	114	Item liber in commendacione antiquorum sapientum 2 fo [. . .
129	115	Item introductorius cosme alexandrini in astrologiam 2 fo les ut ostenderet

Ex altera parte in medio

| 134 | 116 | Summa anglicana asshynden in astrologiam 2 fo iungatur aliquibus |
| **1023** | 117 | Item lincolniensis super libros posteriorum 2 fo per [d]iffe[rencias] |

. . . . .

Item subtus

| **1024** | 118 | Valerius maximus 2 fo vs celius |

Subtus

| *182 | 119 | Virgilius 2 fo assidue |
| ***1025** | 120 | Item liber tragediarum senece 2 fo qui vicit |

In superiori parte librarie in medio sunt duo principales libri theologie

| 28 | 121 | Biblia 2 fo ba. de |
| 36 | 122 | Item Gorram super euangelia 2 fo cristi scilicet |

Additions to List XIII[1]

124–41, additions to Desks 1, 4, 5, 6, are grouped together in the blank space on f. 2ᵛ, col. 2. The rest are additions to the desk lists, ff. 1ᵛ–2ᵛ. 123 makes a third book on the desk 'in medio'.

1026	124	In primo desco Vita iesu 2 fo et completa
1027	125	Item exposiciones super euangelia 2 fo in tabula sinite
***1028**	126	In 4ᵗᵒ dexto Quolibeta sancti thome 2 fo in tabula sanctorum (altered in another hand to brutorum)
1029	127	Item secunda secunde ⎱ 2 fo vt augustinus
		⎰ sancti thome
***1030**	128	Item prima pars secunde ⎰ 2 fo principium
1031	129	Item communis glosa super epistolas pauli 2 fo de fide
***1032**	130	In 5ᵗᵒ dexto Richardus de mediauilla super 4ᵐ sentenciarum 2 fo [An] aqua paludosa
1033–5	131–3	[Item vincentius] 3ᵇᵘˢ voluminibus 2 fo primi [. . . 2 fo secundi [. . . .] gesimus 2 fo tercii [. . .

[1] 50 is another addition which should have been included here.

1036	134	Item doctor subtilis super 3° [. . . . .] 2 fo r[. . .
*1037	135	Iohannes Andree episcopi 2 fo in tabula de Collectis
1038–41	136–9	In 6to dexto 4^{or} volumina alexandri halys
		2 fo primi a spiritu
		2 fo 2^{i} in tabula questio 8^{a}
		2 fo 3^{i} in tabula primo queritur
		2 fo 4^{i} in tabula queritur
*1042	140	Item sermones leonardi de vtino 2 fo [inconu]enienter
*1043	141	Item franciscus petrarcha de Remediis [vtriusque fortune] 2 fo contra omnes
61	29	Item Exposicio iob 2 fo Exquirentes
1043a	33a	Exposicio Io Chrisostomi super Iohannem 2 fo animarum
566	53a	[. . . .] super Sent' 2 fo oris
1044	97	Item Egidius 2 fo licet
1045	99	Item burleus super phisica 2 fo racionem
1046	100	Item Gabriel super metaphisicam 2 fo oritur
1047	123	Item vitas patrum 2 fo in tabula defunctorum

LIST XIV

1048–76 from the Vellum Inventory, ff. 23^{v}–24 (three columns). The third list of books on the theology side of the library is written in a small clear skilful hand with humanistic touches, for example now and then upright *d* and the hat-like mark of abbreviation (⌒). 14 lines take up 50 mm. 178 original entries can still be read or read in part. Perhaps some sixty in all have gone, or thirty in each of the two gaps.

This list probably contained very few books not recorded in List XIII and the additions to List XIII. Of the two surviving books not found in earlier lists **1057** came from Goldwell and **1067** from Richard Topcliffe.

There are only six additions, **1071–6**. The three survivors among them were all Goldwell's.

(f. 23^{v}, col. 1)

Hii libri Subscripti continentur in Bibliotheca Collegii animarum Oxon'. In Theologia et artibus

In primis in Superiori parte primi dextus

554	1	Biblia 2 fo iezraell'
988	2	Item glosa super prologus beati Ieronimi in Bibliam 2 fo numero sub

In media parte eiusdem dextus

96	3	Concordancie 2 fo sicut vestimentum
32	4	Item 3^{m} volumen lire 2 fo pronunciata

| 990 | 5 | Item 5^m volumen lire 2 fo fficaciter |
| 1026 | 6 | Item vita Iesu 2 fo et completa |

In inferiori parte eiusdem dexti

34	7	4^m volumen lire 2 fo non est in eo
991	8	Item 6^m volumen 2 fo secundum carnem
31	9	Item primum volumen 2 fo liber
989	10	Item 2^m volumen 2 fo dati cum dicitur
992	11	Item Gorran super epistolas pauli 2 fo vsque ad

Item subtus eodem dextu

553	12	Biblia anglicana 2 fo In þe begynnyng
1027	13	Item Exposicio super euangelia 2 fo in tabula Sinite
994	14	Item lyra super Iohannem lucam marcum et matheum 2 fo autem invenitur
42	15	Item Hugo de Venna super apocalipsim 2 fo In prima

In superiori secundi dextus parte

*555	16	prima pars biblie 2 fo sciencie dei
*556	17	Item 2^a pars biblie 2 fo vir ille
995	18	Item Holcot super sapiens' 2 fo tare et
*996	19	Item Hugo de sancto victore 2 fo rum

Item in media parte istius dexti

12	20	De quadruplici sensu sancte scripture 2 fo Hebreis
997	21	Item Prosper de vita contemplatiua 2 fo inde tacere
37	22	Item liber de figuris biblie moralizate 2 fo et finaliter
558	23	Item sermones Repyngton' 2 fo est colligacio
*557	24	Item Hugo de Venna super lucam et Iohannem 2 fo ad eam

Ex altera parte eiusdem dextus in superiori parte 2 fo (blank) Hanc scribis[1]

| 48 | 25 | Item 2^a pars quinquagene agustini 2 fo Si vixit |
| 1048 | 26 | Item diuersa opera augustini 2 fo de rebus |

In media parte

1049	27	Augustinus de ciuitate 2 fo disputacio
50	28	Item Augustinus de ciuitate dei 2 fo De pudore
1050	29	Item Claudianus de statu anime 2 fo riora in tabula
25	30	Item Enchiridion Augustini 2 fo minus colendum
1051	31	Item prima pars quinquagene Augustini 2 fo nobis
49	32	Item milleloquium Augustini 2 fo De trinitate

[1] Usually the scribe fitted in the first title of each section after the heading referring to the desk. Here there was not room for a title. He wrote '2 fo' without thinking and then left a blank space. 'Hanc scribis' is in rather larger and perhaps later writing.

In inferiori parte eiusdem dextus

| 562 | 33 | Augustinus de spiritu et anima 2 fo quibus omnia |
| 51 | 34 | Item Augustinus de verbis domini 2 fo sermo eiusdem |

Item subtus eodem dextu

21	35	Innocencius de pontific' et sacerdotal' officio 2 fo domine leuite
39	36	Item Bonaventura super lucam et Iohannem 2 fo non aliorum
561	37	Item Augustinus de caritate 2 fo pergebat
53	38	Item Augustinus de ciuitate dei 2 fo scriptura diuina
26	39	Item Casterdon' super apocalipsim 2 fo vero quod accidit
563	40	Item Augustinus de correpcione et gracia 2 fo dicere
559	41	Item Baconthorp' super libros augustini de ciuitate 2 fo tunc ut dicit

In superiori parte [tercii] dextus

1043a	42	Exposicio crisostomi super Iohannem 2 fo animarum
60	43	Item Gregorius super Cantica canticorum 2 fo vocat
59	44	Item registrum sancti gregorii 2 fo patimur longius
998	45	Item statuta gregorii 2 fo leoni episcopo in tabula

In media parte eiusdem dextus

560	46	Destructorium viciorum 2 fo arrogancia in tabula
400	47	Item crisostomus in opere imperfecto 2 fo eius ostenderetur
1000	48	Item moralia gregorii 2 fo daniel vir in tabula
999	49	Item moralia gregorii 2 fo nam si in tabula

In inferiori parte eiusdem dextus

565	50	Exposicio ac moralizacio trenorum 2 fo signum exterminatum
63	51	Item moralia gregorii a xxi libro 2 fo illius
61	52	Item exposicio iob 2 fo exquirentes

Ex altera parte eiusdem dextus

1001	53	Diuersa opera Ieronimi 2 fo Ieronimus
58	54	Item exposicio Sancti Ieronimi super Marcum Euangelistam 2 fo Iacobus alter
1002	55	Item Commentariolus beati Ieronimi super psalterium 2 fo que sit via

In media parte eiusdem dexti

55	56	Sanctus Bernardus 2 fo congruum videatur
57	57	Item Epistola beati Ieronimi [contra] Rufinum hereticum 2 fo impietatis
*54	58	Item Bernardus super cantica canticorum 2 fo differenter
30	59	Item Histori[a scolastica] 2 fo festinans

*80   60   [Item . . . . 2] fo insuper
*38   60a   [Item . . . . 2] fo esse nemo

· · · · ·

(f. 23ᵛ, col. 2)

In media parte huius dextus[1]

1004   61   Liber Rabani de deo 2 fo incipit
1028   62   Item quodlibeta sancti thome 2 fo sanctorum
1053 63   Item Sanctus thomas super 3ᵐ sentenciarum 2 fo sed per
76   64   Item rabanus de mistica significacione rerum 2 fo arcium
1029   65   Item secunda secunde 2 fo ut augustinus
1005   66   Item ysodorus de summo bono 2 fo cut et reliqua
*19   67   Item ysodorus de ecclesiasticis officiis 2 fo carmine et

In inferiori parte istius dextus

82   68   Liber de Emendacione vite 2 fo cuncta que
67   69   Item dieta salutis 2 fo tamquam infideles
93   70   Item Brodwardyn' de causa dei contra pelagium 2 fo sit
                racione

Item subtus isto dextu

*75   71   Liber omeliarum eusebii emiseni 2 fo et amicus
*1030   72   Item prima pars secunde 2 fo principium
23   73   Item glosa Ieronimi super genesim 2 fo que nostra est
22   74   Item Stephanus archiepiscopus super librum regum 2 fo
                hebrei
1031   75   Item communis glosa super epistolas pauli 2 fo ex fide in
69   76   Item prima pars thome Walden de sacramentis 2 fo prologus
70   77   Item 2ᵃ pars thome Walden' 2 fo nephans perswasionis

In superiori parte 5ᵗⁱ dextus

566   79   Thomas super 4ᵐ sentenciarum 2 fo oris curacionis
*1007   80   Item scotus super 3ᵉˢ primos libros sentenciarum 2 fo rales
                que possunt
1006   81   Item Scotus super 4ᵐ sentenciarum 2 fo consequentis

In media parte huius dextus

1009   82   Hugo de Venna super magistrum sentenciarum 2 fo est de se
91   83   Item petrus de candia 2 fo causabunt
1008   84   Item liber questionum de Fycsshakre 2 fo quia iᵃ principia
13   85   Item Bonaventura super primum et 4ᵐ sentenciarum 2 fo
                enim est precipuus

In inferiori parte illius dextus

84   86   Textus magistri sentenciarum 2 fo an posse in tabula
11   87   Item thomas de cristiana religione 2 fo musicus

[1] This is Desk 4, part 2.

*1032 88 Item Ricardus de media villa super 4^m sentenciarum 2 fo An aqua in tabula

Ex altera parte eiusdem dextus

*567 89 Scotus super 4^m sentenciarum 2 fo et spes
1033 90 Item primum volumen vincencii 2 fo ta iam
1034 91 Item secundum volumen eiusdem 2 fo quadragesimo
1035 92 Item 3^m volumen 2 fo nominis sibi

Item media pars eiusdem

81 93 Quidam fidelis in librum florum 2 fo quia 3^{es}
79 94 Item petrus de aurora super bibliam in versibus 2 fo nam quasi
*73 95 Item Beda de gestis anglorum 2 fo quibusdam in

Item subtus isto dextu

1054 96 Sanctus thomas in prima parte theologie 2 fo cum falso (?)
110 97 Item horologium sapiencie sancti thome 2 fo libet preditus
88 98 Item 3^a pars summe sancti thome 2 fo necessarii sine
*86 99 Item 2^a pars summe sancti thome 2 fo mathematice quantitatis
*77 100 Item liber florum historiarum 2 fo quasi abrahei
71 101 Item liber sancte brigide 2 fo o vere
1055 102 Item formula viuendi 2 fo Item secundum
*1010 103 Item Iulius Solinus 2 fo vrbe roma
1056 104 Item Scotus super 4^m sentenciarum 2 fo vel altera
*20 105 Item eusebius cesariensis de ecclesiastica historia 2 fo de cruciatu
*74 106 Item malesbury de gestis anglorum 2 fo solent

In superiori parte 6^{ti} dextus

570 107 Tabula diuersorum operum 2 fo ascensus
569 108 Item liber sermonum 2 fo in operando
83 109 Item Iacobus Ianuensis in opere quadragesimali 2 fo debemus

In media parte eiusdem dextus

*1042 110 Sermones aurei leonardi 2 fo inconuenienter
*1037 111 Item liber I. Andree episcopi de testimoniis catholicorum 2 fo de collectis
384 112 Item tractatus Iuris ciuilis et canonici 2 fo dicitur esse in tabula
90 113 Item liber veritatis theologie 2 fo gregorius
66 114 Item Distincciones holcott 2 fo sapiens
1011 115 Item Dicta Lincolniensis 2 fo cuteret

In inferiori parte eiusdem dextus

568 116 Hamo super epistolas pauli 2 fo esse humilitatis

Ex altera parte eiusdem dextus

*1057	117	Lactancius de ira dei 2 fo habet
*1043	118	Item franciscus petrarcha de remediis vtriusque fortune 2 fo contra omnes

In media parte eiusdem

27	119	Burleus super libros ethicorum 2 fo ideo sub
*571	120	Item commentum Eustrachii super librum ethicorum 2 fo tum eius
1014	121	Item noua translacio Ethicorum 2 fo quidem et
418	122	Item lactancius de diuinis institucionibus 2 fo celeste pabulum

In inferiori parte eiusdem dextus

*574	123	Questionista super libros ethicorum 2 fo tristiciam
120	124	[. . . . .] ethicorum cum commento [. . .
470	125	Bartholomeus de proprietatibus rerum [. . .
1015	125a	[. . . . . v]ox clamantis [. . .
1038	125b	[. . . . . . . alex]andri de ales [. . .

. . . . .

(f. 24)

In septimi dextus superiori parte

1046	126	In primis Gabriell' super questiones metaphisice 2 fo oritur
1058	127	Item textus philosophie naturalis 2 fo nec leuia
1059	128	Item paulus de venetiis super philosophiam naturalem 2 fo licet fit

In media parte eiusdem

1060	129	Sanctus thomas in diuersa opera 2 fo tradit
575	130	Item commentator in phisicis 2 fo diffinicio vero

In inferiori parte eiusdem

171	131	Egidius de celo et mundo 2 fo seu dimensio
1061	132	Item I. Canonicus 2 fo communia (?) tenet (?)
*121	133	Item burleus super libros phisicorum 2 fo philosophus 3°
*124	134	Item questiones M' Scharp super libros phisicorum 2 fo sine illis
576	135	Item albertus de natura et origine anime 2 fo tatem

Ex altera parte eiusdem dextus

*1016	135	Questionista super paruis naturalibus 2 fo eleuantur
1018	137	Item canonicus super libros phisicorum 2 fo vtrum in quolibet

In media parte eiusdem

123	138	Albertus super diuersa opera 2 fo carnem et
1020	139	Item liber ruralium 2 fo de lenticula
*135	140	Item liber Tholomei 2 fo tatur genus
379	141	Item liber de aspectubus 2 fo libet et

In inferiori parte eiusdem dextus

*572	142	Exposicio super musicam boecii 2 fo vt in epistola
1019	143	Item questionista super metaphisica 2 fo in eo quod quid
1021	144	Item albertus super diuersos libros philosophie naturalis 2 fo et nigram

Subtus isto dextu

577	145	Egidius de anima 2 fo illam rursus
189	146	Item albertus de animalibus 2 fo separatur ex
183	147	Item arismetrica boecii 2 fo que quia

In superiori parte 8^{ui} dextus

185	148	Aggregatorium geomancie 2 fo globo
163	149	Item Theorica planetarum 2 fo sequitur de
139	150	Item theorica M' Campani 2 fo me^{ta} habetur
132	151	Item quatripartitum tholomei 2 fo et potest homo

In media parte eiusdem dextus

130	152	Algorismus 2 fo 4^{or} cicli
583	153	Item Epilogus mappe mundi 2 fo vero numero
*128	154	Item liber de naturis planetarum 2 fo mutacionem
581	155	Item tholomeus in almagesti 2 fo signorum

In inferiori parte eiusdem

| 133 | 156 | Abraham de natiuitatibus 2 fo Et si ad |

Ex altera parte eiusdem dextus

| 134 | 157 | Summa iudicialis de accidentibus mundi 2 fo iungatur |
| 1023 | 158 | Item lincolniensis super libros posteriorum 2 fo per differencias |

In media parte eiusdem

1062	159	Burleus super veterem logicam 2 fo tudinem ad
1063	160	Item scotus super predicamenta 2 fo conceptubus
578	161	Item Boecius in logica 2 fo res subiectas
187	162	Item textus logice 2 fo proprium ut
1064	163	Item boecius de consolacione philosophie 2 fo luminibus
579	164	Item boecius super logicam 2 fo esse uolubile
131	165	Item liber de commendacione Antiquorum 2 fo et scientes
129	166	Item introductorius in astrologiam 2 fo les ut

In superiori parte ultimi dextus

1065	167	Epistole francisci philelfi 2 fo sus vel
1066	168	Item titus liuius 2 fo romanorum
*__1067__	171	Item plautus 2 fo dampna(n)das
1068	172	Item macrobius de sompno scipionis in satur' 2 fo punctum eius

In media parte eiusdem dextus

94	173	Catholicon 2 fo numquam in
1069	174	Item margarita poetica 2 fo epistolis in tabula
1070	175	Item liber metamorphoseos 2 fo redegi

In inferiori parte eiusdem

| *182 | 176 | Liber 2 fo assidue |

Subtus isto dextu

| *1025 | 177 | Tragedie x senece 2 fo qui vicit |
| 1024 | 178 | Item valerius maximus ad Tiberium cesarem 2 fo vs celius |

Additions to List XIV

Additions to the list of books on the upper part of Desk 5 (78), on the upper part of Desk 9 (169–70), and 'subtus' on Desk 9 (179–81).

1071	78	Thomas super 4ᵐ sentenciarum 2 fo et sanctitatem
1072–3	169–70	(*Livy*) in duobus voluminibus
		2 fo primi flumine
		(–2ⁱ) 2 fo vel Roris
*__1074__	179	Item Suetonius 2 (fo) specie in textu
*__1075__	180	Item Petrus candidus de ciuilibus bellis 2 fo Et que
*__1076__	181	Item Laurentius Valla 2 fo huius rei

LIST XV

1077–1125 from the Vellum Inventory, ff. 27–8 (four columns). The fourth list of books on the theology side of the library was written by two scribes, both rather illiterate and the first a poor writer who gave up after no. 10: about nine lines take up 50 mm. The list was probably made to take account of some shifting of books from the law side of the library to the theology side and vice versa. One hundred and sixty-five original entries can still be read or read in part. Perhaps about 36 titles in all have been lost, or 12 in each of the three gaps. Of nineteen books not recorded in earlier lists three survive, all gifts of Goldwell.

The additions, **1097–1125**, include a gift from Nicholas Hals-well, †1528 (**1097–8**), and a Bible printed in 1506–8 (**1107–12**). Also here are the three books chosen for the chained library from the ninety-one given by Archbishop Warham (**651, 677, 698**).

(f. 27)

Subscripti libri continentur In Biblioteca Collegii Animarum ex parte Teologorum et Arcistarum

In primis in medio Bibliotece in dextu indifferenti

28	1	Epistole diui Ieronimi ad Paulinum 2 fo Ba dei cogi
36	2	Item Gorram super Euangelia 2 fo cristi scilicet per

A latere siue parte theologie in superiori dextu supra

554	3	Textus Biblie 2 fo Ierraell'
96	4	Item Concordancie sancti Iacobi 2 fo sicut vestimentum
1026	5	Item Vita Iesu 2 fo et completa
1047	6	Item Ieronimus in libros vitas Patrum 2 fo duxisset ve: in textu
992	7	Item Gorram super epistolas Pauli 2 fo vsque ad extremum 'nunc est in secundo dextu'
991	8	Item Nicholaus de Lira in vi^{to} volumine 2 fo secundum carnem

In media parte eiusdem dextus vt infra

31	9	In primis primum volumen lire 2 fo liber et
1077	10	Item liber sancte Marie de byldewas 2 fo accessibilis est Regiam suscepit
42	11	Item Hugo de Wenna super Apocalypsym 2 fo In prima et tanguntur
34	12	Item liber Ysaie ceterorumque prophetarum de biblia 2 fo Non est in eo sanitas
989	13	Item postylla magistri Nicholai de lyra 2 fo dati cum dicitur
32	14	Item liber Esdrye ceterorumque prophetarum 2 fo pronunciata ante tempus
990	15	Item liber 4^{or} Evangelistarum 2 fo ficaciter inducit
553	16	Item byblya in Anglico sermone 2 fo Cayn and to hys (*entry lined through*)
994	17	Item lyra super 4^{or} Euangelistas 2 fo autem inuenitur
988	18	Item Exposicio prologorum Magistri Nicholai de lyra 2 fo mouetur sub metaphora
37	19	'Item figure biblie 2 fo finaliter'

12 prophetarum] MS. prophetatarum   19 Cf. 25

In 2° dexto

*555	20	prima pars biblie 2 fo sciencie dei absconditi
*556	21	Item 2ª pars 2 fo vir ille
*557	22	Item hugo de Wenna super lucam et Iohannem 2 fo ad eam zacha
26	23	Item Costasay super Apocalysys 2 fo vero quod accidit
12	24	Item liber de 4to sensu 2 fo hebreis in flu
37	25	Item liber de figuris biblie moralizatus 2 fo et finaliter (entry lined through)
*996	26	Item hugo de sancto victore super Ecclesiasten 2 fo rum ad
995	27	Item holcot super sapientiem (sic) 2 fo tare et in textu
558	28	Item sermones kepynton 2 fo est colligatio
39	29	Item bonaventurus super lucam et Iohanem 2 fo non aliorum
997	30	Item prosper de vita contemplatiua 2 fo inde tacere

In alia parte eiusdem

1078	31	Aurelius Augustinus de anime quantitate 2 fo [. . .
1079	32	Item Augustinus de trinitate [. . .
50 or 53	33	Item Augustinus de ciuitate dei [. . .
1080	34	Item Epistole Augustini ad Valensarum [. . .
48	35	Item Augustinus super psalmo octogesimo [. . .
1048	36	Item Augustinus de doctrina cristiana [. . .
563	37	Item Augustinus de correptione ac [gracia . . .

. . . . .

(f. 27ᵛ, col. 1)[1]

61	38	Moralia beati Gregorii 2 fo exquirentes
1082	39	Hugo in didascolon 2 fo dicam que
62	40	Moralia gregorii 2 fo mescit
1083	41	E(x)posicio fratris Iohannis Morawzaus 2 fo corpus
560	42	Destructorium viciorum 2 fo arrogantiam in ta
565	43	Exposicio ac moralizatio tercii capituli terrenorum Ieremie 2 fo signum exterminatum

In alia parte

56	44	Liber historiarum 2 fo vincit pudor
57	45	Pammachius 2 fo impietatis
58	46	Exposicio Ieronimi super Matheum 2 fo Iacobus
*54	47	Liber beati barnardi abbatis in cantica canticorum 2 fo differenter
*1084	48	Auctoritates exposite super pantheologia genesi 2 fo Non loqueris
1002	49	Come(n)tariolus beati Ieronimi super salterium 2 fo Quare fremuerunt Que sit via
1085	50	Quatuor Euangelia glosata 2 fo Abraam

[1] Books in Desk 3.

55	51	Barnardus super missus est 2 fo congruum
*1086	52	Item liber pantheologie 2 fo latrones
*1087	53	Item pantheologia 2 fo cuius racio
80	54	Cato moralizatus 2 fo Insuper
30	55	Historia scolastica 2 fo festinans
47	56	Liber vtilis 2 fo 2^m cum queritur

In 4

*35	57	Exposicio super genesin 2 fo videt hic
22	58	Stefanus Archepiscopus super librum regum 2 fo ebrei
*43	59	Exposicio radulphi monachi super leuiticum 2 fo loquente
44	60	Phalterium glosatum 2 fo tulus non
18	61	Diuersa opera diui Anselmi 2 fo cum igitur
40	62	Communis glosa super xii prophetas 2 fo Annis
46	63	Exposicio vernans super salterium 2 fo In hebreo dicitur
23	64	Glosa super genesi 2 fo que nostra est
69	65	Walden de sacramentis 2 fo nostre patrone
41	66	Communis glosa super ysaiam 2 fo 'ergo' prudens
45	67	Phalterium glosatum 2 fo Itaque veterem
*14	68	Liber Iob glosatus 2 fo omni genere
380	69	[. . . .]leston super phalterium 2 fo ad litteram
1088	70	Parabole salamonis 2 fo 'domino' sunt timoris domini
*1030	71	Prima pars secunde fratris thome de aquino 2 fo principium
1029	72	2^a 2^e 2 fo vt augustinus
76	73	[. . . . . . .] 2 fo artium
	74	[. . . . . 2 fo . . . . .] in tabula

. . . . .

(f. 27^v, col. 2)[1]

1033	75	Speculum historiarum 2 fo ta iam vero
1034	76	Tercia pars speculum historiale 2 fo xlv^s filius
1035	77	Quarta et vltima pars speculum historiale 2 fo nominis sibi
110	78	Horalogium sapientie 2 fo libus predictus
*567	79	Iohannis scotus in 4^{tum} librum sentenciarum 2 fo et spes
11	80	Thomas de cristiana religione 2 fo musicus accipit
1089	81	Conflatus francisci de maronis super 1^m sentenciarum 2 fo quia in
1036	82	Doctor subtilis super 4^m et 3^m sentenciarum 2 fo raciones spirituales
81	83	Liber florum de deo fo 2 quia tres
1090	84	Prima pars summe Magistri henrici de gandauo
79	85	Petrus de aurora 2 fo Nam quasi
1056	86	Doctor subtilis super 4^m sentenciarum fo 2 vel altera
1091	87	Liber de fide et eius obiecto 2 fo signorum vel propter
1055	88	Liber de humilitate 2 fo Item secundum eundem

[1] Books in Desk 5.

In 6° dextu

1011	89	Liber qui incipit Amor multiplicatur 2 fo cuteret
66	90	Liber qui incipit Abhominabitur 2 fo sapiens
568	91	Tractatus hamonis super epistolas 2 fo esse humanitatis
569	92	Liber sermonum super epistolas et Euangelias dominicales 2 fo In operando
570	93	Tabula super flores barnardi 2 fo ascensus est
384	94	Liber in quo continetur tractatus iuris ciuilis et canonici fratris Iohannis de bromyard 2 fo dicitur esse in sanguine
*20	96	Liber Euseybei in eccl(es)iastica historia 2 fo de cruciatibus
1012	97	Liber super epistolas sermones et super Euangeliam parisiensis 2 fo caritas in ta
78	98	Flores theologie 2 fo sionis culpe
90	99	Liber de natura diui(ni)tatis 2 fo gregorius
1041	100	Quarta pars alexandri de ales theologorum monarchie 2 fo sexto queritur
*1042	101	Sermones auree de sanctis fratris leonardi de vtino 2 fo inconuenienter
1038	102	Prima pars summe theoloice Alexandri 2 fo a spiritu sancto
1040	103	3ª pars Alexandri 2 fo primo queritur in ta

In alia parte

27	104	Burleus super libros Ethicorum 2 fo ideo sub doctrina
104	105	Liber de remediis vtriusque fortune 2 fo quia videatur
*1013	106	Liber de regimine principum 2 fo Cum omnis doctrina
1039	107	Liber 2ᵉ partis summe Alexandri 2 fo Questio octaua in ta
*1043	108	Franciscus patriarcha poeta laureatus de remediis vtriusque fortune 2 fo contra omnes
72	109	Tractatus de virtutibus 2 fo sobrietatis
*1037	110	Testimonia excepta de libris chatholicorum patrum a leone papa collecta 2 fo de collectis et
*574	111	Dedicus in libros Ethicorum 2 fo tristiciam
*571	112	Textus Ethicorum cum commento 2 fo tum eius
120	113	Textus Ethicorum cum commento 2 fo igitur eruditus in textu
1014	114	Aristotiles in libros Ethecorum 2 fo quidem et therecum
418	115	Firmiani lactancii diuinarum institucionum aduersus gentiles 2 fo celest'
470	116	Bartholomeus de proprietatibus rerum 2 fo nes quia
*1057	117	Tractatus de ira dei 2 fo habet quod figuram
*1015	118	Iohannes gower 2 fo hic corripit f[. . . .]am

In 7° dextu

576	119	Albertus super libros de anima 2 fo tatem[. . .

110 excepta] MS. expecta

189	120	Aristoteles de animalibus 2 fo separatur ex
575	121	Auarois 2 fo diffinicio
172	122	Libellus de ortu scienciarum 2 fo [. . .
1092	123	[. . . .] Aristotelis 2 fo [. . .
		. . . . .

(f. 28)

In 8° dextu

132	124	Liber astronomie 2 fo et potest homo
139	125	Scriptum super algomasti tholomei 2 fo meto habetur
163	126	Theorica planetarum 2 fo sequitur de tribus
583	127	Cardinalis cameracensis 2 fo vero numero
1093	128	Algarismus 2 fo et duo inst
532	129	Alius liber qui incipit In primis deo gracias 2 fo que proueniunt
1022	130	Scripta diui Iohannis de spira 2 fo et tunc nichil
133	131	Abraam Auenofre de elecionibus 2 fo et si ad
*128	132	Liber de naturis planetarum 2 fo mutacionem
581	133	Almegesti tholomei 2 fo signorum
131	134	Theorica planetarum 2 fo et scientes
129	135	Introductorius Cosme Alexandrini in astrologiam 2 fo les ut
185	136	Compilatorium tocius artis Geometrice 2 fo globo
1262	137	Practica que vocatur lilium 2 fo rat nisi

In alia parte

134	138	Summa iudicialis de accidentibus mundi 2 fo iungatur aliquibus
1264	139	Ysagoge Iohannicii 2 fo nenti
143	140	Auicenna 2 fo capitulum xxv in ta
584	141	Ysagoge Iohannicii ad segni (sic) Galien 2 fo hii vel quia populum
*142	142	Liber morborum 2 fo ciam et accensionem
1023	143	Lyncolniensis in libros posteriorum 2 fo per differencias
579	144	Topica boecii 2 fo esse volubile
1062	145	Burleus super porphurium 2 fo tudinem ad
1063	146	Scotus super vniuersalibus et predicamentis 2 fo conceptibus
578	147	Commentum boetii super porphurium 2 fo res subtus
187	148	Textus porphurii 2 fo proprium
1064	149	Boecius de consolatione philosophie 2 fo luminibus quia
1094	150	Aueroys in librum porphurii 2 fo accidentalis
1095	151	Iohannes de lapide super librum porphurii 2 fo igitur non

In 9° dextu

*147	152	Liber Isac 2 fo nisi discretio
141	153	Almasorius 2 fo receptacula

*140	154	Anchidotarium Nicholai 2 fo q.s. detur
*531	155	Liber de medicinis 2 fo addatur
*1266	156	Opus bartholomei montegani 2 fo C. de frigiditate cerabri
1265	157	Liber canonis 2 fo Capitulum xiii 'ipsum aut'
1263	158	Liber Amphorismorum Iohanni Damasci 2 fo aut sanguine
*146	159	Ysagoge Iohannicii tegni Galieni 2 fo recedit
*535	160	Anathomia henrici de amanda villa 2 fo ossa plurima
*145	161	Rosa medicine 2 fo sanguine exibunt
*537	162	Liber amphorismorum 2 fo de natura morbi est
*530	163	Item alius liber incipiens Capud 2 fo visus debilitas
536	164	Item liber incipiens Galienus 2 fo bitur in qualitate in tex
534	165	Item viaticus 2 fo admisceamus in tex
*585	166	Egidius de vrinis 2 fo subpallidus
		Finis tabule

Additions to List XV

95 is an addition to the list of books in Desk 6. 167–200 are grouped together on f. 28, col. 2, the first seven in one good hand and the rest in another hand. They are additions to Desks 1 (179–86), 2 (187–200), perhaps 4 (174–8), 7 (169–73), and no doubt 9 (167–8).

1096	95	Item liber 2 fo offend'
*1097	167	Item prima pars rasis 2 fo dum et dixit in textu
*1098	168	Item 2ª pars 2 fo Eas

In 7° dextu

1099	169	Argiropolus 2 fo quis vtuntur
1100	170	Tartaretus 2 fo Quod per se
1101	171	Commentator 2 fo Nomen significat
1102	172	Canonicus 2 fo secundus punctus 'deest'
*1103	173	bessarion aduersus calumniatores platonis

In prima parte d'

*1104	174	Opera antonini quatuor voluminibus 2 fo 1 accusatione
*1104a	175	2 fo 2 clesia
*1105	176	2 fo 3 abel quam
1105a	177	2 fo 4 do quia
1106	178	Thomas de yermonthe fo 2 per ad
*1107-12	179–84	Lyra in sex voluminibus impressis ⎫
*677	185	Arretius felinus super psalterium ⎬ In prima classe
*651	186	Biblia ex translacione pagnini ⎭

In 2º dextu ʿin secunda parteʹ

1113	187	Annotaçio 3ª quinquagena ʿAugustiniʹ 2 fo [nia]mus
1114	188	Sermones Augustini 2 fo in tabula adire
1115	189	Augustinus de ciuitate dei cum comment' 2 fo in textu custodibus
1116	190	Augustinus ad romanos 2 fo apostoli
1117	191	Augustini prima quinquagena 2 fo illius
1118	192	2ª quinquagena augustini 2 fo transactum
698	193	6ª pars Augustini 2 fo qua propter

In secundo dextu in prima parte

* **1119–25** 194–200   Hugo cardi[nalis in septem] voluminibus

LIST XVI

1126–1205 from the Vellum Inventory, ff. 32ᵛ–34ᵛ (five columns), and Misc. 230. The fifth list of books on the theology side of the library is written in a current, spreading, and widely spaced hand: seven lines take up 50 mm. The list was made to take account of the books bought by the college in 1544–5. One hundred and twenty-four original entries can still be read or read in part. Perhaps about sixty have been lost, or twelve in each of the five gaps. Most of the losses can be supplied from the hasty and incomplete copy of List XVI made in 1556 to satisfy the Marian Commissioners (Misc. 230).[1] In all, this 1556 list records forty-seven volumes the titles of which are not now to be read in the Vellum Inventory.[2]

Fifty-nine of the seventy-six volumes not recorded in previous lists survive. 1544 is the latest date of printing (**1132**). Entries in the main hand include **1146–8**, bought in 1547–8, but not **1202–4** bought in 1549–50.

---

[1] 'An Inventorye of all the goodes, plate, iewels, money, ornamentę of the churche bookes in the librarie and other stuffe els where wᵗʰin the precincte of yᵉ colledge of Alsowles in Oxford wᵗʰ the Abridgement of the farmes and valew therof etc'. made Anno domini 1556. the xviij day of August, and presentyd yᵉ same yere and day to my lord Legates visitors.' I only got to know of Misc. 230 after I had assigned running numbers and list numbers. To prevent a tiresome amount of alteration **1138a–j, 1141a–d, 1149a, b,** and **1180a** were intercalated and **1206–13, 1228, 1236, 1240** became vacant. 24 a–j, 61 a–l, 93 a–g, 123 a–i, 153 a–i are derived from Misc. 230.

[2] The copyist omitted many of the older books: for example, of nos. 35–60 he records only 36, 37, 44, 51–3, 56–8.

The additions, **1181–1205**, were mainly the gifts of Sir John Mason. Twenty-two of them survive. Only **1181** occurs in Misc. 230.

(f. 32ᵛ)

Libri contenti in bibliotheca collegii animarum ex parte theologie et artium

In dextu indeferenti

| *555 | 1 | Prima pars biblie 2 fo scientie dei |
| *556 | 2 | Secuda pars biblie 2 fo vir ille |

In primo dextu superiore

*1126	3	Biblia roberti stephani 2 fo robertus stephanus
*1107	4	Lyra in 6 voluminibus 2 fo primi quia sunt multi
*1108	5	2 fo 2ⁱ incipit expositio
*1109	6	2 fo 3ⁱ devoti fratres
*1110	7	2 fo 4ⁱ hieronimus
*1111	8	2 fo 5ⁱ incipit prefatio venerabilis
*1112	9	2 fo 6ⁱ incipit prefatio sancti

In prima parte secundi dextus

*677	11	Felinus super spalmos 2 fo clarissimo
*1127	12	Chrisostomus in quinque voluminibus 2 fo 1ⁱ in textu vocarunt
*1128	13	2 fo 2ⁱ omnino
*1129	14	2 fo 3ⁱ turpissime
*1130	15	2 fo 4ⁱ gratiam
*1131	16	2 fo 5ⁱ de timothei
*1132	17	Epiphanius 2 fo in textu nes sumus 'idololatria
*651	18	Biblia pagnini 2 fo dilecti

In secunda parte eiusdem

*1133	19	Opera Tertulliani in vno volu. 2 fo beatus
*1134	20	Opera Eusebii 2 fo in textu ipsius
*1135	21	Ireneus 2 fo in textu tus est
*1136	22	Iosephus 2 fo in textu enim virtutis
*1137	23	[Origines in 2 voluminibus] 2 fo 1ⁱ in ditione
*1138	24	2 fo 2ⁱ [. . .

·   ·   ·   ·   ·

(Inventory of 1556)

| *1138a, b | 24a, b | Ambrosii duo volumina |
| *1138 c–j | 24 c–j | Augustinus in 8 volum. |

(f. 33)

In secunda parte eiusdem[1]

1139	35	Sermones augustini 2 fo peccatores[2]
55	36	Bernardus 2 fo congruum
*996	37	Hugo de sancto victore 2 fo rum admonet
698	38	Sexta pars augustini 2 fo argumentum[2]
*38	39	Thomas super lucam etc' 2 fo esse nemo
*54	40	Barnardus in canticis 2 fo differenter
1140	41	Augustinus ad inquisitiones 2 fo mortui sumus[2]
1048	42	Augustinus de doctrina 2 fo de rebus[2]
79	43	Biblia in carmine 2 fo nam quasi de petra 'iste liber reponitur in 2ᵃ parte 2ⁱ dextus'
*35	44	Isidorus super pentateuchum 2 fo videt
565	45	Opus trenorum 2 fo signum
45	46	Liber in spalmos 2 fo itaque
1141	47	Hugo 2 fo dicant
400	48	Epistole augustini ad Iulianum 2 fo eius ostenderetur[2]
41	49	super esaiam 2 fo ergo prudens
44	50	spalterium glosatum 2 fo tulus non

In prima parte quarti dextus

*59	51	Registrum gregorii 2 fo patimur
60	52	Gregorius in canticis 2 fo vocat
1000	53	Moralia gregorii 2 fo daniel 'in tabula
998	54	Statuta gregorii 2 fo leoni 'in tabula'
999	55	Expositio iob 2 fo nam si illatas
*1104	56	Prima pars antonini 2 fo accusatione
*1104a	57	2ᵃ 2 fo clesia
*1105	58	3ᵃ 2 fo abel
70	59	Walden 2 fo prologus adventum
69	60	Walden 2 fo ab nostre

In secunda parte eiusdem

| *1119 | 61 | Hugonis primum volumen |

. . . . .

(Inventory of 1556)

*1119–25	61, 61a–f	Hugonis vii volum.
1141a, b	61g, h	Thomas Aquinas in 2 partibus
*75	61i	Omelia Eusebii

[1] This is Desk 3.

[2] 35, 38, 41–2, 48 are marked with a cross and are presumably the books referred to in a note in the margin, 'Pro istis quinque et pro alio sexto libro 2 fo imus colendum (**25**) substitutus est hieronimus supradictus'. For this Jerome see the additions to List XVI, below. It is presumably **1214–18** which came in 1558–9.

1141c	61j	Opera Anselmi
*43	61k	Expositio Rodolphi
1141d	61l	Liber sermonum polton

(Vellum Inventory, f. 33ᵛ)

In secunda prima parte quinti dextus

1005	62	Isidorus de summo bono 2 fo cut
*19	63	Isidorus de ecclesiastic' 2 fo carmine
*86	64	Secunda pars Thome 2 fo mathematice
*1042	65	Sermones auree 2 fo inconvenienter
*1086	66	Panthologia 2 fo latrones
*1084	67	Panthologia 2 fo non loqueris
*1087	68	Panthologia 2 fo cuius ratio
1006	69	Ioannes dvns 2 fo consequentis
*1007	70	Ioannes dvns 2 fo rales

In secunda parte eiusdem

1142	71	Aetius 2 fo amplissimis
*1143	72	Antonius musa super aphorismos 2 fo ad serenissimum
*1144	73	Epistole manardi 2 fo reverendissimo
*1145	74	Vesalius de humani corporis fabrica 2 fo ad diuum 'Iste est translatus in sextum'
*1146	75	Galenus grece primum volumen 2 fo de galeni
*1147	76	2ᵐ volumen 2 fo hippocrates typographi
*1148	77	3ᵐ volumen 2 fo plerisque
*531	82	Liber chirurgicus 2 fo addatur
*585	83	Aegidius de vrinis 2 fo subpallidus
1263	84	Aphorismi damasceni 2 fo aut sanguine
1149	85	[. . . .] ius 2 fo cvm aneto (?) 'hic non reperiebatur anno 1550'
1262	86	[. . . .] us 2 fo rat nisi
*145	87	Rosa medicine 2 fo primo 'non repertus anno 155[.]'
1264	90	Ioanitii 2 fo venti
*147	91	[. . . . .] 2 fo [ni]si [. . .
*530	92	[. . . . . .] 2 fo visus
*537	93	[. . . . .] 2 fo de natur[a . . .

. . . . . .

(Inventory of 1556)

534	93a	Constantinus super Apho. Hipp.
532	93b	Avicenna
*1097–8	93c, d	Rasis in 2 partibus
*1149a	93e	Dioscorides
*1149b	93f	Ruellius
1296	93g	Plinius de historia

(Vellum Inventory, f. 34)

In secunda parte eiusdem[1]

*1150	94	Ioannes grammaticus super posteriora 2 fo τέχνον
*1151	95	Ioannes grammaticus super priora 2 fo τὸ περὶ πρότερον
*1152	96	Ioannes grammaticus super libros de anima 2 fo λέγω
*1153	97	Alexander aphrodiseus questiones 2 fo ἦ γῆ
*1154	98	Ioannes grammaticus super libros de generatione 2 fo ἦ ἀὴρ
*1155	99	Ioannes grammaticus super libros physicorum 2 fo σκέναται
*1156	100	Aristoteles latine primum volumen 2 fo de vita
*1157	101	secundum volumen 2 fo clarissimo
*1158	102	Aristo(te)les grece primum volumen 2 fo ἀλέξανδροσ 'iam est in septimo dextu'
*1159	103	2ᵐ volumen 2 fo καστον ἄρα
*1160	104	3ᵐ 2 fo βασιλεύς
*1161	105	4ᵐ 2 fo αἰτίαι
*1162	106	5ᵐ 2 fo δεχαστα 'iam est in septimo dextu'
*1163	108	Theophrastus 2 fo σχήματι 'iam est in septimo dextu'
*1013	109	Regimen principum 2 fo cum omnis
*574	110	Dedecus in libros ethicorum 2 fo tristicia
*571	111	Eustrathius latine super ethica 2 fo tum eius
*572	112	Liber incipiens in nomine sanctę 2 fo ut in epistola
1164	113	Euclides latine

In prima parte septimi dextus

*1164	116	Euclides 2 fo philippus
*1165	117	Alexander aphrodiseus super topica etc' 2 fo κειμένων
*1166	118	Simplicius super libros de celo 2 fo περὶ οὐρανοῦ
*1167	119	Simplicius super libros de anima et 'michael ephesius in' parva naturalia 2 fo τῶν [. . .
1168	120	Plato grece primum volumen 2 fo [. . .
1169	121	2ᵐ volumen 2 fo ἑαυτῷ
*1170	122	Paulus 'de' venetiis 2 fo [. . .
575	122a	Averrois 2° fo [. . .

· · · · · ·

(Inventory of 1556)

*1170a	123a	Pla. latine
1062	123b	Burleus in porphir.
*1043	123c	Franciscus petrarch.
1170b	123d	Geographia Ptolo.
581	123e	Almagest Ptolo.
*1170c, d	123f, g	Sabellicus in 2 volum.
*1359	123h	Quintil. cum comment.
1064	123i	Boetius

[1] This is Desk 6.

(Vellum Inventory, f. 34ᵛ)

133	124	Abraham de divinationibus 2 fo et si 'est furto ablatus
*124	125	Questiones sharpe 2 fo sine illis
1046	126	Gabriel 2 fo oritur
*121	127	Burleus super libros phisicorum 2 fo philosophus

In prima parte octavi dextus

*1075	128	Cḷaụḍiụs Pub candidus de bellis ciuilibus 2 fo et que 'sed magna pars eiusdem est furto sublata'
1303	129	Cicero de oratore 2 fo perraro
*1171	130	Orationes demosthenis 2 fo ἀπὸ στόματοσ
1172	131	Plutarchi vitę 2 fo clarissimo
1173	132	Plutarchi moralia 2 fo reuerendissimo
*1174	133	Chiliades erasmi 2 fo in textu avaro
*1175	134	Opera tullii primum volumen 2 fo positi sui
*1176	135	secundum volumen 2 fo folio quạṛṭọ 14°
*1177	136	Titus livius 2 fo des erasmus

In secunda parte eiusdem

*140	144	Antidotarium nicolai 2 fo q.s.
*1328	145	Varro de lingua latina 2 fo antiqua
1295	146	Boccasius de geneologia deorum 2 fo genuit 'non reperitur
1379	147	Cornucopię 2 fo tabula
1069	148	Margarita poetica 2 fo epistolis
1179	149	Valerius maximus 2 fo philo
1180	150	Quintilianus 2 fo hoc concesserim
1068	151	Somnium scipionis 2 fo vịṛt[ụs] punctum
*1294	152	[Strabo] 2 fo cogitasti

. . . . .

(Inventory of 1556)

*1180a	153a	Calepinus
*182	153b	Vergil.
*1025	153c	Senecæ Traged.
1360	153d	Plautus
*1074	153e	Suetonius
*1076	153f	Valla
*73	153g	Beda de gestis Anglorum
*77	153h	Flores histo.
134	153i	Liber iudiciorum de acciden' mundi

Additions to List XVI

Additions to the lists of books on Desks 1 (10), 2 (25–34), 5 (78–81, 88–9), 6 (107), 7 (114–15, 115a, 123), 8 (137–43, 153).

| 1181 | 10 | Concordantie biblie 2 fo in conc. se dicte sunt |

1085	25	Quatuor Evangelia glossata liber manuscriptus in pergameno 2 fo Abraham
1182	26	Alter liber manuscriptus in pergameno 2 fo [. .] prema [. . .
*1183	27	Iustinus mart' grece 2 fo περι του
79	28	Petrus de aurora 2 fo nam quasi[1]
		In dextu in quo opera Ieronimi[2] locantur in superiori parte eiusdem reponvntur opera dionisii in 4 volu.[3]
*1184	29	in 1° vo 2 fo reverendissimo
*1185	30	in 2° vo 2 fo gotiis occupatum
*1186	31	in 3° vo 2 fo serenissimo
*1187	32	in 4° vo 2 fo christus in
*1188	33	Item basilius 2 fo reuerendo
*1189	34	Item hilarius 2 fo doctissimo
*1190–3	78–81	Galenus latine in quatuor voluminibus
*1194	88	Rondelecius 2 fo privilege
*1195	89	Wotonus de differentiis animalium 2 fo in librum
*1196	107	Themistius grece 2 fo caspa
*1158, *1162, *1163	114–15, 115a	Duo aristotelis volumina et theophrastus ut supra adnotatum est[4]
*1197	123	Necephorus 2 fo ad magnificum
*1198	137	Valerius maximus cum commento 2 fo mortali
*1199	138	Appianus romanarum historiarum 2 fo cælius
*1200	139	Cronicon regum 2 fo nobili
1201	140	Ioannis zonare 2 fo simplicitatem
*1202–4	141–3	Stephani dictionarium in 3^bus voluminibus novum de anno 1543
*1205	153	Horatius 2 fo Ge[orgi]us

LIST XVII

1214–39 from the Vellum Inventory, ff. 50–1 (six columns).[5] The sixth and last list of books on the theology side of the library is written in the large and beautiful humanistic hand of Warden Hovenden: seven lines take up 50 mm. The list was made in 1576 in order to include the gifts of David Pole (List IX). One hundred and thirty-five titles can still be read or read in part. Perhaps about seven titles have been lost in each of the first five gaps, and a few at the end.

All but at most twenty-three of the books recorded in List XVII survive. Among those not recorded before are eleven of

[1] See List XVI. 43, above.   [2] See footnote to List XVI. 35, above.
[3] 29–34 are listed on f. 32ᵛ and again on f. 33.
[4] See List XVI. 102, 106, 108, above.
[5] **1206–13** are vacant numbers.

Pole's, **1214–18** given by William Tucker in 1558 or 1559, **1227**, **1229–30** given by Richard Bartlatt, **1233** given by W. Hone, and **1237–8** given by Mason.
There are no additions.

(f. 50, col. 1)

Hi libri subscripti continentur in Bibliotheca seu Musæo Collegii Omnium Animarum in Oxonia ex parte Theologiæ atque artium Anno Domini 1576 Magistro R. Houenden Custode

In medio Dextu

*555	1	Prima pars Bibliorum scripta in membrana habet in 2 fo scientiæ
*556	2	Secunda pars Bibliorum habet in 2 fo Vir ille

In superiore parte primi dextus

*1107	3	Lyræ pars prima habet in 2 fo De libris
*1108	4	Secunda pars eiusdem habet in 2 fo Prologus hieronymi
*1109	5	Tertia pars eiusdem habet in 2 fo prologus primus
*1110	6	Quarta pars eiusdem habet in 2 fo præfatio beati
*1111	7	Quinta pars eiusdem habet in 2 fo præfatio Nicholai
*1112	8	Sexta pars eiusdem habet in 2 fo præfatio in epistolas

In inferiore parte eius(dem) dextus

*651	9	Biblia Pagnini in quarto in 2 fo Adrianus P.P.
*1126	10	Biblia Stephani habet in 2 fo Robertus Stephanus
*791	11	Nouum Testamentum Erasmi in 2 fo leoni decimo
*793	12	Concordantiæ majores Bibl. in 2 fo Index
*1137	13	Origenis operum pars prima in 2 fo Reuerendissimo
*1138	14	Secunda pars Origenis habet in 2 fo Commentarii

In secundo Dextu parte 1ª sede superiore

*1127	15	Operum Chrisostomi [prima pars habet] 2 fo historiarum
*1128	16	Secunda pars habet [. . .
*1129	17	Tertia pars habet [. . .

. . . . .

(f. 50, col. 2)

*1138g	18	Quintum volumen habet in 2 fo D. Aurelii
*1138h	19	Sextum volumen habet in 2 fo Præfatio
*1138i	20	Septimum volumen habet in 2 fo Præfatio
*1138j	21	Octauum volumen habet in 2 fo D. Aurelii
*1188	22	Opera Basilii magni habent 2 fo Reuerendo

In 3° Dextu parte 1ª sede superiore

*1134	23	Eusebii opera habent 2 fo Index
*1136	24	Iosephi opera habent 2 fo Reuerendo

*823	25	Cyrilli opera habent 2 fo D. Cyrilli
*1135	26	Irenæi opera habent 2 fo Reuerendissimo
*1138a	27	Ambrosii volumen primum habet 2 fo [. . .
*1138b	28	Secundum volumen habet in 2 fo [. . .

In 3° Dextu parte 2ª sede superiore

*1214	29	Primum Volumen Hieronymi 2 fo [. . .
*1215	30	Secundum Volumen Hieronymi 2 fo [. . .
*1216	31	Tertium Volumen habet 2 fo Desy[d . . .
*1217	32	Quartum Volumen habet 2 fo [. . .
*1218	33	Quintum Volumen habet [. . .

In . . . .

| | 34 | Sextum volu[men . . . |

. . . . . .

(f. 50ᵛ, col. 1)

In 4° Dextu parte prima sede superiore

*861	35	Haymo in Paulum habet 2 fo bi coniunctum
*677	36	Felinus in Psalmos habet 2 fo Clarissimo
*854	37	P. Bercharii Dictionarii 1ª pars 2 fo Index
*855	38	Secunda pars habet 2 fo Secundæ partis
*856	39	Tertia pars habet 2 fo Ordo dictionum
1219	40	Scotus in 4ᵐ Sententiarum 2 fo liber quartus
565	41	Moralia in lamentationes Ieremiæ 2 fo signum

In 4° Dextu parte prima sede inferiore

*802	42	Waldensis contra Wicleuistas 1ª pars 2 fo tabella
*803	43	Secunda pars habet 2 fo Reuerendissimo
*804	44	Sacramentale Waldensis habet 2 fo Epistola
1220	45	Summæ Antonini pars 1ª 2 fo habet Præfatio
1221	46	Pars secunda Antonini habet 2 fo Prologus
1222	47	Pars tertia Antonini habet 2 fo Prologus

In 4° Dextu parte 2ª sede superiore

*1119	48	Hugonis Cardinalis pars 1ª 2 fo Prologus
*1120	49	Pars secunda habet 2 fo Proem[ium]
*1121	50	Pars tertia habet 2 fo Prologus
*1122	51	Pars quarta habet 2 fo Prologus
*1123	52	Pars quinta habet 2 fo Prologus

In 4° Dextu parte 2ª sede inferiore

*1124	53	Pars sexta habet 2 fo Epistola
*1125	54	Pars septima habet 2 fo Præfatio
794	55	Micropresbyteron habet 2 fo Amplissimo
*790	56	[. . . . .]tat in Testam. 2 fo In anno[tati]on[es]

1224 57   [. . . . .] 2 fo Inuictissimo
          57a [. . . . .] 2 fo In [. . .
  *43   57b [. . . . .] fo loquent[e]
          57c [. . . . . . .]nus

                    .   .   .   .   .

(fol. 50ᵛ, col. 2)

In 5° dextu parte secunda sede superiore

*1146   58   Galeni Græci pars 1ª 2 fo De Galeni
*1147   59   Pars secunda habet in 2 fo Typographi
*1148   60   Pars tertia habet 2 fo Præfatio
*1195   61   Wottonus de animalibus habet 2 fo In librum
*1144   62   Manardi Epistolæ medicinales 2 fo Reuerendissimo
 1142   63   Ætius medicus habet 2 fo Amplissimis

In 5° Dextu parte secunda sede inferiore

*1190   64   Galeni latini pars 1ª 2 fo Ad illustrissimum
*1191   65   Secunda pars habet 2 fo Hippocratis
*1192   66   Tertia pars habet 2 fo Argumenta
*1193   67   Quarta pars habet 2 fo Cl. Galeni
*1143   68   Ant. Musæ commentarii 2 fo ad serenissimum
*1194   69   Rondoletius de piscibus 2 fo Priuilege
 1225   70   Cato moralizatus 2 fo Et paragrapho
 1263   71   Ioannis Damasceni aphorismi 2 fo aut sang.
 *530   72   Concilia Montagnini 2 fo visus debilitas
 *145   73   Rosa medicinæ 2 fo primo sanguine
 *537   74   Constantinus Afr[icanus in] Hipocratis aphorismos 2 fo de
             natura
 1226   75   Isaacus de arte medicinali 2 fo distinctio

In 6° Dextu parte prima sede superiore

*1227   76   Breuiarium Bartholomæi 2 fo Sed
*1149b   77   Ruellius de stirpibus 2 fo Christianissimo
*1097   78   Rasis primum volumen 2 fo libri totius
*1098   79   Rasis secundum volumen 2 fo eas membro
*1229   80   Continens Rasis primum vol. 2 fo sub litera
*1230   81   Continens Rasis 2ᵐ vol. 2 fo [liber] 27ᵘˢ

In 6° Dextu parte prima sede inferiore

         81a [. . . . . .] 2 fo Clarissimo

                    .   .   .   .   .

(f. 51, col. 1)

*1157   82   Aristotelis latini volumen primum 2 fo Clarissimo
*1156   83   Secundum volumen 2 fo De uita Aristotelis

*1158	84	Aristotelis græci volumen primum 2 fo Ἀριστοτελοῦσ
*1159	85	Secundum volumen 2 fo Ἀριστοτελοῦσ
*1162	86	Tertium volumen habet 2 fo -θέχαστα
*1161	87	Quartum volumen habet 2 fo Ἀριστοτελοῦσ
*1160	88	Quintum volumen habet 2 fo Accidit
1231	89	Dedecus in Ethica habet 2 fo Ethicorum
*1013	90	Ægidius Romanus de reg. principum 2 fo cum omnis
*571	91	Eustratius in Ethica 2 fo tum eius definitio
*572	92	Liber de Musica 2 fo Vt Epistola
*142	93	Gitberti Anglici compendium medicinæ 2 fo ciam et
*147	94	Isaachus de febribus 2 fo nisi discretio boni
*585	95	Ægidii Versus de vrinis 2 fo subpallidus

In 7° Dexto parte prima Sede superiore

*1103	96	Bessarion pro Platone 2 fo de modo dicendi
1164	97	Euclides latinus 2 fo Philippus Melancthon
*1165	98	Aphrodisæus in Topica græce 2 fo pertulit
1232	99	Simplicii græci primum volumen 2 fo Σχολια
*1167	100	Secundum volumen habet 2 fo Franciscus
*1166	101	Tertium volumen habet 2 fo Andreas asulanus

In 7° Dextu parte prima Sede inferiore

***1233**	102	Io. Magister in Aristot. 2 fo iectiua et
*1170	103	Paulus Venetus in physica 2 fo causa per accid.
***1235**	104	Auerrhoes in physicam 2 fo nomen
*1163	105	Theophrastus græce de plantis 2 fo Θεοφράστον
1168	106	Platonis græci volumen primum 2 fo Aldi Pii
1169	107	Secundum habet 2 fo ἑαυτῷ
*1170a	108	Plato latinus habet 2 fo Marsilius ficinus

In 7° Dextu parte secunda Sede superiore

***1237**	109	Gesneri biblioth[. . .
***1238**	110	Secundum Volu[. . .
		. . . . .

(f. 51, col. 2)

In 8° Dextu parte prima sede superiore

*1199	111	Appianus latinus 2 fo Cælius secundus
*1200	112	Pauli Constantini chronicon 2 fo nobili viro
*1171	113	Demosthenes Græce 2 fo Des. Erasmus
1172	114	Plutarchi vitæ latinè 2 fo Clarissimo
1173	115	Plutarchi Scripta latine 2 fo Reuerendissimo

In 8° Dextu parte prima Sede inferiore

*1174	116	Chiliades Erasmi 2 fo Desid. Erasmus
*1175	117	Ciceronis operum 1um vol. 2 fo ad clarissimum

*1176	118	Secundum volumen 2 fo Interpretatio
*1198	119	Valerius Max. et Petrus de Castrovel in Ethica vno vol. 2 fo ad ornatissimum
*1177	120	Titus Liuius 2 fo Des. Erasmus
1201	121	Zonaræ historiæ 2 fo ad magnificum

In 8° Dextu parte secunda Sede superiore

1069	122	Gasparini Barsizii et Stephani Flischi elocutionis præcepta 2 fo Epistolis
1068	123	Macrobius 2 fo Punctum
*1359	124	Quintilianus 2 fo et aliquanto
1180a	125	Calepinus 2 fo Calepinus ortus
1379	126	Cornucopia Perotti 2 fo Tabula cornucopię

In 8° Dextu parte secunda sede inferiore

*140	127	Summa [. . . .] ales 2 fo Q S detur
*1205	128	Horatius cum commento 2 fo G. Fabricius
*1202	129	Stephani Thesauri prima pars 2 fo huius
*1203	130	Secunda pars 2 fo [. . .]ris
*1204	131	Tertia [pars] 2° fo [. . .

. . . . .

LIST XVIII

1241–58 from the Vellum Inventory, ff. 10–11 (single columns on ff. 10 and 10ᵛ: f. 11 nearly empty).[1] This earliest list of books on the law side of the library is in a good hand, but has been badly damaged: eight lines take up 50 mm. Seventy-three titles in this hand can still be read or read in part. Thirteen of them do not occur in List II and are probably therefore additions to the chained library after List II was made.[2]

The additions are **1255–8**, together with nine or ten books which have occurred already in List VI and one book from among those given by Richard Andrew (List IV, **523**). At least one of the additions, **23**, is in a good hand which added to List XXI. The changes to the secundo folios of 9, 10, 65 are in this hand.

(f. 10)

De iure canonico In primo desco

192	1	Vnum librum decretorum 2 fo in textu di facultas
198	2	Iohannem de fanti`cii´s super decret' in prima 2ᵃ parte 2 fo cedat limitato

---

[1] **1240** is a vacant number.

[2] Or fourteen, if **1251** is included. But I have no doubt now that **1251** and **252** refer to the same book.

1241	3	Henricum Bowyke 2 fo quo
*197	4	Primam partem eiusdem 'Fant'' 2 fo 2 3 5 q con
200	5	Petrum de salinis 2 fo de crimine
194	6	Anch' (?) Archidiaconum in rosar' 2 fo ex eodem
224	7	Speculator 2 fo id est multi
221	8	Iohannem andr' super eundem 2 fo vt ibi scripsi

Secundo desco

1242	9	Librum decretalium 2 fo in textu 'corpus et sanguis' (*over erasure*)
1243	10	Innoc' 2 fo 'et contradicentibus' (*over erasure*)
209	11	Primam partem hostiensis in lectura 2 fo fatuum est
210	12	2ᵃᵐ partem eiusdem 2 fo visitat
219	13	Antonium de budreo butreo 'in prima parte' super 2° libro decretalium 2 fo se presentauit
216	15	Primam partem Iohannis de lygn' super decretales 2 fo attendi
217	16	2ᵃᵐ partem eiusdem 2 fo tendit ad
236	17	Summam Reymundi 2 fo est annexum
211	18	Primam partem Iohannis in nouellis 2 fo vltra id
212	19	Secundam partem eiusdem 2 fo scilicet incipiunt
1244	20	Hostiensem in summa 2 fo que uocabatur
213	21	Iohannem in addic' 2 fo quod est materia
414	22	Iohannem andr' super decretales 2 fo incepit

Tercio desco

1245	24	Librum decretorum 2 fo in textu [. . . .] 'que'
199	25	Petrum de salinis 2 fo fendendo
432	26	Tabulam super decreta 2 fo baal 'et est in 2° [. . . . .]t''
229	27	Petrum de Anchorano super sexto 2 fo querit circa
1246	28	Aliam tabulam super decreta 2 fo ecclesie negocii
195	29	Archid' in [. . .] 2 fo Iustius
230	32	[. . .] pe de ancho super cle 2 fo 'dicit' sponsalia
237	33	Willelmum in sacramentalibus 2 fo tario Regis
1247	34	sextum cum doctoribus 2 fo b[. . . . .]s 'Ecce'
1248	36	Librum Clement' cum doctoribus 2 fo in textu [. . . .]us
231	37	Petrum de ancrano super librum Clement' 2 fo de prelacione
1249	38	librum sextum cum doctoribus 2 fo in textu cum nom[. . .
222	39	Tabulam iuris canonici 2 fo monasterii
235	40	Constituciones Iohannis pape vicesimi glosat' per gessellinum 2 fo in [. . .] a canonibus
228	41	[Iohannem in merlcurialibus super quibusdam Regulis iuris 2 fo habetur ipsʋ

. . . . .

8, 9 '2° desco' in margin beside 8 and 'Primo desco' interlined above 9

(f. 10^v)

203	43	Summam Goffr' 'et barth' Brixensis' 2 fo quod non admissis
274	44	Consilia frederici de senis 2 fo de hiis
214	45	Primam partem iohannis in collectar' 2 fo vel vi^{ta}
215	46	2^{am} partem eiusdem 2 fo cum eo
444	47	Barth' super extrauagant' ad repremend' cum aliis tractatibus 2 fo nota de deo
223	48	Reportorium cum diuersis repeticionibus 2 fo defendere 'et est in iii° desco'
6	49	Sampsonem de caluo monte 2 fo Religiosi
208	50	Hostiensem in summa 2 fo naturalis
251	51	2^{am} partem baldi super Cod' 2 fo quia potest
1250	52	Primam partem eiusdem 2 fo ho. queritur 'translatum'
*245	53	Codicem 2 fo in textu mare prospeximus
247	54	2^{am} partem Odefr' super Codice 2 fo et retineo
246	55	Primam partem eiusdem 2 fo liber lege
438	56	Iacobum de Rauenna super Cod' 2 fo in anglia
249	57	Cynum super Cod' 2 fo et ideo
*1251	60	ff vetus 2 fo in textu virum magnificum
254	61	Odefr' super eodem 2 fo intelligenti
	61a	[. . . . .] 2 fo [. . .
273	62	Barth' super ff veteri 2 fo hic.l.qu[.] faciunt
268	63	Barth' super Cod' 2 fo nec dicitur
244	64a	Codicem 2 fo co[mposicione]m
1252	65	ff' vetus 2 fo in textu 'excerpsimus' (*over erasure*)
1253	66	[. . . . .] ff infor' et prima parte f[. . . . .] 2 fo de iure docueri (?) doci (?) (*entry cancelled*) 'Modo est in eleccione sociorum'
*259	67	ff infort' 2 fo in textu ro eius
257	68	Iacobum de b[. . .] super ff' vet' 2 fo consuetudo
255	70	Odefr' super ff veteri in prima parte 2 fo de vsu [. . .] (*entry cancelled*) 'Modo est in eleccione sociorum'
256	71	2^{am} partem eiusdem 2 fo in iure
272	73	Barth' super ff inforc 2 fo priuilegium
*264	74	ff nouum 2 fo in textu predii
261	75	Reynerium in lectura super ff' inforc' 2 fo soluto
260	76	ff inforc' 2 fo in textu ex die
271	77	2^{am} partem barth' super ff nouo 2 fo placuerit
375	78	Primam partem eiusdem 2 fo vt restituas
269	79	[. . . . .] Barth' super ff nouo 2 fo sed quid prohibet
1254	80	[. . . .] et nouo 2 fo in tabula do de hered' instituend'
	81	[. . . . .]uitur[. . .

. . . . .

79 In another hand

(f. 11)

263	82	Iacobum de Rauenna super libello 'institucionum' 2 fo et iure l.i vel 2° in anglia et hoc dicit glosa
239	83	Paruum volumen' 2 fo in textu tim ab inicio (*entry cancelled*)
371	84	Item vnum doctorem cum albo coopertorio 2 fo et ff ad l ro de 'Odefr' super ff nouum 2 fo et ff ad l Ro de iac' 'et est in sexto desco' (*entry cancelled*)

Additions to List XVIII

Additions to the lists of books on Desks 2 (14, 23) and 3 (30, 31, 35, 42), and on other desks.

593	14	Item anton' de butrio in 2ᵃ parte 2 fo 2ᵉ partis vencione partium
*594	23	Libellus componendi instrumenta 2 fo pater pie manum
595	30	Petrum de Anchorano super viᵗᵒ 2 fo stipendium
596	31	Prothodosinus de ordine iudiciario 2 fo lent C de [. . .
597	35	Antonium de Butrio 'super 4ᵗᵒ' 2 fo Vt dato
598	42	Item Iohannem in nouella [. . . . .] 2 fo [. . . .] gestum et est ex dono [. . .
1255	58	Cynus super Cod' 2 fo notatur ergo
1256	59	Barth' super ff vetus 2 fo sit docendum
523	64	Willelmus de Cunys 2 fo glo. que. illud
1257	69	Barth' super ff inforc' 2 fo vt plenius
1258	72	Barthol' super ff ve 2 fo [. .] a de [. . .
257	85	Lectura super ff veteri 2 fo consuetudo (*entry cancelled*)
606	86	Antonium de butrio super primo decretalium 2 fo fal quam
608	87	Antonium super 5ᵗᵒ 2 fo antequam denuncietur
607	88	Antonium super 3° 2 fo deponuntur
605	89	Anto (*sic*)

LIST XIX

1259-1304 from the Vellum Inventory, ff. 3-4ᵛ (four columns). The second list of books on the law side of the library is in the same hand as List XIII and follows it immediately. One hundred and seven original entries remain and are legible or partly legible. Only eight of them have not occurred in previous lists. One of the eight, a copy of Bartholomaeus Montagnana given by John Racour, †1487, has claims to be the printed book which has been longest in the college library (**1266**).

The long list of additions, **1267-1304**, is set out like the additions to List XIII. Five of the seven survivors were gifts of James Goldwell, †1499.

(f. 3, col. 1)

Ex parte legum

In media parte primi dextus cathenantur In primis

*197	1	Iohannes de fawnt super decret' 2 fo 2.3.5
198	2	Item alia pars eiusdem 2 fo cedat limitato
192	3	Item decreta 2 fo di facultas in textu

Inferius

1242	4	Liber decretalium 2 fo corpus et sanguis in textu

Subtus

1241	5	Henricus Bowyk 2 fo quo frustra
224	6	Item Wyllelmus in speculo 2 fo id est multi v'
194	7	Item Archidiaconus in Rosario 2 3 fo na. ¶ ex non scripto
200	8	Item lectura petri de salinis 2 fo de crimine in tabula

In secundo dextu

In medio cathenati sunt hii libri subscripti.

219	9	Lectura secundi libri dec' domini Antonii de butrio 2 fo se presentauit.
593	10	Item alia pars eiusdem lecture 2 fo vencione parcium
605	11	Item alia pars eiusdem 2 fo tollitur contrarium

In inferiori parte

209	12	Prima pars hostiensis 2 fo futurum 'fatuum'
210	13	2ª pars hostiensis 2 fo visitat

Subtus

221	14	Speculum iuris editum per dominum Guilelmum duranti cum addicionibus per dominum Iohannem Andree insertis 2 fo vt ibi scripsi.
414	15	Item addiciones super 5m librum decretalium edite a Iohanne Andrea 2 fo incepit credo
216	16	Item liber 1us Iohannis de lynyno 2 fo attendi et est spissus papiro
213	17	Item liber diuersorum tractatuum 2 fo quod est materia
217	18	Item apparatus super 3m 4m et 5m libros Iohannis de lynyno 2 fo tendit
601	19	Item prima pars abbatis super 2m librum decretalium 2 fo ac si clerici
600	20	Item 3ª pars eiusdem 2 fo Nota ibi
1243	21	Item prope fenestram primus liber Innocencii 4ti 2 fo et contradicentibus
606	22	Item liber cuius 2 fo incipit fal quam gram[. . .

Ex alia parte huius dextus in medio

236	23	Summa Raymundi de casibus 2 fo est adnexum
211	24	Item Nouella domini Iohannis Andree 2 fo vltra
432	25	Item liber continens tabulam legum 2 fo baal
212	26	[. . . . .] de nouella 2 fo s. incipiunt
234	26a	[. . . . .] fo doctoribus
1244	27	[. . . . .] 2 fo que vocabatur

(f. 3, col. 2)

Subtus

*594	28	In primis vnus liber 2 fo pater
223	29	Item liber alius de papiro 2 fo defendere
1259	30	Item liber concordie discordancium canonum 2 fo primumque
228	31	Item Iohannes in mercurialibus cum aliis contentis 2 fo habetur
598	32	Item nouella Iohannis andree 2 fo diserte gestum

Ex altera parte huius dextus In superiori parte

607	33	Magnus liber papiri 2 fo deponuntur

In media parte

225	34	Reportorium Magistri Guillelmi duranti 2 fo docuerunt
274	35	Item consilia frederici de senis 2 fo de hiis
*308	36	Item Chislynden super clement' 2 fo alia conclusio
237	37	Item liber qui dicitur sacramentale Guilelmi de hauduno 2 fo tario regis

Inferius

229	38	In primis liber spissus papiri 2 fo queritur circa
595	39	Item petrus de anchorano 2 fo stipendium
226	40	Item liber sixtus cum doctoribus 2 fo id est confessione

In 4to dextu in superiori parte.

444	41	Tractatus Alexandri de ancilla 2 fo nota de deo

In media parte

203	42	Quedam Summa cum aliis contentis 2 fo quod non
222	43	Item tabula iuris canonici 2 fo monasterii
220	44	Item commentum super 4^m librum decretalium secundum franciscum de zabarellis 2 fo dicto capit'

Inferius

202	45	liber decretalium glosatus 2 fo damnamus

Subtus

520	46	[Lib]er papiri 2 fo li vi

599	47	[Item] Abbas super librum decretalium 2 fo iusti qui
603	48	Item Abbas super 4to et 5to 2 fo [e]cc[le]si[a]
232	49	Item Apparatus domini Guillelmi de monte Auduno super const[itucionibus] clement' 2 fo ipse tamen
231	50	Item petrus de anchorano 2 fo de prelacione
6	51	Item hostiensis in lectura abbreuiat' 2 fo relig[iosi]
235	52	Item constituciones Iohannis pape xxii° 2 fo a cano[nibus]
602	53	Item abbas super 3° decretalium 2 fo nobiliori
518	54	Item vnus spissus et paruus liber papiri 2 fo differre
205	55	Item apparatus decre(talium) nouissimarum gregorii decimi 2 fo di C. con[. . .]nt

Ex altera parte in medio

215	57	Vnus liber 2 fo cum eo
214	58	Item alius 2 fo vel vi xc
218	59	Item lectura karoli super decretal' 2 fo [. . .
5	60	Item hostiensis in lectura 2 fo [. .]all[. . .

Inferius

	60a	E[. . .
9?	61	Item secunda pars hostiensis [. . .

. . . . .

(f. 3^v, col. 1)

In media parte

438	62	Iacobus de Rauenna 2 fo in anglia
1256	63	Item Bartholomeus super ff veteri 2 fo sit docend'
244	64	Item liber Codicis 2 fo composicionem in textu

Inferius

254	65	Lectura domini Odofredi ff vet 2 fo intellegenti

In 6to dextu in media parte

257	66	Lectura super ff veteri 2 fo consuetudo
256	67	Item secunda pars Odofredi super ff veteri 2 fo in iure ap'

Inferius

371	68	Carriarius super ff nouum 2 fo et ff ad .l.

Subtus

265	69	ff vetus nouum 2 fo opida in textu
271	70	Item Bartholus super ff nouo 2 fo placuerit
269	71	Item Alexander de ancilla cum aliis 2 fo sed quid prohibet
1252	72	Item ff vetus 2 fo excerpsimus in textu
272	73	Item Bartholus super ff inforciat' 2 fo priuilegium
375	74	Item Bartholus super ff nouo 2 fo vt restituas

62–5 These were in Desk 5   71 siue (?) hic nichil bene (?) *in margin*

Ex alia parte superius

| *264 | 75 | ff nouum 2 fo predii nunciauit |
| 260 | 76 | Item Ro[. . .]ll' super ff inforciat' 2 fo ex die (*entry cancelled*) |

In media parte

| 1257 | 77 | Bartholus super ff inforciat' 2 fo vt plenius |
| 260 | 78 | Item ff inforciatum 2 fo ex die |

Inferius

| *259 | 79 | ff inforciatum 2 fo ro eius |

In septimo dextu superius

| *240 | 80 | [. . . . .] 2 fo dicit azo |

In media parte

*266	81	Summa azonis 2 fo de hereticis
1260	82	Item reportorium super lecturis domini barth' et consiliis et questionibus per eum disputatis 2 fo species [a]b altera
1254	83	Item dynus super ff inforciato et ff nouo 2 fo do de hered' in tabula

Inferius

| 239 | 84 | [Instituta] glosat' 2 fo tim ab inicio |

Subtus

263	85	[. . . . .] institucionum 2 fo et hoc di[cit]
204	86	[. . . . .] 2 fo decreto
		[. . . . .] glo [. . .

. . . . .

(f. 3^v, col. 2)

Inferius

1261	87	Pupilla oculi 2 fo fuerat per miraculum
*147	88	Item liber febrium ysaac 2 fo nisi discrecio
1262	89	Item lilium medicine 2 fo rat nisi
1263	90	Item libellus aphorismorum Iohannis damac' 2 fo aut sanguine in textu

Subtus

| *142 | 91 | Liber Gilberti Anglici 2 fo ciam et accensionem |
| *145 | 92 | Item Rosa medicine 2 fo i° sanguine |

Ex alia parte in medio

| 141 | 93 | Liber almansoris cum aliis 2 fo receptacula |

Inferius

| **1264** | 94 | Liber Iohannicii in tegni Galieni 2 fo venti |
| 532 | 95 | Item Auicenna in summa 2 fo que proueniunt |

75 [. . . .] m' super ff [. . . . .] *in margin*   87–95 No doubt books in Desk 8

In fine librarie superius

| 534 | 96 | Breuiarium domini constantini 2 fo admisceamus |
| **1265** | 97 | Item liber canonis et (*sic*) 2 fo capi. xiii in tabula |

In medio

| *535 | 98 | Anathomia magistri henrici de amandavilla etc' 2 fo ossa plurima |
| *531 | 99 | Item liber quarundam distinccionum in medicinis 2 fo addatur farine etc' |

Inferius

*1266	100	Liber Bartholomei montagnane 2 fo C de frigi(di)tate
*530	101	Item alius magnus liber scriptus in papiro 2 fo visus debilitas in tabula
*585	102	Item paruus liber egidii de vrinis 2 fo liber collegii

Subtus

143	103	Auicenna 2 fo capitulum xxv
*140	104	Item Aphorismi Iohannis damac' [cum] commento ysidori 2 fo tangit causam q s detur
584	105	Item ysagoge Iohannicii in tegni galieni 2 fo hii [. . .] quia

Additions to List XIX

56, 56a are added to the list of books in Desk 4. 106–42, additions to Desks 1–5 and 8, are grouped together on f. 4, which was originally blank. The missing part of the leaf probably contained additions to Desks 5, 6, and 7.

| | 56 | Item liber decretalium 2 fo [. . . |
| | 56a | Item liber decretorum 2 fo [. . . |

(f. 4)

In primo desco

*1267	106	Speculum consciencie 2 (fo) in tabula defensores ex dono etc'
1268	107	Liber decretorum 2 fo Sil' ex dono etc'
1269	108	Casuarius super decreta 2 fo Sue culpe ex dono etc'

In 2° desco

1270	109	Consilia abbatis 2 fo Aliquem ad bellum in tabula
1271	110	Item disputaciones abbatis 2 fo c. pastoralis
*1272	111	Item prima pars reportorii Brixens' (2 fo) nare quemlibet
*1273	112	Item 2ª pars reportorii eiusdem (2 fo) Quod faciendo

In 3° desco

| **1274** | 113 | Ioannes in Nouella super Sexto 2 fo Iure iª de consecratione |
| **1275** | 114 | Item conclusiones rotales 2 fo in tabula de commissionibus |

| 1276 | 115 | Item Consilia frederici 2 fo possit |
| *1277 | 116 | Item Cardinalis super Sexto 2 fo So secundam pau |

In 4° desco

1279	117	Prima pars Abbatis 2 fo S[. . .]ca
1280	118	Item reportorium aules (?) 2 fo Actor
1281	119	Item Iohannes de turrecremata super ecclesiastica potestate 2 fo in tabula Ca 64°
1282	120	Item tractatus de potestate ecclesiastica 2 fo de[. . .
1283	121	Item Godfr[edus] in summa 2 fo constitucio[. . .

In quinto desco

1284	122	Prima pars Saliceti super codice 2 fo quid Subiectum
1285	123	2ª pars eiusdem 2 fo quia omnia
1286	124	3ª pars Baldi super C. 2 fo te iustum
1287	125	Prima pars Bartholi super C. 2 fo contradicat
1288	126	2ª pars eiusdem 2 fo Ergo
*1289	127	[Rep]ortorium Antonii (2 fo) hic et ibi
*1290	128	[. . . . .] W Vrbasche 2 fo tator[um]

. . . . .

(f. 4ᵛ)

In vltimo dextu

1291	129	Iosephus in antiqua historia 2 fo fuit
1292	130	Item prima pars plutarchi 2 fo gloriam
1293	131	Item 2ª pars eiusdem 2 fo ea tempestate
*1294	132	Item strabo 2 fo cogitasti
1295	133	Item Bocacius 2 fo in tabula genuit
1296	134	Item plinius 2 fo Item
1297	135	Item Quintilianus 2 fo proinde
1298	136	Item Questiones tusculane tullii 2 fo studia
1299	137	Item Nonius marcellus 2 fo tollere
1300	138	Item Epistole leonardi aretini 2 fo leonardus
1301	139	Item oraciones tullii 2 fo duces
1302	140	Item Rhetorica trapezuncii 2 fo que ad
1303	141	Item Tullius de oratore cum commento 2 fo perraro
1304	142	Item Rhetorica tullii 2 fo creacione

LIST XX

1305–28 from the Vellum Inventory, ff. 24ᵛ–25 (three columns). The third list of books on the law side of the library is in the same admirable hand as List XIV and follows it immediately. It is the best preserved of the law lists in the Vellum Inventory.

120, 121 were added later

One hundred and sixty-two original entries remain and are legible or partly legible. Of surviving books not entered in previous lists, **1325** and **1326** were given by Goldwell, and **1319–23** by Thomas Mors, †1501.
163–4 are the only additions.

(f. 24ᵛ, col. 1)

Hii libri Subscripti continentur In Bibliotheca collegii animarum Oxon' Ex parte legum

In primis in superiori parte primi dextus

*1267	1	Speculum consciencie 2 fo defensiones
1269	2	Item casuarius super decreta 2 fo sue culpe
*197	3	Item Iohannes de Fawnt super decret' 2 fo 2. 3. 5
198	4	Item 2ᵃ pars I. de Fawnt 2 fo cedat
192	5	Item decreta 2 fo di Facultas

Item in media parte huius dextus

1242	6	Liber decretalium 2 fo corpus et sanguis

Item subtus isto dextu

1241	7	Henricus Bowyk 2 fo quo frustra
224	8	Item Wyllelmus in speculo 2 fo id est multi v'
194	9	Item Archidiaconus in Rosario 2 fo ex eodem volumine
200	10	Item lectura petri de salinis 2 fo de crimine in tabula
1268	11	Item liber Decretorum 2 fo sill' ex Dono

In superiori parte 2ⁱ dextus

1270	12	Consilia abbatis 2 fo aliquem ad

In media parte huius dextus

219	13	Lectura 2ⁱ libri Dec' Domini Antonii de butrio 2 fo se presentauit
593	14	Item alia pars eiusdem lecture 2 fo vencione per
1271	15	Item Disputaciones Domini Nicholai abbatis 2 fo .c. pastoralis
605	16	Item alia pars prioris lecture 2 fo tollitur contrarium

Item in inferiori parte istius dextus

209	17	Prima pars hostiensis 2 fo Fatuum
210	18	Item 2ᵃ pars hostiensis 2 fo visitat

Ex altera parte eiusdem dextus

236	19	In primis Summa Raymundi de casubus 2 fo est adnexum

In media parte

212	20	2ª pars I de novella 2 fo 5. incipiunt
432	21	Item liber continens tabulam legum 2 fo bal. xxii
211	22	Item Novella domini Iohannis Andree 2 fo vltra id
1244	23	Item Summa de titulis decretalium 2 fo que vocabatur

Item in inferiori parte

| 234 | 24 | Franciscus de Zarabellis super clement' 2 fo Doctoribus |

Item subtus eodem dextu

1243	25	Primus liber Innocencii 4ᵗⁱ 2 fo et contradicentibus
*1272	26	Item prima pars Reportorii Brixens' 2 fo nare quemlibet 'athenas'
*1273	27	Item 2ª pars eiusdem reportorii 2 fo quod faciendo
601	28	Item prima pars abbatis super 2ᵐ librum decretalium 2 fo ac si clerici
600	29	Item 2ª pars eiusdem 2 fo Nota ibi
606	30	Item alius liber 2 fo fal quam
221	31	Item Speculum Iuris per dominum gwylelmum duranti cum addicionibus 2 fo ut ibi scripsi
213	32	Item liber diuersorum tractatuum 2 fo quod est materia
216	33	Item liber 2ᵘˢ I. de lynyno super libr' decretalium 2 fo attendi quod
414	34	Item addiciones super 5ᵐ librum decretalium 2 fo incepit
217	35	Item apparatus super 3ᵐ 4ᵐ et 5ᵐ libros I. de lynyano 2 fo tendit ad

In superiori parte tercii dextus

597	36	Antonius de butrio super 4ᵐ librum 2 fo ut dato
*1277	37	Item cardinalis super 6ᵗᵒ 2 fo So secundum pau'
1274	38	Item I. in nouella super 6ᵗᵒ decretalium 2 fo Iure iª

In media parte istius dextus

196	39	Liber paruus 2 fo cautela
195	40	Item Archidiaconus in rosario 2 fo iustius cum
199	41	Item Petrus de Salinis Super Decret' 2 fo fendendo
233	42	Item 2° libri concathenati vnius 2 fo suum motum
1305	43	Item alius 2 fo posicione testator

In inferiori parte istius dextus

604	44	Constituciones prouinciales 2 fo condentis
596	45	Item liber paruus domini prothodosini apparatus 2 fo lent .C.
1306	46	Item 2° libri simul cathenati vnius 'prima pars dominici' 2 fo inhonestis
1307	47	Item alterius 'secunda pars dominici' 2 fo secundum Io.
608	48	Item antonius de butrio 2 fo antequam

Ex altera parte eiusdem dextus

1275	49	Conclusiones rotales 2 fo de commissionibus
1276	50	Item consilia frederici 2 fo possit
607	51	Item magnus liber in papyro 'videlicet Antonius de butrio 2 fo deponuntur

In media parte eiusdem

237	52	Liber qui dicitur sacramentale 2 fo tario regis
*308	53	Item chislenden' super clement' 2 fo alia conclusio
274	54	Item consilia frederici de senis 2 fo de hiis
225	55	Item Reportorium M' gwylelmi duranti 2 fo docuerunt

In inferiori parte eiusdem

229	56	Liber spissus papiri 2 fo queritur circa
595	57	Item petrus de anchorano 2 fo stipendium
226	58	Item liber sextus cum doctoribus 2 fo id est confessione

Item subtus eodem dextu

223	59	Tabula auctoritatum 2 fo defendere
*594	60	Item alius liber papiri 2 fo pater
1259	61	Item liber concordie discord[ancium . . . . .]m 'decretorum' 2 fo primumque
228	62	Item Iohannes [in] merc[urialibus . . . . . .] 2 fo habetur
598	63	Item Nou[. . . . .] 2 fo diserte gestum
1247	64	[. . . . .] 2 fo ecce sum

. . . . . .

(f. 24ᵛ, col. 2)

1282	65	Item tractatus de potestate eccl(es)iastica 2 fo deum omne
602	66	Item abbas super 3° decretalium 2 fo nobiliori
603	67	Item abbas super 4ᵗᵒ et 5ᵗᵒ 2 fo ecclesia
231	68	Item petrus de anchorano 2 fo de prelacione
205	69	Item apparatus decretalium nouissimarum gregorii 2 fo di .c.
208	70	Item Summa de titulis decretalium 'hostiensis in summa' 2 fo naturalis
520	71	Item liber papiri 'videlicet Io Caldri' 2 fo ly vi et
232	72	Item apparatus domini Gwyelmi de monte Auduno super constituc' clement' 2 fo ipse tamen
6	73	Item hostiensis in lectura abbreuiat' 2 fo religiosi
235	74	Item constituciones Iohannis pape xxii° 2 fo a canonibus
1283	75	Item Godfredus in summa 2 fo constitucionum
518	76	Item vnus spissus et paruus liber 2 fo differre 'deest'
1309	77	Item [. . . . .] 2 fo [. . . (*entry erased*)

65–77 were in Desk 4

In superiori parte 5ᵗⁱ dextus

| 1286 | 78 | 3ª pars baldi super codice 2 fo te iustum |
| 268 | 79 | Item lectura bartholi super codice 2 fo nec dicitur continere |

In media parte eiusdem dextus

247	80	Secunda pars odofredi 2 fo et retineo
246	81	Item odofredus de nouo codice componendo 2 fo liber .l.
1285	82	Item 2ª pars saliceti super C. 2 (fo) que omnia
1255	83	Item summa cini 2 fo notatur ergo

In inferiori parte eiusdem dextus

| *245 | 84 | Codex domini Iustiniani 2 fo mare prospeximus |
| 249 | 85 | Item lectura cini 2 fo et ideo |

Ex altera parte eiusdem dextus

| 1287 | 86 | Prima pars Bartholi super C. 2 fo contradicat |
| 523 | 87 | Item lectura gwylelmi de cimio 2 fo glo quia illud |

In media parte eiusdem

438	88	Iacobus de Ravenna 2 fo in anglia
1256	89	Item Bartholomeus super ff veteri 2 fo sit docend'
1288	90	Item 2ª pars Bartholi super C. 2 fo ergo quod
254	91	Item lectura domini Odofredi super ff veteri 2 fo intelligenti

In inferiori parte eiusdem

| *1289 | 92 | Reportorium Antonii 2 fo hic et ibi |

Subtus isto dextu

1250	93	Baldus super tres libros codicis 2 fo Translatum in
1284	94	Item prima pars saliceti super codice 2 fo quid subiectum
*1251	95	Item digestum vetus 2 fo virum magnificum
*1290	96	Item conclusiones W. Urbasche 2 fo torum quod
1286	97	Item 3ª pars Baldi super C. 2 fo te iustum

In superiori parte 6ᵗⁱ dextus

1310	98	Bal (super) 5ᵉ libros C. 2 fo distancia
1311	99	Item C. vetus de tortis 2 fo a conferentibus 'in glo'
1312	100	Item liber Institucionum 2 fo et viii vel
1313	101	Item ff vetus 2 fo a fulgere 'in glo'

In media parte eiusdem dextus

| 1314 | 102 | Bal' super 6ᵗᵒ 8° 7° et 9° C. 2 fo si / Quarum |

Item ex alia parte eiusdem dextus

| *264 | 103 | Novvm ff 2 fo predii nunciauerit |

78 occurs again as 97

| 261 | 104 | Item liber domini Renardi super ff Inforciato 2 fo ex die salutis |

In media parte eiusdem

1315	105	Nouum ff 2 fo labeo non
260	106	Item ff inforciatum 2 fo ex die
1257	107	Item Barthol^{us} super ff inforciat' 2 fo ut plenius
1316	108	Item Singularia lodowici cum diuersis tractatibus bart' 2 fo qui sit

In inferiori parte eiusdem dextus

| **1317** | 109 | Prima pars veteris ff 2 fo excepto |

Subtus isto dextu

1318	110	Bal super 2ª parte veteris ff et super librum feodorum 2 fo in quolibet
***1319**	111	Item Bal. super prima parte veteris ff 2 fo cia illi viri
***1320**	112	Item Bal. super novum ff et inforc' 2 fo quod si quis
***1321**	113	Item prima 2ª et 3ª partes consiliorum Bal. 2 fo peruenerunt ad
***1322**	114	Item 4ª et 5ª partes consiliorum Bal. 2 fo mulier
***1323**	115	Item libri 7 petri de Ferrariis super ff 2 fo de clausul' in tabula

Item in superiori parte 7^{mi} dextus

| *240 | 116 | Iohannes Faber 2 fo dicit azo |

In media parte eiusdem

*266	117	Summa azonis 2 fo de hereticis
1260	118	Item reportorium super lecturis d' Barth' et consilibus et questionibus per eum disputatis 2 fo species ab
1254	119	Item Dynus super ff inforciato et ff novo 2 fo do de heredit'

Ex altera parte eiusdem dextus

***1324**	120	2ª pars Calderini 2 fo potest
1325	121	Item vocabularius iuris 2 fo aboletur
*267	122	Item petrus Iacobi de aureliato 2 fo superiorem

In media parte eiusdem

| 258 | 123 | Petrus in repeticionibus super ff veteri 2 fo consuetudinario |
| ***1326** | 124 | Item prima pars reportorii calderimi 2 fo celebrare |

Subtus isto dextu

239	125	Instit' glosata 2 fo tim ab inicio
1327	126	Item [An]gl's super institut' 2 fo nisi probetur
*242	127	Item [Iohannes] de platea 2 fo 5° nota ibi [. . . . .] rer[um . . .] dic

. . . . . .

(f. 25)

*531	128	Item liber quorundam distinccionum in medicinis 2 fo addatur
143	129	Item avicenna 2 fo C xxi in tabula
1262	130	Item lilium medicine 2 fo rat nisi
532	131	Item auicenna in summa 2 fo que proueniunt
141	132	Item liber almansoris cum aliis 2 fo receptacula

In inferiori parte eiusdem dextus

| *1266 | 133 | Liber bartholomei montagnane 2 fo .C. de frigiditate |
| 1265 | 134 | Item liber canonis 2 fo .'C'. xiii in tabula |

Subtus isto dextu

534	135	Breuiarius domini constantini 2 fo admisceamus
375	136	Item prima pars lecture domini Bartholomei super ff nouo 2 fo ut restituas
256	137	Item 2ª pars odofredi super ff vet' 2 fo in iure
257	138	Item lectura super ff vetus 2 fo consuetudo
269	139	Item alexander de ancilla 2 fo sed quid
536	140	Item galienus 2 fo bitur in qualitate
*535	141	Item Anathomia M' Henrici de amandavilla 2 fo ossa plurima
*530	142	Item liber magnus scriptus in papiro 2 fo visus debilitas
*145	143	Item rosa medicine 2 fo i° sanguine
*537	144	Item liber amphorismorum 2 fo de natura morbi
*142	145	Item liber gilberti anglici 2 fo ciam et accensionem
584	146	Item Isagoge Iohannicii in tegni galieni 2 fo hii vel quia
*140	147	Item amphorismi I. damasceni 2 fo q.S. detur.
1263	148	Item libellus amphorismorum I. damasceni 2 fo aut sanguine
146	149	Item ysagoge Iohanicii et (?) tegni galieni 2 fo recedit exterius
*585	150	Item exposicio super solo 2 fo subpallidus

In superiori parte Vltimi dextus

| 1295 | 151 | Bocasius de geneologia deorum 2 fo genu[it] |
| 1296 | 152 | Item plinius 2 fo Item |

In media parte eiusdem

1291	153	Iosephus in antiqua historia 2 fo fuit sufficiens
1292	154	Item prima pars plutarchi 2 fo gloriam
1293	155	Item 2ª pars eiusdem 2 fo ea tempestate
*1294	156	Item strabo 2 fo cogitasti

Item subtus eodem dextu

| 1304 | 157 | Rethorica tullii 2 fo ꝟt creacione |
| 1301 | 158 | Item oraciones Tullii 2 fo duces |

128–50 were in Desk 8

1300	159	Item epistole leonardi Arratini 2 fo leonardus
1299	160	Item Nonius marcellus 2 fo tollere
1298	161	Item Questiones tusculane tullii 2 fo studia
1297	162	Item quintilianus 2 fo proinde
		'Nota quod desunt omnes libri M' holt'
1303	163	'Item Tullius de oratore 2 fo perraro'
*1328	164	'Item varro de lingua latina 2 fo Antiqua'

LIST XXI

1329–79 from the Vellum Inventory, ff. 28ᵛ–29 (four columns). The fourth list of books on the law side of the library was written after (soon after?) List XV, which ends on the recto of f. 28. It is in a smaller and more expert hand than XV: twelve lines take up 50 mm. The occasion of the new list was the rearrangement of the law side, which seems to have taken place in 1512 or 1513. As a catalogue XXI is the best in the Vellum Inventory. One hundred and eighty-one of the original entries are legible or partly legible. Of books which have not occurred in previous lists **1332–4** were gifts of John Holt and John Cole and **1357** and **1359** came from Goldwell.

Of the additions, **1361–79**, and the volumes of Durand's Speculum which replaced **1332–4**, only **1376–7** survive: these were given by Michael Wogan, † after 1514.

(f. 28ᵛ, col. 1)

Subscripti libri continentur in bibliotheca ex Parte Legum

Primo in dextu Superius

*1329	6	Archidiaconus super decreta 2 fo Intentio eius
192	7	Decreta 2 fo Di facultas in textu
195	8	Archidiaconus super decreta 2 fo Iustius cum
1268	9	Decreta 2 fo simul rebus in textu
223	10	Distinctiones Iohannis Caldrini 2 fo defendere
199	11	Petrus de Salinis super decreta 2 fo fendendo

Inferius

1329a	13	'Io de Ymola 2 fo ergo et'[1]
1330	14	Decreta 2 fo dampnandus in tabula
1269	15	Casuarius super decreta et decretales 2 fo sue culpe
*197	16	Prima pars Iohannis Fawnnte super decreta 2 fo 235
198	17	Secunda pars Iohannis fawnnt 2 fo cedat
194	18	Archidiaconus super decreta 2 fo ex eodem

[1] See 83.

237	19	Guillelmus in sacramentalibus 2 fo tario regis
236	20	Summa Raymundi de casibus 2 fo est adnexum
*1290	21	Conclusiones Guillelmi Vrbache 2 fo torum quod
1281	22	Iohannes de turrecremata super ecclesiastica potestate 2 fo [. . . . .] in tabula (*entry cancelled*)
1282	23	Cancellarius parisiensis super ecclesiastica potestate 2 fo deum omne

Secundo in dextu Superius

603	25	Abbas super 3° decretalium 2 fo ecclesia ut
1331	26	Abbas super 4° et 5° decretalium 2 fo preterea
***1332**	27	Prima pars Speculi cum reportor' 2 fo accessoria 'trina'
***1333**	28	Secunda pars Speculi 2 fo Innuit 'dierum'
***1334**	29	Tercia pars Speculi 2 fo possum 'par' (*entry cancelled*)

Inferius

1335	30	Decretales 2 fo et litteris in tabula
1336	31	Abbas super 1° decretalium 2 fo sciencia
1337	32	Abbas super 1ª parte 2ˡ libri 2 fo par [. . .
1338	33	Abbas super 2ª parte 2ˡ libri 2 fo condi[. . .
1339	34	Abbas super 3ª parte 2ˡ libri 2 fo necessario
1340	35	Prepositus super 4° decretalium 2 fo affectus
1275	36	Conclusiones rotales 2 fo de commissionibus in tabula
520	37	Conclusiones rotales 2 fo l. vi
1271	38	Nicholai abbatis Siculi disputaciones 2 fo c pastoralis

Ex altero eiusdem dextus latere Superius

599	40	Abbas super 1° decretalium 2 fo iusti qui
601	41	Abbas super 2° decretalium pro 1ª parte 2 fo ac si clerici
600	42	Abbas super 2° decretalium pro 2ª parte 2 fo nota ibi
602	43	Abbas super 3° decretalium 2 fo Nobiliori
603	44	Abbas super 4° et 5° decretalium 2 fo ecclesia

Inferius

1241	45	Henricus Bowyc 2 fo suffra
216	48	Iohannes de Ligniano super 1° et 2° decretalium 2 fo attendi
217	49	Iohannes de Ligniano super 3° 4° et 5° decretalium 2 fo tendit
1247	50	Guido archidiaconus super vi° decretalium cum Mandagoto et aliis 2 fo ecce cum
1270	51	Abbatis consilia 2 fo aliquem in tabula
220	52	Franciscus de zarabellis super 4° decretalium 2 fo dicto c
1243	53	Innocentius super [. . . .] 2 fo et contradicentibus

[Tercio in dextu Superius]

| 6 (?) | 54 | [. . . . .]us et in textu |
| | 54a | [. . . . .] in tabula |

·   ·   ·   ·   ·

(f. 28ᵛ, col. 2)

Ex altero latere eiusdem 3ⁱ dextus Superius

1341	55	Reportorium petri Brixensis pro 1ᵃ parte 2 fo athenas
*1273	56	Reportorium eiusdem pro 2ᵃ parte 2 fo quod faciendo
203	57	Godfridus de trano in summa super decretalibus 2 fo quod non admissis
128	58	Karolus in lectura super decretalibus 2 fo Io. an.
274	59	Questiones et consilia frederici 2 fo de hiis que
1276	60	Questiones et consilia frederici impressa 2 fo possit exigere in tabula
1244	61	'Summa hostiensis 2 fo in textu qui vocabatur'

Inferius

214	62	Iohannes Collectanus super 1° et 2° decretalium 2 fo vel vi xc
215	63	Iohannes Collectanus super 3° 4° et 5° decretalium 2 fo cum eo
211	64	Iohannes Andreas in Novella super 1° et 2° decretalium 2 fo vltra id
212	65	Iohannes Andreas in Novella super 3° 4° et 5° decretalium 2 fo sed incipiunt
213	66	Iohannes Andreas in Nouella super decretalibus 2 fo quod est materia
414	67	Iohannes Andreas in Nouella cum addicionibus super decretal' 2 fo incepit credo
205	68	Innocentius super decretalibus 2 fo di .c.

Quarto in dextu Superius

1274	70	Iohannes andreas in nouella super vi° decretalium 2 fo iure ii 'per inv'.
595	71	Petrus de anchorano super vi° 2 fo stipendium (*entry cancelled*)
229	73	Petrus de anchorano super vi 2 fo querit circa 'salutis'
598	74	Iohannes andreas in novella super vi 2 fo diserte
*1277	73	Franciscus cardinalis de zarabellis super Clementinas 2 fo So secundum pau
234	76	Franciscus cardinalis de zarabellis super Clement' 2 fo doctoribus

Inferius

226	78	Iohannes andreas super vi et Sextus liber ipse in medio libri 2 fo id est confessione
1307	79	Dominicus pro 1ᵃ parte super vi 2 fo secundum Io. an.
*1306	80	Dominicus pro 2ᵃ parte super vi 2 fo inhonestis
228	81	Iohannes in mercurialibus cum tabula questionum mercurialium 2 fo habetur

233	82	Paulus de lyzariis super constit' Clement' 2 fo suum motum
1329a	83	Iohannes de Imola super clement' 2 fo Ergo et (*entry cancelled*) 'quia supra in primo dextu' 'iam in supremo **dextu**'
231	84	Petrus de anchorano super clement' 2 fo De prelatione
*308	85	Reportorium Chyselden' super clement' 2 fo alia conclusio
232	86	Guillelmus de monte auduno super clement' 2 fo ipse tamen

Ex altero latere dextus 4^i Superius

*1267	88	Speculum consciencie Arnoldi quod gnotosolitos appelatur 2 fo defensiones in tabula
221	89	Speculum iudiciale Guillelmi Duranti cum suppletione Io. an. 2 fo vt ibi scripsi
225	90	Speculum iudiciale Guillelmi Duranti 2 fo docuerint
224	91	Speculum iudiciale Guillelmi Duranti 2 fo id est multi
604	92	Guillelmus Lynwod 2 fo condentis [. . .
235	93	Constitutiones Iohannis Pape glosate 2 fo a canonib[us in] tex[tu]

Inferius

1344	97	Reportorium Iohannis Bertachini pro prima parte vtriusque iuris 2 fo abbatis consensus
1345	98	Reportorium eiusdem pro 2^a parte vtriusque iuris 'aureum' 2 fo iusti et 'hic et'
*1326	99	Reportorium Caldrini prima in parte 2 fo celebrare
*1324	100	Reportorium eiusdem in 2^a parte 2 fo potest
222	101	Tabula iuris canonici et ciuilis 2 fo monasterii
1325	102	Vocabularius iuris vtriusque 2 fo aboletur
432	103	Tabula report' legum vtriusque iuris 2 fo baal xxii
196	104	Reportorium aliud [. . . .] incertum est 2 fo cautela in tabula

Quinto in dextu Superius

1310	105	Baldus super prima parte Codicis 2 fo distancia
1314	106	Baldus super 2^a parte Codicis 2 fo fi [. . .
1346	107	Bartholus super prima parte Codicis 2 fo [. . .
1347	108	Bartholus super 2^a parte Codicis [. . .
1348	109	[. . . . .] super 1^a parte Codicis [. . .

. . . . . .

(f. 29, col. 1)

Ex altero eiusdem 5^i dextus latere Superius

1252	113	ff vetus 2 fo excerpsimus in textu
254	114	Odofridus super ff vet' 2 fo intelligenti
523	115	Guillelmus de Cluuio super ff vet' 2 fo glo quia
*1321	116	Prima 2^a et 3^a pars consilii Baldi 2 fo peruenerunt
*1322	117	Quarta et 5^a pars consilii Baldi 2 fo Mulier

Inferius

1313	118	ff vetus de tortis 2 fo gum cognomen in textu
*1319	119	Baldus super 1ª parte ff veteris 2 fo tia illi
1318	120	Baldus super 2ª parte ff veteris 2 fo in quolibet
1349	121	Bartholus super 1ª parte ff veteris cum autent' 2 fo si ver-beratum
1350	122	Bartholus super 2ª parte ff veteris et 3^bus libris C. 2 fo presumuntur
239	123	Paruum volumen cum autent' 2 fo tim ab in textu

Sexto in dextu Superius

1351	124	Bartholus super 1ª parte ff Noui 2 fo ar. sª
1352	125	Bartholus super 2ª parte ff Noui 2 fo cum in eis
1353	126	Bartholus super 1ª parte ff Infortiati 2 fo data vt
1354	127	Bartholus super 2ª parte ff Infortiati 2 fo ab ea iª
1254	128	Ç'D'ynus super ff Infort' et Nouum 2 fo 'do' de heredibus in tabula

Inferius

1355	129	ff vetus 2 fo anno nostras in textu
1356	130	ff nouum 2 fo Nunciationem in textu
*1320	131	Baldus super 2ª parte ff Noui 2 fo Quod si quis
260	132	ff Infortiatum 2 fo ex die in textu
261	133	Ranerius super ff Infort' 2 fo Soluto
371	134	Galiocus super quibusdam titulis et Odofridus super ff nouo 2 fo et ff ad l

Ex altero latere eiusdem 6^i dextus Superius

1275	137	Cynus super Codice 2 fo notatur ergo
268	138	Bartholus super C 2 fo nec dicitur
1256	139	Bartholus super ff vet' 2 fo sit docendum
1260	140	Bartholus super ff No' 2 fo species ab
1257	141	Bartholus super ff Infort' 2 fo vt plenius 'surripitur'

Inferius

*245	142	Codex 2 fo Mare in textu
*1251	143	ff vetus 2 fo virum in textu
*264	144	ff Nouum 2 fo predii in textu
*259	145	ff Infortiatum 2 fo Ro eius in textu
1250	146	Baldus super 1º 2º et 3º Codicis 2 fo translatum
1286	147	Baldus super 3ª parte Codicis 2 fo te iustum
257	148	Iacobus Bu (sic) super ff vet' 2 fo consuetudo
256	149	Odofridus super 2ª parte ff veteris 2 fo in iure

Septimo in dextu Superius

*240	151	Faber super Institut' 2 fo dicit azo
*342	152	Iohannes de platea super 3^bus libris insti. 2 fo hoc nota

243	153	Iohannes de platea super vltimo instit. 2 fo in glo
238	154	Paruum volumen 2 fo rerum in textu
2	155	Iacobus de Beluiso de vsibus feodorum 2 fo hic loquitur
*1357	156	Bartholus super 3^bus libris C et vsibus feodorum 2 fo strumenti

Inferius

*266	157	Azo in Summa 2 fo de hereticis
1327	158	[. . . . .] super Instit' 2 fo nisi probetur
263	159	[. . . . .] super Instit' 2 fo et hoc dici[t]
	159a	[. . . . .] 2 fo homines

. . . . .

(f. 29, col. 2)

Inferius secundo ex latere Septimi dextus

1315	160	ff Nouum 2 fo Labio non in textu
*267	161	Petrus Iacobus de aureliato in practica ad formandos libellos de accionibus 2 fo Superiorem
204	162	Roffridus beneuentanus de ordine iudiciorum et qualiter concipiantur libelli 2 fo Decreto
*1323	163	Iohannes Petrus de ferrariis in practica 2 fo De Clausulis in tabula
1358	164	Breuiloquus 2 fo dracęna

Octaui dextus Superius

1072	165	Titus liuius de bello punico 2 fo flumine
1073	166	Titus liuius de vrbe condita 2 fo vel roris
1070	167	Apuleus de asino aureo 2 fo redegi 'caret'
*1294	168	Strabo 2 fo cogitasti
1069	169	Margarita poetica 2 fo epistolis in tabula

Inferius

***1359**	170	Quintilianus 2 fo et aliquanto
1297	171	Quintiliani alius liber 2 fo proinde de
*1328	172	Varro de ligua latina 2 fo ambages in tabula
1066	173	Titus liuius 2 fo romanorum
1024	174	Valerius maximus 2 fo vs celius
*1074	175	Suetonius 2 fo vltimus in tabula
*1010	176	Solinus 2 fo vrbe roma

Ex altero latere eiusdem dextus 8^i superius

1068	178	Somnium scipionis 2 fo punctum eius
1295	179	Boccatius de genelogia deorum 2 fo genuit abantem in tabula
*1075	180	Appianus de ciuilibus romanorum bellis 2 fo et que
*1025	181	Seneca in tragediis 2 fo qui vicit

Inferius

1304	182	Rethorice tullii 2 fo creatione
1298	183	Questiones tusculane tullii 2 fo studia gloria
1301	184	Orationes tullii 2 fo duces quibus
1303	185	Tullius de oratore 2 fo perraro
1299	186	Nonius marcellus 2 fo tollere pati 'surripitur'
*182	187	Virgilius 2 fo assidue tremebat
*1076	188	Laurentius valla 2 fo cuius rei
1360	189	Plautus 2 fo teneo quid

Vltimo dextus Superius

*77	190	Flores historiarum 2 fo quasi abrahei
1291	191	Iosephus 2 fo fuit sufficiens
*73	192	Beda de gestis anglorum 2 fo quibusdam
74	193	Malmesbury de gestis anglorum 2 fo solent
1065	194	Francisci philelfi epistole 2 fo sus vel
1300	195	Leonardus de studiis et litteris 2 fo leonardus 'desunt'

Inferius

1296	196	Plinius 2 fo Item panetium
1292	197	Campanus de vitis principum 2 fo gloriam superavit
1293	198	Alius liber Campani 2 fo ea tempestate
94	199	Catholicon 2 fo numquam

Additions to List XXI

Additions to the lists of books on Desks 1 (1–5, 12), 2 (27a, 28a, 46, 47), 3 (69), 4 (72, 77, 87, 94–6), 5 (110–12), 6 (135–6, 150), 8 (177).

1361	1	Repertorium Montalui
1362–5	2–5	Abbas in 4^or voluminibus
1366	12	Decisiones rote
1367	27a	(*See List XXI. 27 and note to* **1332**)
1367a	28a	(*See List XXI. 28 and note to* **1333**)
202	46	Decretales 2 fo dampna[mus]
1368	(39), 47	Decretales 2 fo firmiter[1]
1369	69	Constituciones prouinciales [. . .] linwod 2 fo iuxta inte (?)
1370	72	Philippus francus 2 fo sane
1371	77	Franciscus Sabarella super Clement' 2 fo vna in princ'
1372	(24), 87	Sextus 2 fo vel in parte[2]

194–5 'desunt' applies to both 194 and 195

[1] Entered twice. The first entry, after XXI. 38, cancelled.

[2] Entered twice. The first entry, 'Sextus cum Clementinis 2 fo vel in parte in textu', after XXI. 23, cancelled.

1372 a–c	94–6	Bartachinus in tribus voluminibus
1373	110	Baldus super feodis
1374	111	Paulus super digestum vetus
1375	112	Iason super digestum vetus
*1376	135	Odifridus super ff ve 2 fo trahuntur
*1377	136	Item alius Odifridus super ff ve 2 fo pactis
1378	150	Casus Bug' super Iure ciuili 2 fo tate nec
1379	177	Cornucopu 2 fo in tabula cor(n)ucopie

For 1373–1375: } in 5° dextu in 2° latere

LIST XXII

1380–1455 from the Vellum Inventory, ff. 35–7 (five columns), and Misc. 230. The fifth list of books on the law side of the library is the companion to List XVI, but not in the same hand, though, like it, spreading and widely spaced: six lines take up 50 mm. Entries in the original hand of 117 books remain legible or partly legible. Most of the gaps can be filled from Misc. 230 (cf. the notice of List XVI), which lists thirty-two volumes not now recorded in the Vellum Inventory because of damage to the lower parts of ff. 35–7. Forty of the eighty-three volumes not recorded in previous lists survive. 1544 is the latest date of printing (**1393–7**), as in List XVI.

Of the additions (**1432–55**) **1434**, **1448**, and **1451–3** came from Cox, **1432** from Weston, **1436** from Stone, and **1442–3** from Dalby. Some of these additions were certainly in the library before 1556, but they are not listed in Misc. 230.

(f. 35)

Iesus

Libri contenti in bibliotheca collegii animarum ex parte Iuris

In primo dextu

Integrum opus Iuris civilis sine glosis in 6 voluminibus

1380	1	In 2 fo ff veteris didissimi
1381	2	In 2 fo ff Infortiati postea
1382	3	In 2 fo ff Novi reficienti
1383	4	In 2 fo Codicis Nicenam
1384	5	In 2 fo Autent' modo
1385	6	In 2 fo 3 libr. cod. ram libertatem

Integrum opus Iuris Civilis cum glosellis in 5 voluminibus

1386	7	In 2 fo ff veteris vacue
1387	8	In 2 fo ff infortiati amissam

1388	9	In 2 fo ff Novi ignorans
1389	10	In 2 fo Codicis superiorem
1390	11	In 2 fo autent' diem
*1391	12	Budeus [in] pandect' in vno volumine 2 fo piis 'Weston dedit'
1392	13	Alciatus 2 fo propter

Opus Iuris Civilis integrum manuscriptum in 4 voluminibus

*1251	14	2 fo veteris de bonorum
*259	15	2 fo Infortiati quod raro
*264	16	2 fo Novi in provinciali
*245	17	2 fo Codicis duodecimo

In secundo dextu superioris partis

Bartholus in Integrum Ius civile in 5 voluminibus

*1393	18	2 fo ff veteris amplissimo
*1394	19	2 fo ff infortiati bartholi
*1395	20	2 fo ff Novi bartholi
*1396	21	2 fo Codicis poma
*1397	22	2 fo Consiliorum parmensis
*1398	23	Decius in vno volumine [. . .
*1399	24	Statuta anglorum [in 2 voluminibus 2 fo 1^i . . .
*1400	25	[2 fo 2^i . . .

. . . . .

(Inventory of 1556)

*1400a	25a	Consil' Alexandri
*1400b–d	25b–d	Alexander de Imola in 3 volum.
*1400e–i	25e–i	Albericus in 5 volum.

(Vellum Inventory, f. 35^v)

In Tertio dextu superioris partis

Zasius in 5 voluminibus

1401	26	2 fo Instit. de actionibus remota
1402	27	2 fo ff veteris mox adito
*1403	28	2 fo ff Novi hoc pactum
1404	29	2 fo Consiliorum quod se
1405	30	2 fo Intellect' singularum vis aliquando
*1406	31	Klyng super Instituc' in vno volumine 2 fo rem intellectum
*1407	32	Angelus in 3 voluminibus 2 fo ff veteris autem se
*1408	33	2 fo ff Novi siationis
*1409	34	2 fo Codicis die

In Tertio dextu Inferioris partis

| *1377 | 36 | Odofredus in ff vet' in 2 voluminibus 2 fo 1^i pactis |
| *1376 | 37 | 2 fo 2^i trahuntur |

'Iste **Odofridus** translatus est in primam partem quinti dextus'

1284	38	Salicetus super Codic' in 2 voluminibus 2 fo 1 quid subiectum
1285	39	2 fo 2 quia omnia
1410	40	Iason in tribus voluminibus 2 fo veteris cont'
1411	41	2 fo ff Novi sed aduerte
1412	42	2 fo Codicis quando

'Isti tres libri Iasonis deperditi erant eo anno quo dati erant de [. . . .]s et is habet vol[. .] deb[. . .]'

'Pro hoc Iasoni hic ponitur alius novus Iason in quinque voluminibus'[1]

In 4° dextu superioris partis

*1413	43	Baldus super feudis in vno volumine 2 fo cludendo
*1321	44	Consilia baldi in 2 voluminibus 2 fo 1 pervenerunt
*1322	45	2 fo [2] mulier '[. . . . . . .]'
*1414	46	[Consilia Io. de] Immola 2 fo [. . . .] rat[. . .
*1414a–e	46a–e	[. . . . .]minibus
		[. . . . .] ill[. . .

. . . . .

(Inventory of 1556)

*1414a–e	46a–e	Baldus in 5 vo.

(Vellum Inventory, f. 36)

Paulus castrensis in 4 '5ᵉ' voluminibus

*1415	47	2 fo ff veteris istius glo
*1416	48	2 fo ff Infortiati secus
*1417	49	2 fo ff Novi nomine domini
*1418	50	2 fo Codicis sic preceptum

In quinto dextu superioris partis

1367	52	Speculum guilelmi duranti in 2 voluminibus 2 fo 1 omisso
1367a	53	2 fo 2 dierum
*1376–7	54, 54a	'odofredus huc translatus est'[2]
257	56	Iacobus butrigarius manuscripta 2 fo consuetudo
258	57	Petrus in repeticionibus super ff veteri 2 fo consuetudinario
1419	58	Alius liber manuscriptus sine nomine super ff vet 2 fo Iurare ap[. . .
1316	59	Singularia domini lodovici pontani 2 fo qui sit in (?) modo (?)
*522	60	Cinus [super] codic' 2 fo istius civitatis
1255	62	Summa Cini 2 fo notatur

In quinto dextu inferioris partis

1420	64	Tabula prepositi 'super 4 decretalium' 2 fo affectus

[1] Cf. List XXVII at 1547–8.   [2] Cf. 36, 37.

*1421	65	Feli[nus super] decret' in [2] voluminibus 2 fo 1 25 folio
*1422	66	2 fo 2 et d
269	67	Alexander de ancilla 2 fo Sed quid
216	68	Ioannes de liniano in 2 voluminibus 2 fo 1 attendi
217	69	2 fo [2] tendit

· · · · ·

(Inventory of 1556)

1422a	69a	Decretal'
1422b	69b	Decius super Decret'
1422c–g	69c–g	Abbas pan. in 5 volum.

(Vellum Inventory, f. 36ᵛ)

1270	70	Consilia abbatis 2 fo aliquem
1271	71	Disputaciones abbatis 2 fo ¶C pastoral' 'perd (?) Anno 1557' 'iste liber reperitur'
606	72	Antonius de butrio in 5 voluminibus 2 fo 1ⁱ fal quam
605	73	2 fo 2ⁱ tollitur
593	74	2 fo 3ⁱ ventione
219	75	2 fo 4ⁱ se presentauit
1423	76	2 fo 5ⁱ v c

In sexto dextu inferioris partis

220	82	Franciscus de Zarabel super 4ᵐ decretalium 2 fo dicto c.
205	83	Innocentius super decret' 2 fo di c.
1244	85	Summa hostiensis 2 fo q vocabatur
9	86	2ᵃ pars hostiensis 2 fo debet
5	89	Prima pars hostiensis 2 fo alia 'hic liber non reperitur'
6	90	Apparatus hostiensis 2 fo religiosi 'non reperitur 1563'
214	92	Prima pars coletani [. . .
215	93	2ᵃ pars coletani 2 fo cum eo
1424	94	Novella Ioannis andree 2 fo s[. . . .]rori

In septimo dextu superioris partis

274	95	Consilia frederici 2 [fo] de hiis
*594	97	Concordia 2 fo pater 'et nota quod iste liber vltimo anno non erat repertus et est [. . . .] iuris civilis' (*addition cancelled*)
*1290	99	Guilelmus horbache 2 fo torum
*267	100	Liber instrumentorum petri Iacobi 2 fo superiorem
1425	102	Opusculum de verborum et rerum significatione 2 fo pla[. . .] dat (?)
	104	[. . . . .] 2 fo quod [. . .
	105	[. . . . .] 2 fo [. . . .] ta

· · · · ·

(Inventory of 1556)

1283	105a	Summa Godfridi
1425a	105b	Barto. super 2 collationem
1370	105c	Philippus Francus super 6°
*240	105d	Io. Faber super Inst.
*1425b	105e	Decisiones Rote
1425c	105f	Pe. de Ancharano

(Vellum Inventory, f. 37)

Dominicus in 2bus voluminibus

1306	106	2 fo 1ⁱ secundum Ioannem 'glo patet'
1307	107	2 fo 2ⁱ inhonestis 'dum de' (entry cancelled)
226	109	Textus libri sexti 2 fo in consti id est confessione
1247	110	Apparatus guydonis 2 fo ecce
1426	111	Textus libri sexti 'cum comment'' 2 fo mis qui

Octauus dextus superioris dextus (sic)

*1323	113	Practica Ioannis ferarii 2 fo ac et
*1357	117	Baldus de pace 2 fo strumenti
1427	118	Constituciones prouinciales 2 fo ipsi gloria (entry cancelled)
*197	119	Prima pars Ioannis fawet 2 fo 2 3
198	120	2ᵃ pars 2 fo seda[t]
*1329	123	Archidiaconus 2 fo [. . .
1330 (?)	124	Textus decretorum 2 fo [. . .
243	125	Ioannes de platea [2 fo in] glo
1428	126	[. . . . .] 2 fo pres[. . .
210	127	[. . . . .] hostiensis 2 fo visitat

'nota desunt anno 1557'

*1326	128	[. . . . . . .] pars iᵃ 2 fo celebrare
*1324	129	[. . . . .] 2 fo potest
*1429	130	Prima brixensis 2 fo temporalibus
*1273	131	[2ᵃ pars] 2 fo 'quod' faciendo
*1272	132	3ᵃ pars 2 fo athenas
1430	133	T[. . . . .]et' 2 fo vel solus 'est in 1ᵃ parte eiusdem dextus'

In inferiori parte octaui dextus

1378	134	Casus bug' 2 fo tate
1431	135	I[. . . .] platea 2 fo hominis (?)
242	136	Iohannes platea 2 fo ho[. . .
*1431a	137	Angelus [. . .

. . . . .

(Inventory of 1556)

| ***1431a** | 137 | Angelus super Inst |
| **1431b** | 137a | Azo |

1431c	137b	Libellus de ordine iudiciorum
1431d	137c	Speculi 2ª pars
1431e	137d	Boleus super Inst.
***1431f**	137e	Piro

Additions to List XXII

Additions to the lists of books on Desks 3 (35), 4 (51), 5 (55, 61, 63), 6 (77–81, 84, 87–8, 91, 96, 98, 101, 103), 7 (108, 112), 8 (114–16, 121–2).

***1432**	35	Tractatus angeli de maleficiis 2 fo tractatus
***1433**	51	2 fo consiliorum. Abbas[1]
***1434**	55	Lucas de penna 2 fo tabula tabella
***1435**	61	Repetitiones Iohannis baptiste 2 fo etiam in
***1436**	63	Decisiones rote 2 fo capitulum

Item adhuc in 6° dextu in prima parte

1437	77	Constitutiones ottonis 2 fo in con[2]
1438	78	Provincialis linwood 2 fo a. hec
***1439**	79	Lamfrancus 2 fo cum pena 'iste non inuenitur' (*entry cancelled*)[3]
1440	80	Consilia frederici de senis 2 fo prescrip presumpt' 'iste non reperitur' (*addition cancelled*) 'isti duo reperti anno 1557'[4]
***1439**	81	Liber diuersorum tractatuum 2 fo cum pena
1441	84	Bartholomeus Zosimus de except' 2 fo vulgo
***1442–3**	87–8	Adiectus Io(a)nnes Andree in duobus voluminibus ex dono magistri dalb[y] 2 fo erant quedam
***1444**	91	Liber diuersorum tractatuum 2 fo prescriptibilis
***1445**	96	Tertium volumen conciliorum domini barbatii 2 fo sus in
***1446**	98	Concilia oldradi 2 fo incipit tabula 'D Mugge'
1447	101	[. . . . . .] super [dec]ret' 2 fo [. . .
***1448**	103	[Singularis Re]petitio ludouici romani 2 fo ordinariam
***1449**	108	Dominicus super sexto 2 fo rentur
1450	112	Repetitiones azonis 2 fo dum de

Ioannes de turrecremata super ca [. . .] dec' in 3bus voluminibus

***1451**	114	2 fo 1ⁱ reuerendi pientia
***1452**	115	2 fo 2ⁱ reuerendi quia sicut
***1453**	116	2 fo 3ⁱ [Peru]tilis niunt hic

---

[1] A fifth volume of Paulus Castrensis: cf. XXII. 47–50.
[2] 77–80 are bracketed and 'cox' is written against the bracket.
[3] Entered twice: cf. XXI. 81.
[4] The two finds were XXI. 79 and 80.

| **1454** | 121 | Baldus super 2° decretalium 2 fo [. . . .]ari |
| ***1455** | 122 | Repetitiones domini nicholai de milis 2 fo fines |

LIST XXIII

1456–67 from the Vellum Inventory, ff. 48ᵛ–49ᵛ (five columns). The list was made in 1575 in order to include the gifts of David Pole and is in the same hand as the Pole list (IX): eight lines take up 50 mm. Entries of 107 books remain legible or partly legible. All but at most twenty-three of them survive. Among those not recorded before are **1456** given by John Weston in 1565, **1458**, **1459**, **1463** given by Richard Mugge, **1465** given by William Pigot in 1575, and **1466** given by Robert Mowsherst in 1575.

There are no additions.

(f. 48ᵛ, col. 1)

Subscripti libri continentur in Bibliotheca Collegii omnium animarum in Oxonia ex parte legum ‘1575 magistro R. Houenden custode’

In primo dextu Superius

| 1392 | 1 | Alciatus super tt de summa trinitate, suprasancte ecclesie, edendo, in ius vocand’, pact’, transact’, quinque pedum prescrip. Eiusdem paradox dispunct’, de eo quod interest, in tres lib. C. pretermissorum, declamatio vna. de stipul. diuisionibus, in 12m lib. ff. Parerg. Iuris et in tt de verborum significatione vno vol. in 2 fo ampliss. |

Corpus Civile in text’ sex vol.

1380	2	primum habet in 2 fo tituli
1381	3	secundum habet in 2 fo titulorum
1382	4	Tertium habet titulorum digesti
1383	5	quartum habet Index
1384	6	Quintum habet ampliss.
1385	7	Sextum habet in 2 fo puram
*1391	8	Budæus in pandecta In 2 fo At qui

Inferius

Corpus Civile cum glossis quinque vol.

1386	9	Primum habet in 2 fo Vacue
1387	10	Secundum habet in 2 fo Amissam
1388	11	Tertium habet in 2 fo Ignorans
1389	12	Quartum habet in 2 fo Superiorem
1390	13	Quintum habet in 2 fo diem

121 *Perhaps* confirmari

*1251　14 ⎫
*259　15 ⎬ Quatuor lib. manuscript. in pergam.
*264　16 ⎪
*245　17 ⎭

In secundo dextu ex parte dextra superius

*1397　18　Consilia Bartoli In 2 fo parmensis
1456　19　Barbatius super tt de officio del. off. leg. de off. ord. ʻeiusdem consilia' vno vol. In 2 fo famosissimi
*1398　20　Decius super tt si cert. pe. et duobus lib. C. vno vol. In 2 fo acutissimi

Statuta aliquot Regni duobus vol.

*1399　21　Primum habet in 2 fo A renovation
*1400　22　Secundum habet in 2 fo Abbetour

Inferius

Bartolus super C ff no. Infort. et vet. quatuor vol.

*1396　23　Primum habet in 2 fo Poma
*1395　24　Secundum habet in 2 fo Bartoli
*1394　25　[Tertium habet in 2 fo Ba]rtoli
*1393　26　[Quartum habet in 2 fo amplissimo]

. . . . . .

(f. 48ᵛ, col. 2)

1401　27　Zatius in tt de Act' inst. et paraticla in primam partem ff vet' vno vol. In 2 fo Nobili
*1406　28　Kling super inst. et Zatius super tt de iust. et iure leg. iurisd. omnium iud. quod quisque iur. si quis ius dic. non obt. de in ius voc. et de edendo vno vol. 2 fo Rem
1405　29　Intellectus singulares Zatii 2 fo Quamuis
1402　30　Zatius in tt si cer. pet. ff. 2 fo in titt
1404　31　Eiusdem consilia 2 fo Domino Bonifacio

Inferius

Angelus de perusio super C: ff: no: Infor: et vet. tribus vol.

*1407　32　primum habet in 2 fo lectura
*1408　33　secundum habet in 2 fo Incipit
*1409　34　Tertium habet in 2 fo Index
*1432　35　Tractatus maleficiorum Angeli et Alberici In 2 fo Tractatus
*1403　36　Zatius in tt de ver. ob. ff. 2 fo Lecturæ

Ex parte sinistra superius

*720　37　Iason super C. In 2 fo Ad illustrissimam
*727　38　Cynus super C. In 2 fo Incipit lectura

Salycetus super C duobus voluminibus

*725　39　primum habet in 2 fo Incipit tertia
*726　40　secundum habet in 2 fo Commentaria

27–44 were in Desk 3

Inferius

Iason super ff. vet. Infor: vna cum eiusdem repertorio quatuor vol.

*721	41	primum habet in 2 fo Ad illustrissimum
*722	42	secundum habet in 2 fo Iasonis
*723	43	tertium habet in 2 fo Iasonis mayni
*724	44	quartum habet in 2 fo Iasonis

In quarto dextu ex dextra parte

	45	C[. . . . .] 2 fo Excellentiss[. . .
	46	[. . . . .] Preposit[. . .

. . . . .

(f. 49, col. 1)

*1416	47	Tertium habet 2 fo Incipit lectura
*1417	48	Quartum habet 2 fo Incipit
*1418	49	Quintum habet 2 fo Vtilis

In quinto dextu ex dextra superius

*733	50	Speculum durandi duobus vol. primum habet 2 fo Repertorium
*734	51	secundum habet 2 fo Incipit
*1435	52	Repetitio L. diem functo. De eff. ass. ff. per Io. Baptistam cum aliis vno vol. 2 fo etiam in
*1434	53	Lucas de penna super 10m 11m et 12m lib. C 2 fo Libratum
*1377	54	Odofredus super ff. vet. duobus vol. primum habet in 2 fo In nomine
*1376	55	Secundum habet 2 fo Contrahuntur
*1444	56	Tractatus Bauldi Novelli de dotibus et dotatis mulieribus. practica papiensis. Margarita nova Bauld. et singularia seu repertorium Bauldi et singularia Angeli vno vol. 2 fo incipit
1316	57	Singularia Pontani vna cum diuersis tract' Bart' vno vol. 2 fo q[ui s]it

Ex sinistra parte superius

*738	58	Innocentius super decretal' 2 fo Apparatus
*737	59	Prepositus super decretal' 2 fo reverendi
*735	60	Anchoranus super decretal' duobus vol. primum habet 2 fo lectura
*736	61	secundum habet 2 fo [. . . . . .]tilis
	62	[. . . . .] tales 2 fo [. . .

. . . . .

(f. 49, col. 2)

*744	63	Secundum habet 2 fo De Iudiciis
*745	64	Tertium habet 2 fo In nomine

Inferius

*749	65	Panormitanus quatuor vol. primum habet 2 fo In dei
*750	66	Secundum habet 2 fo Incipit
*751	67	Tertium habet 2 fo Incipit lectura
*752	68	Quartum habet 2 fo Reuerendi
*748	69	Provinciales constitut. 2 fo Tabula

Ex sinistra parte superius

		Io. Andreas 'super decretal'' duobus vol.
*1442	70	Primum habet 2 fo Incip[it] novella
*1443	71	Secundum habet 2 fo De vita
*753	72	Distinct. Bowicki 2 fo venerabilibus
*754	73	Barbatius de prestant. Card. 'de offic. delegat. et off. ord. Anto. prepostit (sic). super decretal' et Alexandri super lit. de appellat.' 2 fo Ad reverendissimum

Inferius

*1458	74	Ieminianus super sexto 2 fo Clarissimi
*755	75	Philippus francus super sexto 2 fo Clarissimi
*1459	76	Anchoranus super sexto 2 fo summo Iuris
1460	77	Sextus decret. 2 fo Circa

In septimo dextu ex dextra superius

*1461	78	Geminianus Dominicus de Sancto geminiano super decret' 2 fo Divinum
*760	79	Prepositus super causis 2 fo Commentum
*759	80	Archidiaconus super decret' 2 fo Reuerend[i]
*758	81	Prepositus super distinct' 2 fo Repertorium
1462	82	Decreta 2 fo C (?) [. .]noma

Inferius

*1463	83	Zabarell in Clement' 2° fo francisci
*757	84	Bonifacius super Clement' 2° fo non ideo
*1464	85	Repetitiones Azonis super [decreto] 2 fo] famos[issimi]
*756	86	Arch[idiaconu]s [. . .

. . . . . .

(f. 49ᵛ, col. 1)

*1439	87	Lanfrank' de Ar. (?) 2 fo cum pena
1271	88	Disputationes Nic. ab. siculi 2 fo c. past
*1357	89	Bauldus super pace Constant' manuscript. 2 fo Instrumenti
*761	90	Summa Angelica 2 fo Epistola

Inferius

| | | Repertorium Pet. Brixiensis tribus vol. |
| *1429 | 91 | Primum habet in 2 fo temporalibus |

*1272	92	Secundum habet 2 fo mare
*1273	93	Tertium habet 2 fo quod
*1326	94	Repertorium Caldrini duobus vol. primum habet 2 fo cele-brare
*1324	95	Secundum habet 2 fo potest
*762	96	Singularia Romani cum aliis vno vol. 2 fo Index
*1455	97	Repertorium nicolai de milis 2 fo fines

Ex sinistra parte superius

*240	98	Ioh.Faber in pergam. manuscrip. 2 fo dicit
1371	99	Franciscus Zabarell' super Clement' 2 fo vna
*267	100	Petrus Iacobus super inst. 2 fo Christianiss. manuscrip. 2 fo superiorem

Inferius

*1465	101	Minsingerus super inst. 2 fo Christianiss.
*1466	102	Ioh. Faber super inst. 2 fo Repertorium
*776	103	Iason super tt de Act. inst. 2 fo Eximii
*197	104	Ioh. de Faunt super vndecem causis manuscrip. 2 fo verba
1270	105	Consilia abbatis 2 fo Aliquem
*594	106	Concordia facta per Ioh' Cant' Archiepiscopum inter Regem Angliæ et Regem Franciæ in pergam. manuscrip. 2 fo pater
*1290	107	[Conclusi]ones Willelmi Horbach manu[scrip. . . .

.   .   .   .   .[1]

LIST XXIV

1468–1543 from the Vellum Inventory, ff. 25[v] and 26[v]. A list of books circulating among the fellows in the early sixteenth century, nos. 1–39 written on f. 25[v] and nos. 40–100 on f. 26[v] in probably a different hand: f. 26[r] is blank. Each of the two gaps may have contained some twenty entries. Of the remaining titles 23 have occurred in previous lists, 14 in List II, 6 in List IV, and 3 in List V.

Thirteen of the fifteen survivors are printed books, nine of them Goldwell's gifts. One of the two surviving manuscripts occurs in List V (**538**). It strayed from All Souls and was bought back in 1938.

(f. 25[v])

Hii sequentes Collegii animarum libri. sunt inter socios eiusdem collegii concurrentes in theologia et artibus et gramatica

| **1468** | 1 | In primis Bartholomeus de proprietatibus rerum 2 fo Angelicam |

[1] Only a few titles are missing. The second column is blank.

540	2	Item Gilbertus anglicus 2 fo se non est
*538	3	Item officiorum liber 2 fo amribasius
542	4	Item liber pract' 2 fo iste est paruus
*1469	5	Item questiones scoti super primum sentenciarum 2 fo persona quam
*1470	6	Item questiones scoti super 2ᵐ sentenciarum 2 fo potest esse
1471	7	Item liber de vita cristi 2 fo quia lumine
		Item opus scoti super 4ᵒʳ libros sentenciarum
1472	8	2 fo prime partis agenti naturali
*1473	9	2 fo 2ᵉ partis completa racio
1474	10	2 fo 3ᵉ partis humane
*1475	11	2 fo 4ᵉ partis de securi
*1476	12	Item addiciones super eosdem libros sentenciarum 2 fo scilicet essenciale
*1477	13	Item glosa super psalterium 2 fo que docet
1478	14	Item opus trivium 2 fo ab infancia
*1479	15	Item sermones Guilberti tornacensis 2 fo blandi
*1480	16	Item sermones leonardi de Vtino 2 fo in festo
1481	17	Item liber sentenciarum 2 fo transieris
1482	18	Item opus Mathei 2 fo non negaret
1483	19	Item Biblia 2 fo vxores
29	20	Item scolastica hystoria 2 fo quia tenent
1484	21	Item doctor subtilis super iiiiᵗᵒ libro sentenciarum 2 fo probacio maioris
*1485	22	Item tercium volumen de lira 2 fo et modesti sumus
1486	23	Item psalterium 2 fo sionem verus cum commento
1487	24	Item Boetius de consolacione philosophie 2 fo vidisset admouit
1488	25	Item Bessarius 2 fo veritate
1489	26	Item sermones Augustini de verbo domini 2 fo quot habes
1490	27	Item Eusebius super Ecclesiastica historia 2 fo Genadius
*1491	28	Item lira super Evangelium 2 fo mutacionem
1492	29	Item lactancius 2 fo tibi deus
1493	30	Item Cicero 2 fo rem istam iampridem
1494	31	Item Epistole francisci 2 fo enim et grauia
1495	32	Item Biblia 2 fo testimonia quasi
*1496	33	Item ambrosius de officiis 2 fo approbans
1497	34	Item glosa super psalterium 2 fo vel quia
*1498	35	Item laurencius Vall' 2 fo sancte ac religiose
1499	36	[Item . . . .] 2 fo [. . . . .]rgo

.   .   .   .   .

(f. 25ᵛ, col. 2)

1500	37	Item magister historiarum 2 fo emitte spiritum tuum
1501	38	Item primus liber de anima 2 fo Item arguitur quod sciencia

| 1502 | 39 | Item Vincencius in lucarium (?) 2 fo cedes rapinas |

(f. 26ᵛ, col. 1)

350	40	In primis ff vetus 2 fo promittentibus
507	41	Item ff inforc' 2 fo tuiciorem fundum
436	42	Item Codex 2 fo istorum etenim
381	43	Item paruum volumen 2 fo generaliter
1503	44	Item legenda sanctorum 2 fo petimus
1504	45	Item pupilla occuli 2 fo carecteres
1505	46	Item vocabulest' 2 fo et est focio (?)
1506	47	Item Casuarium super C 2 fo certis capitull'
1507	48	Item Abbat' super 4ᵗᵃᵐ et 5ᵗᵃᵐ 2 fo florentina
1508	49	Item Clement' 2 fo ordine hoc
1509	50	Item Casus Bernardi 2 fo vt qui propter
1510	51	Item Clement' cum doctore 2 fo per studia
514	52	Item Casus Bernardi super decretales 2 fo futura tantum
300	53	Item sextus cum doctore 2 fo In quo
1511	54	Item prima pars Bartholi super inforc' 2 fo de dote
1512	55	Item prima pars Bartholi super ff vet' 2 fo havet (?)
1513	56	Item 2ᵃ pars Bartholi super inforc' 2 fo potest
1514	57	Item Innocencius super decretales 2 fo non potest
1515	58	Item prima pars abbatis super primo libro 2 fo Inst'
1516	59	Item prima pars super primo libro 2 fo At si
1517	60	Item 2ᵃ pars super 1º libro 2 fo c.licet
1518	61	Item hodifre[dus] super ff vet' 2 fo de vsusc'
1519	62	Item decreta 2 fo concessa
1520	63	Item Aparatus Io Andree 2 fo cum super sex
283	64	Item decretales 2 fo Illud potissimum
1521	65	Item Sextus cum clementinis 2 fo in tex antiquorum
1522	66	Item Codex 2 fo cusantes
1523	67	Item ff vetus 2 fo latas
353	68	Item ff inforc' 2 fo pidicinas
441	69	Item ff n(o)uum 2 fo opus nunciari
1524	70	Item paruum volumen 2 fo et perpetua
1525	71	Item Tullius de [. . . .]s 2 fo deliberacionem

.   .   .   .   .   .

(f. 26ᵛ, col. 2)

500	72	Item vi liber decretalium 2 fo quia consuetudo
287	73	Item Apparatus Innocencii 2 fo C Sicut tres contra 1ᵃ
1526	74	Item Bartholus super 2ᵃ parte ff noui 2 fo vt (?) l quod dicimus
1527	75	Item Bartholus super 2ᵃ parte ff noui 2 fo erant
1528	76	Item ff nouus 2 fo lieri vel
323	77	Item paruum volumen 2 fo elementa in quibus
1529	78	Item ff inforc' 2 fo mariturus

1530	79	Item Clement' 2 fo innodate
1531	80	Item Decreta 2 fo nomine
*1532	81	Item Tullius de officiis 2 fo ornate dicere
1533	82	Item Abbas super iii° decretalium 2 fo nobiliori
516	83	Item godfredus In summa 2 fo virtutes
1534	84	Item virgilius 2 fo textus quamuis multam
1535	85	Item orthographia Iohannis Aretini 2 fo orthographie
1536	86	Item Tullius de finibus bonorum et malorum 2 fo citari fecit
497	87	Item Decretal' 2 fo proprietates
357	88	Item ff inforc' 2 fo Si fundus
1537	89	Item Baldus super C 2 fo hoc queritur
1538	90	Item Sextus decretalium 2 fo et beringarium
331	91	Item paruum volumen 2 fo citum est
1539	92	Item Bartholus super ff vet' (2 fo) hi l
1540	93	Item clement' 2 fo hactenus impediti
293	94	Item hostiensis in prima parte lecture 2 fo sumpsit
294	95	Item hostiensis in 2ª parte lecture 2 fo huius glose
*411	96	Item decreta 2 fo Illud cornell'
510	97	Item Innocencius super decretalibus 2 fo quod omnes
1541	98	Item Archidiaconus super decret' 2 fo rellege est
1542	99	Item rofredus in libell' 2 fo ea que sunt
1543	100	Item lucanus 2 fo magne tuam

LIST XXV. ACCESSIONS, 1577–1600

The care taken in inscribing books from 1575 (**1465, 1466**) onwards, and the evidence provided by the Benefactors' Register and the college accounts allow us to draw up a chronological list of accessions in the last quarter of the sixteenth century, which is likely to be complete and reliable in so far as it is concerned with gifts. The gifts of 1575 and 1576 are in the Vellum Inventory, together with those of some later years. The rest can be collected from the inscriptions in the books themselves and, in the case of Richard Franklyn's gift, from the accounts for 1598–9. The books acquired by purchase are a different matter. The tradition of not writing inscriptions in these books did not change in Hovenden's time. There is no contemporary *ex libris* in the two books bought, as the accounts tell us, in 1587–8, nor in the volumes of Concilia (**975–9**), even though these were bought with money provided by benefactors. Books were bought for £1. 6s. 4d. in 1576–7 and for £4. 17s. 6d in 1595–6, but we do not know what they were. One of them may have been the Budaeus, List XXVIB. 9.

B1576–7. y purchase. See List XXVII at 1576–7.

1577. Two volumes by bequest from Thomas Carpenter: will in University Archives, Registrum GG, f. 229, proved 16 August 1577.

*1. J. Weckerus, Syntaxes utriusque Medicinae.
*2. Epitome Operum Galeni per A. Lucanam.

1584. Eight volumes from Francis Milles. See **980–7**.

1586. One volume from Thomas Lucke,† 26 November 1586.

*1. Basilii opera graece.

1586–7. Five volumes bought with money given. See **975–9**.

1587. Three volumes from Richard Master.
*1. Avicenna, Liber canonis.
*2, 3. C. Gesner, Historia animalium.

1587–8. Two volumes bought.
*1. Strabo, Rerum geographicarum libri octo.
*2. Novum Testamentum Theodori Bezae.

1588. One volume from Robert Dow, †10 November 1588.

*1. A. Ortelius, Theatrum orbis terrarum.

1592. Eleven volumes by bequest from Henry Jones, †1592.

*1–9. Repetitiones in varia juris consultorum responsa.
*10–11. A Beroius, Commentarii in Decretalia.

1592. One volume from Thomas Boys, 12 April.

*1. J. B. Nicolaus, Regularum juris tomi duo.

1593. One volume by bequest from Stephen Lynch, †12 January 1592/3. Will in University Archives, Registrum GG, f. 270ᵛ.

*1. L. Caelius Rhodiginus, Lectiones antiquae.

1595–6. By purchase. See List XXVII, 1595–6.

1598. Four volumes from Robert Master.

*1–4. U. Zwinglius, Opera.

1598. Four volumes from Robert Porter.

*1–4. H. Zanchius, Opera.

1598. Four volumes from Robert Hovenden, 30 November.

*1–4. J. Bertachinus, Repertorium.

1598–9. Fifteen volumes from Richard Franklyn.

*1–5. Bibliotheca sanctorum patrum, ed. M. de la Bigne.
*6–14. M. Flacius Illyricus, Historia ecclesiastica.
*15. Sixtus Senensis, Bibliotheca sancta.

1599. One volume from William Hendley, 13 March.

*1. (a) J. Pecham, Perspectiva communis.
(b) Euclides, etc.
(c) J. Stöffler, Elucidatio astrolabii.
(d) Georgius Peurbachius, Theoricarum novarum textus.

1599. Twelve volumes from Francis Milles.

*1–6. Biblia glosata.
*7, 8. P. Melancthon, Opera.
*9. M. de Azpilcueta, Consilia.
*10–12. J. Mascardus, De probationibus.

1600. Eighteen volumes from Francis James.

*1–18. Tractatus ex variis iuris interpretibus collecti.

LIST XXVI. ACCESSIONS NOT INCLUDED IN LISTS I–XXV

A. GIFTS OF KNOWN DONORS, 1438–1592

Some of the books listed here are recorded no doubt in the Vellum Inventory, but cannot be identified there with any certainty, for example John Lovelich's and Robert Est's. Others, not many I think, will have been entered in parts of the Vellum Inventory which have been destroyed. Probably the largest number are books which were not placed in the chained collection. For such books List II, *c.* 1440 and List XXIV, s. xvi in., are our only evidence, apart from contemporary bindings with no chainmark on them, or a chainmark in a position which suggests that chaining took place only after 1597–8.[1] The list could be arranged chronologically. Dates of acquisition are sometimes doubtful, however, and I have thought it better to arrange the names of the donors alphabetically and to reserve a chronological order for the summary list, XXVIII.

John Alexander, †*c.* 1520, gave a manuscript:

*1. Alexander de Hales, Expositio librorum de anima Aristotelis.

Richard Bartlatt, †by 21 January 1557, gave a manuscript:

*1. Johannes de Mirfeld, Breviarium Bartholomaei,

Stephen Barworth, †by May 1511, gave a printed book:

*1. Albertus Magnus, De animalibus.

John Betts, †1501. His will, P.C.C. 3 Blamyr, 19 August 1501, proved 12 September 1501, records a gift of seven volumes:

I bequeth to All Sowlen Collige in Oxforde

(1–3) my booke called Pantholegia conteyned in (iii) volumes
(4) my booke called Almasorium conteyned in x part*is*
(5) my booke diuisio Rasis

---

[1] Goldwell 1 with the six-nail mark, and Derlyngton 1, Goldwell 4, Warner 3, and Weston 1 with the chainmark at the foot (F1) were presumably chained in the library before 1597–8. Alexander 1, Bartlatt 1, Cockys 1, Gaunt 1, 3, Goldwell 7, and Warner 1 have never been chained. Bisshop 1, Goldwell 5, Halswell 1, Honywood 1, and Stone 1 were chained in a position (HS1 or HS2) which was rarely used before 1597–8. Cf. Appendix III.

(6) my booke callid liber Antedodarii Rasis et Experimentorum et Sinomorum Rasis

(7) and my booke callid Anetomia.

Thomas Bisshop, †after 1497, gave a manuscript:

*1. Constitutiones provinciales Angliae, etc.

Thomas Bloxham, †1473. His will, P.C.C. 9 Wattys, 1 April 1473, proved 25 May 1473, provided that such books as Merton College wanted were to go to the library there and the rest to be sold 'preter vnam bibliam pulcram quam lego Collegio Animarum'.

William Broke, †1525, gave a printed book:

*1. Dominicus de S. Geminiano, pars ii super Sextum.

William Byconyll, †1448. His will, Reg. Stafford, Lambeth, f. 167, 3 November 1448, proved 19 November 1448, records a gift of sixteen manuscripts:

*(1, 2) Lego domino Iohanni Byrkhed duo volumina mea de vita Cristi et fidei sue committo quod post decessum suum eadem volumina restituet collegio Animarum . . .

Lego collegio Animarum . . .

(3-6) Nicholaum de Lyra in quatuor voluminibus cum prohemio
(9) Decreta mea
(8) Librum meum decretalium paruum dum tamen consensus Iohannis Elmeregge senioris omnino interueniat
(9) Librum meum sextum cum duobus doctoribus
(10) Librum meum Clementinarum cum doctoribus

Volo quod restituantur collegio Animarum

(11) Henricus Bowhik in vno volumine
(12) Ianuensis in vno volumine
(13) Franciscus de Sabarell' super Clement' in papiro
(14) Petrus de Crescentiis
(15) vnus liber habens plura contenta qui incipit 2° folio [not entered]
(16) Bartholomeus de proprietatibus rerum

Richard Caunton, †1465. His will, P.C.C. 9 Godyn, 17 June 1465, proved 25 July 1465, has the following clause: 'Item I will that my cousyn doctor Oweyn lloyd haue a corse of Ciuyll of myn' to occupye terme of his lif and afterwarde he to leue it to All' Soulyn' collage of Oxenforde for euermore.'

John Cockys, †1546, gave three printed books in addition to the nine included in Vellum Inv.

*1. Innocentius IV, Apparatus decretalium.
*2. Johannes Antonius de S. Georgio, Super quarto libro Decretalium.
*3. (a) Johannes Andreae, Novella super sexto libro Decretalium.
    (b) Johannes de Imola, Super Clementinis.

Joan Croxford gave a Bible in 1457–8: see List XXVII. 1457–9.

William Derlyngton, †1525, gave a manuscript:

*1. Biblia sacra.

John Druell, †1487. His will, P.C.C. 1 Milles, 17 September 1486, proved 6 March 1487, records a bequest:

(1) Quolibetum doctoris subtilis 2 fo essencia non est
(2) Alium librum compendium morale de quibus(dam) dictis antiquorum 2 fo dein*de* adhibita.
(3) et librum Dialogorum Gregorii.

Robert Est, †1493. By will, 10 April 1493, proved 18 August 1493 (printed in *Test. Ebor.* iv. 84–6), he left money to All Souls and also:

Eidem collegio lego

(1–5) v volumina domini Abbatis
(6, 7) ac duo volumina domini Dominici de sancto Gemminiano super Sextum
(8) ac unum volumen domini Bald' super Codicem.

Richard Gaunt, †by September 1519, gave five printed books:

*1. Alexander Carpentarius, Destructorium vitiorum.
*2. Johannes Duns Scotus, In secundum librum Sententiarum.
*3. Johannes Duns Scotus, In tertium librum Sententiarum.
*4. Johannes Duns Scotus, In quartum librum Sententiarum.
*5. Johannes Lathbury, In Threnos Jeremiae.

James Goldwell, †1499, gave three manuscripts and six printed books in addition to the manuscripts and printed books included in Vellum Inv.:

*1. Thomas Elmham, Vita et Gesta Henrici V.
*2. Repertorium juris utriusque, A–I.
*3. Formulare epistolarum.
*4. Willelmus Durand, Rationale divinorum.
*5. P. Comestor, Historia Scholastica, pars 2.
*6. Johannes Duns Scotus, In quartum librum Sententiarum.
*7. N. de Lyra, Postillae in Bibliam, pars 1.
*8. Quintus Curtius, etc.
*9. Franciscus Savonensis, De sanguine Christi, etc.

Nicholas Halswell, †1528, gave a manuscript:

*1. Liber Serapionis aggregatus.

Robert Harlow, †1476. The Benefactors' Register, p. 2, records *Thomas* Harlow's gift of three books:[1]

(1) Johannes Canonicus
(2) Lyra super Evangelia
(3) Biblia

[1] Emden, *BRUO*, p. 876, notes that Robert Harlow is named Thomas in error in Warden of All Souls College MS. 3.

Robert Honywood, †22 January 1523, gave a manuscript:

*1. Johannes de Turrecremata, In Psalterium.

Thomas Kaye, †1572. His will in Univ. Archives, Registrum GG, f. 219ᵛ, records that he bequeathed to All Souls 'Opera Aristotelis cum theophrasto greco to be cheyned in their librarie'.

Thomas Kent, †1469. For the terms of his will see Emden, *BRUO*, p. 1038. It seems unlikely that any of the twenty-eight law books listed by Emden came to All Souls.

John Lovelich, †1438. His will, 26 August 1438, proved 10 September 1438 (*Registrum Chichele*, ii. 562), includes a bequest of five legal manuscripts:

Item lego

(1) unum parvum volumen
(2) unum codicem
(3) unum Digestum vetus
(4) et Digestum forciatum
(5) unum Librum Sextum cum Clementinis in vno volumine novo collegio domini archiepiscopi Cantuariensis in Oxonia vocato collegium animarum omnium fidelium defunctorum.

John Mason, †1566, gave seven printed books (the seventh known only from the Benefactors' Register) in addition to the sixteen included in Vellum Inv.:

*1. Valerianus Bolzani, Hieroglyphica.
*2. Simplicius, In praedicamenta Aristotelis.
*3. W. Lazius, Commentarii reipub. Romanae.
*4, 5. J. Nauclerus, Chronicon.
*6. D. Erasmus, Tomus primus Paraphraseon in Novum Testamentum.
7. Leovitii ephimerides.

Richard Mugge gave, presumably in 1550–1 (see List XXVII, 1550–1), a printed book, in addition to the four printed books included in Vellum Inv.:

*1. Philippus Francus, Lectura super Sexto Decretalium.

Philip Polton, †22 September 1461, gave a manuscript:

*1. Petrus de Palude, De causa immediata ecclesiasticae potestatis; etc.

John Racour, †1487, gave a manuscript, in addition to the two manuscripts and the printed books included in Vellum Inv.

*1. Chirurgia Rogerii, etc.

John Saunder, †1485. His will in Eton College Register 1457–1536, pp. 116–17, 3 June 1485, proved 21 October 1485, contains a bequest to All Souls of two books in addition to the book 'ex propria manu' included in Vellum Inv.

(**1016**): Preterea lego Collegio animarum omnium fidelium def' in Oxon' libros specificatos inferius videlicet . . .

(1) librum dictum Io. Canonici ex propria manu
(2) et Textum Ethicorum.

He asks that **1016** should be chained, but makes no reference to the chaining of the other two books.

Edmund Shether, † in or after 1543, gave a printed book:

*1. (a) J. de Sacrobosco, Sphaera mundi.
    (b) Cl. Ptolemaeus, Almagestum.

Thomas Spray, †1455. The notice of him and his bequests to All Souls in the margin of Vellum Inv., f. 10 (cf. also his will in *Registrum Cancellarii*, i. 351, and *Mun. Acad.* ii. 660) ends with the words 'Cum duobus libris videlicet

(1) Sermones vicarii beate marie magdalene 2 fo [*blank*]
(2) et alio libro dicto Manipulus curatorum 2 fo [*blank*]

Walter Stone, †by May 1519, gave a manuscript, in addition to the six printed books included in Vellum Inv. (**1415–18, 1425b, 1436**):

*1. Prosdocimus de Comitibus, De ordine judiciario, etc.

Richard Topclyffe, †after 1485, gave a printed book and, according to the Benefactors' Register, p. 3, two other books, in addition to the book recorded in Vellum Inv. (**1067**):

*1. (a) Sallustius.
    (b) Plautus.
  2. Duns super 4 lib. sententiarum.
  3. Textus moralis philosoph.

William Tucker. For his gift of the eleven-volume 1529 edition of Augustine in 1558–9 see the note to **1218**.

William Warham, †1532, gave a manuscript and a printed book not included in List VII or in the Benefactors' Register.

*1. Bernardus; Robertus, prior Sanctae Frideswidae.
*2. P. Blesensis, Epistolae.

John Warner, †1565, gave four printed books:

*1. Mesue cum expositione Mundini.
*2. (a) Galeatius de S. Sophia, Opus medicinae.
    (b) Liber Rasis ad Almansorem.
*3. L. Fuchsius, De natura stirpium.
*4. Euclides latine.

John Weston. In addition to **1432** and **1456** he is credited in the Benefactors' Register (p. 7) with the gift of two printed books which are extant and bear his name but no college *ex libris* and one (no. 1) which, if extant, has no inscription:

*(1) Albertus de stat:
*(2) Decretalia Gregorii
*(3) Sextus Decretal:

Another book with his name but no college *ex libris* is

*(4) Casus longi super ff. Veteri Viviani Bononiensis (etc.).

Thomas Wyche, †by September 1475, gave, according to the Benefactors' Register, p. 3:

(1) Prima pars summae Henrici de Gandavo
(2) Questiones Fishaceri
(3) Liber Decretalium

B. BOOKS FROM UNKNOWN DONORS OR BY PURCHASE

1–5 are manuscripts. 6–11 are printed books.

*1. T. Rudborne, Breviarium Chronicorum.
*2. J. Gadesden, Rosa medicinae.
*3. J. de Deo, Casus Decretalium.
*4. Medica quaedam.
*5. Constitutiones Clementinae.
*6. M. Socinus, Tractatus de Citacionibus (*et al.*).
*7. Eusebius, Historia Ecclesiastica per Rufinum.
*8. N. Perottus, Cornucopia.
*9. G. Budaeus, Commentarii Linguae Graecae.
*10. J. Ruellius, De natura stirpium.
*11. Index in tomos omnes operum divi Hieronymi.

C. BOOKS RECORDED BY JOHN BALE

Bale visited All Souls a little before or a little after 1550. He gives 'Ex collegio Animarum Oxon' as his source for ten titles in his notebook of writings by English authors.[1] Six of them, under the names Henricus Huntendunensis, Joannes Gower, Joannes Rocheforth, Joannes Sharpe, Mattheus Florilegus, and Nigellus de Werekere, refer to manuscripts still at All Souls (MSS. 37, 85, 97, 98). One under Guilhelmus Malmesburiensis, may refer to a now missing manuscript of the Gesta Regum or possibly to the one which still remains at All Souls as a fragment

---

[1] *Index Britanniae Scriptorum*, ed. R. L. Poole and M. Bateson, Oxford, 1902.

of four leaves (**74**). One, under Thomas Rudborne, is likely to refer to the manuscript entered above in List XXVIʙ (no. 1). The other two titles are

> (p. 38) Bartholomeus quidam,
> Sermones edidit, li. 1. 'Tollite iugum meum super vos, Notandum quod', etc.
>
> (p. 491) Chronicon 'Stephani Eyton' de Edwardo secundo Anglorum rege, li. 1. 'Post mortem toti mundo deflendam Edwardi primi inclyti regis, successit', etc.

D. BOOKS RECORDED IN THOMAS JAMES'S *ECLOGA* (1600)

In 1600 Thomas James published a list of forty-three manuscripts at All Souls.[1] It is far from being a complete list, since there were at least sixty-six manuscripts at All Souls at this date. Thirty-five of James's titles are identifiable with manuscripts now in the library. One, no. 21, refers to a manuscript which has strayed (**145**) and one, no. 17, to a now missing manuscript (**1263**). Nos. 32 and 42 are likely to be MSS. 49 and 51. No. 36 'Incerti Auctoris opuscula, in Iure Canonico' is probably one of three manuscripts, 53, or 54, or 62. The other three are:

> 6. Grammatica Latina, incerto auctore. Pr. Cum sæpe mecum.
> 28. Speculum regiminis habens duas partes.
> 35. Silius Italicus.

---

[1] *Ecloga Oxonio-Cantabrigiensis*, pp. 45–7. Forty-four manuscripts as numbered, but 40, 41 are one.

LIST XXVII. EXTRACTS FROM COLLEGE ACCOUNTS, 1437–1600

All extracts are from the account rolls of the college, except at 1437–41 and 1545–6. The rolls, drawn up annually by the two bursars, cover a year beginning on All Souls Day, 2 November. Normally two copies of each roll were prepared, one on paper and one on parchment. Either one or other survives, and sometimes both, for all but a couple of dozen years between 1446–7 and 1599–1600. The gaps are mostly in the last four decades of the fifteenth century. For these forty years there are over twenty rolls in existence, but many of them are more or less defective and only fourteen are actually dated.[2] Outside this period the only gaps seem to be at 1507–8, 1511–12, 1548–9, 1565–6, 1566–7, and 1569–70.

Even if there were no gaps one could not write the history of the library from the accounts. It would not be possible to say that so many books were bound and so many were chained, since these figures would include chapel-books, and small payments, e.g. for chaining, may often not have been separated out by the bursars, but lumped with other unspecified payments. So, too, expenses of the fabric and fittings are concealed in payments to tilers, plumbers, and joiners, or in the unfruitful phrase 'ut patet per billam'. On the important matter of book buying it seems safe to say that books were bought now and then, even if the accounts do not mention it (cf. **571**). The large purchase in 1544–5 escapes the bursars' accounts altogether, but

[1] The rolls are kept now in the Bodleian, those up to 1600–1 in boxes marked DD c. 275–87.

[2] The dated rolls are for 1460–1, 1461–2 (Recepta only), 1462–3, 1465–6, 1467–8, 1469–70, 1473–4, 1479–80, 1480–1, 1481–2, 1483–4, 1489–90, 1492–3, 1494–5. Most of the undated rolls are in DD c. 275. Here nos. 1–3, 6, 8a–c, 9, 11–15, all on paper, belong in this forty-year period. Some of them can be assigned probably to particular years, 1463–4? (no. 3), 1464–5 (nos. 11+1), 1466–7 (no. 12), 1468–9 (no. 13). DD c. 278 contains a headless roll for, probably, 1498–9: another bit of it may be DD c. 275, no. 4. A fragment of an early roll is apart from the rest as Misc. 219. In going through the rolls again after an interval of twenty years I have been unable to find one to which I assigned the date 1472–3. In my extracts the bracketing of a year date shows that the roll is headless and does not bear a date in a contemporary or near-contemporary hand. The contemporary date is that in the heading to the roll. I am not sure that the date which occurs also sometimes in the margin at the end of the roll is strictly contemporary.

was large enough to be mentioned specifically in the accounts of the chest in the tower. Smaller purchases too may have been paid for out of tower money. And purchases may be concealed 'in pede computi': that 'bille allocate' were for books is only openly stated in 1547–8 and 1549–50.[1] In reply to questions All Souls said in 1545–6[2] that they spent on an average £1 a year on buying books and on other library expenses. This is very much more than appears in the accounts.

(Building accounts,[3] f. 2ᵛ, 1437.) 7s. 6d. 'pro vectura xlix librorum Oxon' destinat'. ponderanc' iiiᶜ xiiˡⁱᵇ' et i quart' '.
(Building accounts, f. 41ᵛ, August 1440.) 4s. 'Ric. Tyllok Ioynoʳ ad faciend' le deskes in libraria'.
(Building accounts, f. 51, between 1 Nov. 1440 and 2 Feb. 1441.) 2s. 4½d. for candles bought 'pro le Ioynores operant' circa le deskes in libraria fact' '.

1448–9. *In variis expensis et reparacionibus.* 2s. 4d. 'pro cariag' librorum london' et amigdal' '. . . . 3s. to Henry Bath 'pro vectura 8 librorum et ali' '. 1s. to John Prat 'pro cathenacione 5 librorum'.

1449–50. *In variis expensis.* 8d. 'vectori pro vectura libri Ianuensis a lond' '. 2d. 'pro reparacione libri phisicorum alberti'. 2d. to Prat 'pro cathenacione cuiusdam questioniste inter libros philosophie'. 8d. 'vectori exon' pro port' Gower a magistro Drwse'.
   Circa Reparaciones. 12d. to Prat 'pro ligatura Willelmi in speculo'.

1450–1. *Allocaciones Capelle.* 11d. 'pro opere Pratt circa emendaciones variorum librorum tam in librar' quam in Capella vna cum diuersis signaculis Colleg' abscissis a diuersis libris'.
   In variis expensis. 6d., 3 Aug., 'Pratt pro emendacione certorum librorum'.

1452–3. *Reparaciones.* 2d. to Pratte, 31 Dec., 'pro reparacione Baldi in vtroque volumine et textus Codicis'. . . . 6d., 25 Sept., 'pro pelle vitulino ad reparand' libros'. 2d., Oct. 1, 'pro pelle ouina ad cooperiendum vnum librum Clementino-rum'. . . . 7d. 'Io. Pratte in parte solucionis pro reparacione diuersorum librorum xii die Septembris per Custodem'. 2s. 'Radulpho pro tribus cathenis ad libros prec' cathene viii *d*' x die Iunii per eundem'.
   Varie expense. 8d., 16 Dec., 'pro cathenacione librorum dat' per M. Couper'. 4d. to Pratte, 21 Jan., 'pro emendacione vnius quaterni Bartholi et imposicione alterius quaterni ff. veteris et pro cathenacione vnius libri dat' per M. W. Griffith'.

---

[1] See below under these years. The loss of the roll for 1548–9 is unfortunate.
[2] Valor of 37 Henry VIII: P.R.O., Augmentation Office, E. 315/441, f. 81. The return from All Souls College states that expenditure on the library was 'pro empcione et Renouacione ac emendacione librorum et graduum voc' dexis in Bibliotheca communibus annis xxˢ in toto per annum prout patet'.
[3] MS. 401 (LR 5. b. 3).

1456–7. *Reparaciones infra Collegium.* 3*s.*, 23 July, 'Iohanni Bokebynder pro emendacione et ligacione librorum hoc anno in parte solucionis'. 2*s.*, 12 Aug., 'eidem Iohanni pro eodem labore'.

1457–8. *Capella.* 1*s.* 11*d.* 'Thome filio stac' pro ligacione et coopertura 2^{orum} librorum et catenacione libri vi^{ti} in libraria'. . . . 1*s.* 4*d.*, 30 June 'Iohanni Bokebynder pro ligacione Antonii super iiii^{to} libro decretalium et cathenacione Odefredi'. . . . 3*s.* 'pro xxvi pellibus pargameni xii die Iulii pro Custodiis librorum in ecclesia et libraria'.

Varie expense. 4*d*, 27 May, 'pro emendacione et cathenacione 1 libri dat' a magistro Io. Dryell'. . . . 2*s.* 4½*d.* 'pro vino et cibariis ex bursa custodis Iohanne Croxford et aliis eodem tempore quo dedit bibliam et vestiment' Collegio'.

(1458–9). *Varie expense.* 4*d.* 'pro catenacione Antonii super quartum librum decretalium'.

1459–60. *Reparaciones infra collegium.* 3*s.* 4*d.* 'pro ligacione librorum M. Roberti Est et Goldwell' '. 2*s.* 6*d.* 'Magistro lumbury pro ligacione librorum'.
Varie expense. 9*d.* 'vni adducenti librum sextum a(pu)d Tenbury ad Stanlake'.

1460–1. *Varie expense.* 3*s.*, 3 July, 'pro vectura librorum per Iacobum Cariour'. . . . 3*s.*, 3 Oct., 'pro vectura librorum collaturum per M. Kees'. . . . 3*s.* 4*d.* 'Iohanni Beke p̄ri Milwyn' pro deliberacione libri decretalium Custod' apud Tedbury'.

1462–3. *Varie expense.* 1*s.* 8*d.*, 4 April, 'pro reparacione vnius libri'.

(1463–4.) *Varie expense.* 4*s.* 4*d.* 'pro diuersis cathenis emptis'.

(1464–5.) *Varie expense.* 7*d.* 'pro catenacione et emendacione quinque librorum'. . . . 2*s.* 'vni dawber emendanti hostium in libraria'.

1465–6. *Varie expense.* 5*d.* 'pro duas vangis ad mundandam librariam'. 10*d.* 'pro ligacione vnius libri (*entry cancelled*).
(*Reparaciones infra Collegium.*) 2*s.* 'pro liga' libri codicis in libraria', 1*s.* 8*d.* 'pro emendacione libri sexti et aliorum librorum' (*entry cancelled and marked with a cross*). 4*s.* 'pro ligacione librorum in collegio diuersis temporibus'.

(1466–7.) *Regard'.* 1*s.* 8*d.* 'duobus seruientibus Magistri Northfolk adducentibus libros collegio datos'.
Reparaciones infra Collegium. 1*s.* 5*d.* 'pro ligatura vnius libri iuris ciuilis'. . . . 2*d.* 'pro incathenacione petri de Ankarano'. . . . 6*d.* 'pro vna cathena et incathenacione vnius libri M. Eliot'. 2*s.* 'pro ligatura petri de ankarano'. 2*s.* 8*d.* 'pro ligatura duorum librorum arcistarum'.

1467–8. *Varie expense.* 10*d.* 'pro vectura libri Hugonis de Viennia'.
Reparaciones infra collegium. 1*s.* 1*d.* 'pro ligacione libri logicalis'.

(1468–9.) *Varie expense.* 2*d.* 'pro reparacione vnius libri codicis existentis apud Stacionarium'. 4*s.* 4*d.* 'pro diuersis reparacionibus et cathenacione librorum in libraria et choro'.
Reparaciones infra Collegium. 2*s.* 8*d.* 'pro ligatura duorum librorum vnius decretal' et cardinalis super vi^{tum}'.

1470–1. *Varie expense.* £1 'Magistro Badkock pro libro philosophie'.

(1472–3.) *Regard'.* 4d. 'vectori deuonie pro adducione 2ᵒʳᵘᵐ librorum'.
   Reparaciones infra collegium. 2s. 6d. 'pro reparacione in libraria'.

1479–80. *Reparaciones infra Collegium.* 4d. 'pro cathenacione duorum librorum in libraria'.

1480–1. *Reparaciones infra Collegium.* 6s. 8d. 'pro 2ᵇᵘˢ duodenis cathenarum pro libraria'. 1s. 'pro ligatura Anthonii in libraria cathenati'.
   Varie expense. 1s. 8d., 30 June, 'pro vectura biblie'. . . . . 2s. 'pro vectura sex voluminum hantton' Antonie ex dono Magistri Wyntyrborne'. . . . . 1s. 7d. 'pro cathenacione octo voluminum in libraria posit''. . . . 3d. 'pro cathenacione trium voluminum in libraria posit' '. 1s. 6d. 18 Dec., 'pro vi cathenis'. 10d. 'pro reparacione vnius libri et cathenacione eiusdem'. £1 'solutis Burs' arcium pro lathbury super libros trenorum imprimendo et emendo pargamenum'.

1481(–2). *Varie expense.* 6d. 'pro vectura 3ᵘᵐ librorum August' ex dono M. Wynterborne'. . . . 2d., 28 July, 'pro vectura vnius libri de astronomia'. . . . 1s. 8d. 'pro vectura x librorum ex dono M. Goldvyn iii die Ianuarii'.

1489–90. *Reparaciones infra Collegium.* 2s 8d. 'petro ligatori librorum pro ligacione 2ᵒʳᵘᵐ librorum'.

1494–5. *Reparaciones infra collegium.* 3s. 1d. 'pro cathenis librorum'. . . . 2s. 4d. 'pro ligatura voluminis decretalium et 2ⁱ voluminis dominici super sexto'.
   Varie expense. 6s. 4d. 'pro vectura 8 librorum eboraco oxon' ex legat' Magistri Est'. . . . 8d. 'pro apposicione cathenarum v voluminibus et clausoriis eorundem'.

(1498–9.) (*Varie expense.*) 2s. 4d. 'savtre pro cathenacione librorum dat' [. . . . . .] M. Mors'.

1502–3. *Varie expense.* 1s. 'sawtre pro cathenacione librorum'. . . . 4d. 'pro vectura libri ex dono M. Stokes a Wyndsor' ad londinium'. . . . 2s. 'Radulpho pro vectura librorum Magistri Stokes et alterius'. . . . 3s. 'pro novem cathenis pro libris cathenandis'.
   Post festum. 4d. 'pro vectura libri diuersorum operum ex dono Magistri doctoris Mors'.

1504–5. *Reparaciones in colegio.* 3s. 8d. 'pro ligatione diuersorum librorum in bibliotheca'.
   Varie expense. 1s. 1d. 'pro Catinacione librorum et pro stater' '.
   Regardis. 1s. 8d. 'famulo Magistri Bettis ferente libros colegio'.
   Post festum. 4d. 'Sawtre pro cathenacione librorum'.

1506–7. *Reparaciones infra.* 4d. 'carpent' pro emendacione scannorum in bibliotec' '.

1508–9. *Reparaciones infra.* 16s. 'pro 4ᵒʳ ly dosyn cathenarum'. 2d. 'pro reparacione hostii bibliothece'.

Varie expense. 4s. 4d. 'walkare pro vectura librorum quos dedit M. Cole'. . . .
4*d.* 'penhur pro mundacione bibliotece'. . . . 4*s. 8d.* 'pro cathenacione librorum'.

1509–10. *Reparaciones infra. 8d.* 'pro cathenacione iiii librorum'.

1512–13. *Reparaciones infra. 6s. 5d.* 'laborantibus circa librariam et Cubiculum
M. Ryche'.
Post festum. 13s. 4d. 'Magistris leceter et haklet pro Catenacione librorum in
Ordine'.

1513–14. *Varie Exspense. 4d.* 'pro reparacione vnius libri Iuris in custodia M'
haklet'.

1517–18. *Varie expense. 1d.* 'pro reparacione libri in bibliotheca'.

1518–19. *Varie expense. 7s.* 'Cornyshe pro emendatione librorum'.

1520–1. *Reparaciones infra. 1s. 9d.* 'liganti libros et coopertura eorundem'.

1522–3. *Reparaciones infra. 8d.* 'pro chathenacione librorum in capella et
bibliotheca'.

1523–4. *Reparaciones infra. 12d.* 'pro tegulis ad reparacionem claustri et biblio-
theci'.

1524–5. *Reparaciones infra. 1s. 9d.* 'pro ligatura quinque librorum in bibliotheca'.

1525–6. *Varie expense. 6d.* 'pro mundacione librarie'.

1526–7. *Varie expense. 1s.* 'Henrico bokebynder construenti librum registri'.

1527–8. *Reparationes infra. 1s. 3d.* 'pro coopertura librorum in bibliotheca'.

1530–1. *Reparationes infra. 5d.* 'pro reparatione Valerii Maximi'.

1533–4. *Varie expense. 8d.* 'pro corbe ad vehendos libros domini cant' a londino'.
. . . 4*s.* 'pro cista empta ad portand' libros domini Cantuar' '. 8*d.* 'pro sera ad
eandem et vectura ad diuersorium tabellarii'. 11½*d.* 'pro canvas pro mappis
stramine ad libros et cingulo pro sagittis'. . . . 9*s. 6d.* 'frewen pro vectura librorum
domini cantuar' et etiam racemorum'.

1538–9. *Varie expense. 2s.* 'fabro pro libris reponendis in liberario'.

1539–40. *Varie expense. 4d.* 'Matthẹo evans pro inscriptione librorum de heresi
condempnatorum'.

1540–1. *Reparationes intrinc'. 4d.* 'fabro ferrario cathenanti librum statutorum
et cathenam reparant' '. . . . £7. 6*s.* 0½*d.* 'pro reparationibus super librariam
factis hoc anno'.
Varie expense. 12d. 'vehenti libros a magistro Ryche donatos'. . . . 19*s. 2d.*
'dewe pro vectura liberate et librorum'. 4*d.* 'pro vectura harum rerum ad
diuersorium dewe'. . . . 3*s. 4d.* 'Arundell ementi quadragesimales pisces ceram et

alias res, nec non laboranti circa librorum a doctore cok*is* donat' vecturam in partem expens' suarum'.

1541–2. *Rep(ar)ationes.* 3*s.* 2*d.* 'fabro ferrario cathenanti libros in Biblitheca'.

1542–3. *Varie expense.* 2*d.* 'ad figendum librum statutorum in librario'.

1544–5. *Reparaciones infra.* 5*s.* 3½*d.* 'pro reparacione bibliothece magistri (*sic*) fuller vt patet per eius billam' . . . 12*d.* 'fabro ferrario pro reparacione serarum in communi bibliotheca et laboranti circa cathenacionem librorum ibidem'.

Varie expense. 8*d.* 'famulis garbronde bibliopole vt melius expolirent libros emptos ex commune ęre collegii hoc anno'.

1545–6. *Variæ expensæ.* 4*d.* 'lotrici mundanti bibliothecam'. . . . 5*d.* 'fabro ferrario cathenanti in bibliotheca communi'. 4*d.* 'pro emundatione bibliothecæ ad pustulationem decani iuristæ'. 3*s.* 4*d.* 'pro cathenatione librorum ex dono Magistri Cooxe'.

(Accounts of the common chest in the upper chamber of the tower, Archives, DD c. 369, f. 17.) Memorandum that the book*is* newe bowght for the librari by master bullyngham and master heryng amownt to the svm of £36. 12*s.* 4*d.* the whyche svm they have receyued ageyn of thys cofer the xiiii^th day of november in the xxxvii^th yere of our souereigne lorde the kyng.

1546–7. *Reparationes intra.* 4*s.* 'pro duodecim Clavibus ad ostium communis bibliothece'.

Variæ expense. 4*d.* 'lotrici emund' bibliothecam'.

1547–8. *Reparationes infra* (altered to *intra*). 4*d.* 'pro clavi ad ostium bibliothece pro eodem Freacke'.

In pede computi. Deinde tamen in finali computo predicti computantes (*the bursars John Hering and John Gibbon*) satisfecerunt et soluerunt predictam summam collegio in billis iuste allocatis . . . £11. 17*s.* 0½*d.* . . . Bille allocate . . . continebant pro omnibus operibus Augustini £4 et pro operibus Iasonis £3 et pro operibus Galeni £2. 10*s.* 0*d.* et pro cathenis 2*s.*[1]

1549–50. *Recepta.* £1. 6*s.* 8*d.* 'pro veteribus libris venditis magistro garbrande'.

Reparaciones intra. 1*s.* 'pro emundatione librarii et cubiculi custodis lotrici'.[2]

Varie expense. 4*d.* 'Garbrand eo quod posuit libros in bibliotheca'.

In pede computi. Deinde tamen in finali computo predicti computantes (*the bursars Thomas Abbot and Thomas Chamber*) satisfecerunt et soluerunt predictam summam Collegio. videlicet in dictionario stephani posit' in bibliotheca £2. 12*s.* 0*d.* . . .[3]

1550–1. *Varię expensę.* 1*s.* 10*d.* 'pro vectura mantice et librorum doctoris Bartlet a Londino eodem tempore (*the time of the May progress*)'. . . . 2*s.* 6*d.* 'pro vectura librorum collegio datorum ex dono D. Mugge'. . . . 8*d.* 'lotrici pro emundatione bibliothecę'. 2*s.* 4*d.* 'Garbrando pro cathenis et suis laboribus in reponendo libros D. Mugge et D. Bartlet in librario'.

---

[1] The total sum in question was a credit balance of £12. 18*s.* 5½*d.*

[2] Perhaps the warden's library is meant.

[3] The total sum in question was a credit balance of £4. 1*s.* 4*d.*

1551–2. *Variæ expensæ. 4d.* 'lotrici mundanti bibliothecam'.

1552–3. *Reparationes intrinsec'. £4 (sic)* 'pro clave ostii librarii pro Den'. . . . 10d. 'pro duabus clavibus ostii librarii pro cubiculo Mʳⁱ Bedell et Champenyse'.
   Variæ expensæ. 4d. 'lotrici mundanti bibliothecam communem'.

1553–4. *Reparationes intrinsecæ. 5d.* 'pro clave bibliothecæ pro Mʳᵒ Jhones'. . . . *£2. 10s. 9d.* 'Tegulatori reparanti bibliothecam (etc.)'.
   Variæ expensæ. 2s. 8d. 'pro cathenatione librorum in Bibliotheca'. . . . *4d.* 'pro mundatione Bibliothecæ'.

1554–5. *Reparaciones intrinsecę. 10d.* 'pro emendacione tigni in bibliotheca'.

1555–6. (*Variæ expensæ.) 6d.* 'pro mundatione Bibliothecæ'.

1558–9. *Variæ expensæ. 8d.* 'mundanti Bibliothecam'. . . . *£1. 3s. 7d.* 'pro vectura librorum dat' collegio per magistrum Tucker'.

1559–60. *Reparaciones intrin'. 6s.* 'Stile tegulatori et famulo suo per quatuor dies circa bibliothecam'. *£2. 13s. 2d.* 'plumbario operanti circa orientalem partem bibliothece'.

1561–2. *Varie Expense. 1s. 4d.* 'lotrici mundanti bibliothecam'.[1]

1567–8. *Variæ expen'. 6d.* 'pro catenacione libri in bibliotheca'.

1571–2. *Variæ expensæ. 4s.* 'pro papiro ly riall pro libro collegii'. *1s.* 'pro ligatione eiusdem'. *4s.* 'pro ligatione lib' regist' indentur' '. *6s. 10d.* 'pro papiro pro ii libris regist' '. *1s. 6d.* 'pro papiro ad conficiendum libri regist' pro nominibus sociorum'. *10d.* 'pro ligatione eiusdem'. . . . *1s. 6d.* 'pro ligatione et catena libri statutorum'.

1572–3. *Varię Expensę. 17s. 2d.* 'for a statute booke to the Subwarden'.
   Recepta. £4. 4s. 0d. 'for parchment bookes'.

1574–5. *Recepta. 19s.* 'pro libris pergamenis'.
   Variæ expensæ. 18s. 9d. 'dat' cavye for cheynynge lxxv bookes 3d ly booke'. *10s.* 'pro ly bindinge of Panormitan in quatuor vol.'.
   Summa equitancium. £6. 2s. 2d. 'pro expensis mousherste fetchinge the bookes from Peterboroughe per Billam'.

1575–6. *Recepta. £5* 'ex legato magistri Andree Kingesmill quondam socii ad libros emend' '.
   Variæ Expensæ. 1s. 4d. 'pro reparatione librorum et catenarum in Bibliotheca'.
   1576–7. *Variæ Expensæ. £1. 6s. 4d.* 'Magistro Garbrand for Bookes'. *3s.* to 'Cavie for chening xii bookes'. *2s. 6d.* 'for bynding Innocentius'.

---

[1] There are special payments of 13s. 4d. in 1559–60 'lotrici propter paupertatem' and in 1562–3 'matri ferryshe olim lotrici propter paupertatem' and a payment of 6d. 8d. in 1563–4 'Oven ob laborem et sumptus impensos in pauperculam nostram lotricem vulgariter vocatam mother Ferrys nuper defunctam'.

1578–9. *Reparationes intra.* 2*d.* 'for chaining yᵉ statute book'.

1580–1. *Variæ expensæ.* 7*s.* 'for newe binding 3 vol. of the Civil Course'.

1583–4. *Variæ expensæ.* 11*d.* 'for Royall paper for yᵉ newe Bible'. 36*s.* 'to dominicke for bindinge yᵉ same'. 10*s.* 'to Jhon frenchman toward yᵉ makinge of bosses and claspes for the same'.

1584–5. *Reparationes intra.* 3*s.* 4*d.* 'for cheining x bookes in the librarie'.
Variæ expensæ. 10*s.* 'for making bosses and claspes for the great byble'. . . . 7*s.* 'for chaynes xii for the librarie'.

1586–7. *Recepta.* £2 'for the legacie of one Mʳ Bastard sometyme Canon of Worcester giuen the Colleg'. £3 'given to the College by D. Jones canon and late Chauncelor of Welles'.
Variæ expensæ. £6. 13*s.* 6*d.* 'for the general counsails in Venise print. v volums to the Library whereof iii¹' was giuen by Mʳ doctor Jones Chancelor of Welles, xls. by Mʳ Bastard prebendary of Worcester 'late fellowe' the rest viz' xxxis. vid. paied by the College'. (The paper copy of the account adds that the expenses were for 'buieng, binding, bossing the generall Councells'.) 3*s.* 4*d.* 'for five chaynes to the saide five bookes'.

1587–8. *Reparationes intra.* 5*s.* 8*d.* 'for plaisteringe the librarie and sweepinge the hall wall'.
Variæ expensæ. £2. 4*s.* 0*d.* 'for Beza his annotations one the new Testament et Strabo gręce et latine vt patet per billam Garbrand'. 4*s.* 'for eight chains for the Councels'. 3*s.* 8*d.* 'for chaininge of xi bookes in the librarie'.

1589–90. *Variæ Expensæ.* 1*s.* 2*d.* 'for mending the booke of Martirs and the chaine to it'. 8*s.* 'for a new pagnins bible for the haule'. 1*s.* 'for a lether couer for the same'.

1591–2. *Reparationes intra.* 3*s.* 6*d.* 'for carieng of books from London' being geaven to the Colledg by doctor Johns'.
Variæ expensæ. 2*s.* 8*d.* 'for binding of a booke for the librarie'. . . . £1. 10*s.* 6*d.* 'for binding ix books wᶜʰ doctor Johns did geave to the Colledg iiis. 4*d.* the booke and vi to the bookbinders man'. 1*s.* 1*d.* 'for rioll' paper to be sett before the books'. 1*s.* 6*d.* 'for claps to the same and setting them in the librarie'. . . . 2*s.* 4*d.* 'to the freanchman for putting on plates on the books wᶜʰ doctor Johns bestowed'. . . . 4*s.* 'for a dozen of chaens for doctor Johns his books'. 7*s.* 'for binding to Lawe books'. 8*d.* 'for claps for them'. 6*d.* 'for chayning them'.

1593–4. *Variæ Expensæ.* 4*s.* 6*d.* 'for new bindinge and mending the booke of accountes about the buildinge of the colledge'.

1595–6. *Varię expensæ.* 4*s.* 8*d.* 'for binding ii lawe books vz Cynus et Lanffrancus'. . . . £4. 17*s.* 6*d.* 'for certaine books to be putt in yᵉ librarie bought of Mʳ Kisby'.

1596–7. *Reparaciones intra.* £9. 8s. 6d. 'for waynscott and Clayboord for the Library 23 waynscotts and 60 Clayboords'. . . . £2 'for the Carryage of the waynscotts and Clayboord from London to Burcott'. 1s. 3d. 'for the wharfage of the same'. 10s. 'for the cariage of the same at ii loades from Burcott to Oxford'. 1s. 'for the cariage of ii peeces of Waynscott from Burcott more which was left behind'. . . . 11s. 4d. 'for a peece of Timber for the Library'. . . . £2 'to Garrett for ii peeces of Timber for the library'. 4s. 'to a Carpenter for squaring the same tymber be iiii daies'. 10s. 'for Cariage of the same tymber at 3 loades at iiis. iiiid. the loade'. . . . £2. 3s. 8d. 'for 600 and a quarter of boards for the Library at viis. the hundred'. 5s. 'for the Cariage of them from Brill'. . . . £1. 2s. 9d. 'for 300 and a quarter of oake boards at viis. the hundred for the library'. . . . £24. 10s. 6d. 'to the Joyner for worke in the library vt patet per billam'. . . . £37. 7s. 5½d. 'for charges in the Library Mr Wardens kytchen and other places vt patet per llabim'.

Variæ expensæ. 10s. 'to the Joyner for his iourney to London for the waynscott'. . . . 3d. 'for carryeng the dust out of the library when the Joyner wrought there'.

1597–8. *Reparationes intra.* £7. 10s. 4½d. 'to the smith for worke done for Mr Warden and the Library vt patet per billam'. 3s. 8d. 'to the carpenter and his man for two dayes in the library at the vsuall rate'. 3s. 6d. 'for studes to dub the upper end of the wale in the librarye'. . . . 5s. 4d. 'for 8 bushell of lime for the library at 8d.'. 1s. 4d. 'for 2 bushell of haire for the library at 8d.'. . . . 3s. 4d. 'for on planke and two elme boordes for the pendentes in the librarye'. . . . 5s. 4d. 'for on quarter of haire for the library'. . . . £1. 0s. 6d. 'for boord and tymber for the Library vt patet per billam'. 6s. 'for 6 dayes to the carpenter in the librarye'. . . . 2s. 8d. 'for half a quarter of haire in the library'. . . . 6s. 'for the carpenter 6 dayes in the librarye'. 4s. 6d. 'to the carpenter 4 dayes and a half there'. 2s. 'for a peece of timber for the statues in the Librarye'. 1s. 4d. 'to a labourer for 2 dayes in the Lybrarye'. 4s. 6d. 'to the Carpenter 4 dayes and a half in the Librarye'. 8s. 6d. 'for a carpenter 8 dayes and a half in the Librarye'. 3s. 6d. 'to Stiles for 3 dayes in the library and a half day in Sr Ingram's studye'. 8s. 'for a peece of Walnut tree for the personages in the Librarye'. 6s. 'for two doz. of quarters for wainscott in the Librarye'. 1s. 'for the use of cloathes to couer the deskes in the librarye'. . . . 2s. 6d. 'to Thornton for 2 daies worke and an half in the librarye'. . . . 8d. 'for a bushell of haire for the librarye'. 9s. 'for a doz. of clawboordes for the librarye'. 2s. 6d. 'for 15 yardes of quarters for the librarye'. . . . 25s. 4d. 'for 38 bushells of lime at 8d. for the librarye'. 1s. 3d. 'to Stiles his man for a day and half in the librarye'. . . . 2s. 'to the carpenter two dayes in the librarye'. . . . 18s. 'for 200 of boordes for the librarye'. 15s. 'for foure score and ten yardes of quarters to make wainscot for the librarye'. 4s. 6d. 'for six clawboordes to make crests for the worke in the library'. . . . 7s. 'to the carpenter 7 dayes in the librarye'. . . . 4s. 'for culleringe and varnishinge the pillers in the Librarye'. . . . 6s. 'to David for 4 dayes in the Librarye'. 4s. 6d. 'for half a doz. of clawbordes for the Librarye'. 2s. 6d. 'for 30 fote of halfinch bordes for the librarye'. . . . 3s. 6d. 'for 3 bush: of lime to white the Librarye and horse hire to fetch the same at Abbington'.

2s. 6d. 'for a carpenter two dayes and a half in the Librarye'. . . . 9s. 'for 100 oken bordes for the librarye'. . . . 4s. 'for 6 bush: of haire for the Librarye at 8d.'. . . . £1. 7s. 0d. 'to Mʳ Garbran for 300 fote of bordes for shelves for the librarye at ixs.'. 6s. 'to the plaisterer for 6 dayes at the walles and silinge at the Entry into the librarye'. 4s. 'to his man for 6 dayes there'. £28. 12s. 6d. 'to Pearson for 229 yardes of fretworke at 2s. 6d. the yarde'. £6. 12s. 4d. 'alowed to Pearson for the carvar in the librarye'. 10s. 'alowed to Pearson for alteringe the armes'. £1. 16s. 0d. 'for whitinge the Librarye'. £59. 9s. 2s. 'to the ioyners for their worke in the library vt patet per billam'.

Variæ expensæ. 9s. 2d. 'to the carpenter and his man 5 dayes in the Librarye'. . . . 1s. 'for sawinge a walnut tree for the statues of the librarye'. . . . £1. 2s. 4d. 'for claspes and eyes for the Library bookes'. . . . 2s. 'for a pound of wire to chaine bookes'. 12s. 'for 3 dozen payre of claspes'. 3s. 'to two women for 3 dayes a peece for washinge the library and the glasse'. . . . 7s. 9d. 'for 7 doz of claspes for the librarye bookes wᵗʰ the carriage'. . . . £1. 8s. 0d 'for 7 doz of chaines for the library at iiiis.'. £1. 4s. 'to Dominicke for bindinge bookes'. £9. 19s. 4d. 'to Dominicke for 92 dayes worke for himself and his man at 2s. 2d. the daye'. £13. 17s. 3¼d. 'for nayles'. . . . 8d. 'for Sutton one day for carring Rubbedge out of the librarie'.

1598–9. *Variæ expensæ.* £3. 14s. 6d. 'for lathes for the librarye'. £6. 3s. 6d. 'for Domynicke and his man 57 dayes at iis. iid. the daye'. 1s. 4d 'to Domynicke for his man two dayes'. £3. 18s. 6d. 'for stuffe from the beginninge of Domynicke working here vt patet per billam'. . . . £1. 0s. 0d. 'to Domynicke for bindinge seven books in fol. in borde'. 3s. 'to the same for bindinge one other booke'. 13s. 6d. 'for 3 dozen of chaines of Domynicke'. 1s. 'for wiar'. 8s. 'for 2 dozen of Chaines of Brimi Carier'. . . . 7s. 8d. 'for nayles for the claspes of the books and to Domynicke for 3 dayes worke and a half'. . . . £4 'to Sampson for payntinge the Librarye'. . . . £1. 18s. 2d. 'for the bindinge of the bookes gyven by Mʳ Richarde Francklin and claspinge and a chest to bringe them'. . . . 10s. 'to Domynicke to buy leather to cover the bookes wᶜʰ Mʳ Mills gave the colledge'. . . . £2. 4s. 0d. 'to Domynicke for bindinge Mʳ Mills his bookes'. . . . 8d. 'for washinge the librarye'.

1599–1600. *Variæ expensæ.* 3d. 'for bringinge clasps from London'. 5s. 'to dominicks man for 5 dayes in Chaininge Mʳ Mills his books'. 7s. 6d. 'for 3 doz of plats' . . . . 7s. 'for clasps for the books'. 6d. 'for cariage of tractatus Doctorum to the Sarasins heade'. 15s. 'for bindinge them'. 7s. 6d. 'for caryinge them to Oxon'. 4d. 'for bringinge them to the Colledge'. . . . £1. 12s. 0d. 'for viii dozen of chaines at iiiis. the dozen' . . . 13s. 4d. 'for a stamp for the Colledge books'. . . . 5s. 'for a doz. of chaines for the library'. 3s. 9d. 'for a doz. and a half of plates for the newe books there'. 1s. 8d. 'for ii dayes worke for the same'. . . . 5s. 5d. 'for bindinge Zanchius his works given by Mʳ Porter'. . . . 1s. 'for chaininge four books in the library'.

LIST XXVIII. CHRONOLOGICAL TABLE OF ACQUISITIONS BY GIFT AND PURCHASE, 1438–1576[1]

This list is entirely by reference back, except at 1438, 1441, 1461, 1469, 1481–2, 1493, 1502, 1507, and 1545, where reference is to wills containing bequests of unspecified books to All Souls.

† before a date shows that the donor died in this year, but his gift may have been earlier. Some bequests may have reached their destination some years after the death of the donor (cf. Betts at 1501 and 1504–5). With the two obvious exceptions before 1500 and with the exception of Edmund Shether and Robert Weston after 1500 all the donors up to and including Richard Bartlatt (1550–1) are included in *BRUO*.

1438. John Lovelich. List XXVIA.

1438. Henry Penwortham. Will, 27 September 1438 (*Reg. Chichele*, ii, 574–6): Item lego . . . Henrico Cantuariensi Archiepiscopo pro collegio suo in vniuersitate Oxoniensi libros meos vsque ad summam xl\a marcarum. ***75**, ***77**, ***182** are of this gift.

1439. Thomas Gascoigne. ***59**.

1440. John Lyndfeld. Will, 28 October 1440, proved 5 November 1440 (*Reg. Chichele*, ii. 576–7): Item lego collegio animarum Oxonie libros meos iuris ciuilis et canonici meliores ad valorem viginti librarum. Cf. ibid. ii. 38. Cf. ***266**.

1440. King Henry VI. **1–27** (List I).

†1441. John Southam. ***245**.

1441. Reginald Kentwoode. Will, 15 September 1441, proved 23 December 1441 (*Reg. Chichele*, ii. 589–91): Item lego et uolo omnes libros meos quod habeo ex propriis de iure canonico et ciuili nouo collegio Omnium Sanctorum domini Cantuariensis archiepiscopi Oxonie situato.

By †1443. Richard Andrew, †1477. ***43**, ***54**, ***80**.

†1443. Henry Chichele. **95, 208, 415**: cf. **97–8**.

1448. William Byconyll. List XXVIA.

1449–50. – Drwse (probably Ralph Drew, †by June 1456). List XXVII. Cf. ***1015** (List XIII).

---

[1] For acquisitions in the years 1577–1600 see List XXV.

†1451. Peter Partridge. **187–91** (List II).

1452–3. Robert Cowper, †1452. List XXVII.

1452–3. William Griffith. ***1010** (List XIII). List XXVII.

1455. Thomas Spray. List XXVIA.

1457–8. John Druell. ***572** (List VI). List XXVII. Cf. **470–1** (List II).

1457–8. Joan Croxford. List XXVII.

†1459. Walter Hopton. ***574** (List VI).

1460–1. Roger Kees. List XXVII.

1461. Philip Polton. List XXVIA. Will, 17 September 1461 (*Registrum Cancellarii*, ii. 80–5: to All Souls College 'duos libros facultatis sacre theologie ad usum studencium in eodem'.

1465. Richard Caunton. List XXVIA.

†1466. John Stokes. **558, 598** (List VI): cf. **607–8** (p. 22).

1466–7. John Norfolk, †1467. **472–96** (List III). List XXVII.

1469. Thomas Kent. Cf. Emden, *BRUO*, p. 1038. It is not likely that these books came to All Souls.

1470–1. See List XXVII for the purchase of a book.

1471. Richard Andrew. **497–529** (List IV).

1473. Thomas Bloxham. List XXVIA.

†1475. Thomas Wyche. List XXVIA.

†by August 1476. Robert Harlow. List XXVIA. Cf. **573** (List VI).

1480–1 and 1481–2. Thomas Wynterborne. ***557** (List VI). List XXVII.

1481–2. William Goldwyn. **530–40** (List V). List XXVII. Will, 2 June 1482, proved 14 June 1482 (P.C.C. 5 Logge): to the Collage of all soulen in Oxenforde . . . all his book*is* of Fysyk there to be chayned in the commyne librarie for euirmore'.

1483. William Elyot, master of Godshouse, Portsmouth. ***594** (List VI).

1483. William Folowys. ***996** (List XIII).

1484. John Grafton. ***1042** (additions to List XIII).

1485. John Saunder. ***1016** (List XIII). List XXVIA.

After 1485. Richard Topclyffe. ***1067** (List XIV). List XXVIA.

1487. John Druell. List XXVIA.

†1487. John Racour. **584**, ***585** (List VI), ***1266** (List XIX). List XXVIA.

1490. Robert Elyot. *1007 (List XIII).

1493. William Potman. Will 8 Febr. 1493, proved 18 Aug. 1493 (*Test. Ebor.* iv. 78–83): to All Souls College 'xii libros manu mea in secundis et tertiis folios assignatos'.[1]

1494–5. Robert Est, †1493. Lists XXVIA, XXVII. Cf. **599–603** (List VI).

1466–94, in the wardenship of John Stokes. All books in Lists IV (see above, 1471), Va (see above 1481–2, William Goldwyn), Vb, c (gifts of William Denis and of Richard Salter, †1519), and VI.[2]

By *c.* 1495. Thomas Lay. *1013 (List XIII).[3]

1498–9. Thomas Mors. List XXVII. Cf. at 1502–3.

†1499. James Goldwell. *1028, *1030, *1032, *1037, *1043 (additions to List XIII). *1057 (list XIV). *1074–6 (additions to List XIV). *1084, *1086, *1087 (list XV). *1103 (additions to List XV). *1272–3, *1289, *1290, *1294 (additions to List XIX). *1324, *1326, *1328 (List XX). *1357, *1359 (list XXI). *1429? (List XXII). *1470, *1473, *1475, *1476, *1477, *1480, *1485, *1491, *1496, *1498, *1532 (List XXIV). List XXVIA (nine books).

†1501. John Bettis. List XXVIA. Cf. at 1504–5.

1502. John Seymour. Will, 20 September 1500, proved 15 October 1502 (P.C.C. 20 Blamyr): 'Item Collegio animarum Oxon . . . tribus libris de theologia videlicet de melioribus'.

1502–3. Thomas Mors, †1501. List XXVII. Of the five books from Mors now at All Souls, *1323 is probably the book 'diversorum operum' received in 1502–3, and *1319–22 are probably the books received in 1498–9.

1502–3. John Stokes, †1503. List XXVII.

1504–5. John Bettis. List XXVII. Cf. at 1501.

†1507. John Game. *1235 (List XVII).

1507. William Eliot, provost of St. Edmund's, Salisbury. Will proved 19 March 1507 (P.C.C. 21 Adeane): to All Souls College all his books 'Iuris Ciuilis et canonice Rethorice et Poetrie'.[4]

---

[1] Antwerp, Plantin–Moretus Museum 67, P. Comestor, Historia Scholastica, secundo folio *et factum est*, belonged to Potman, but is not so inscribed.

[2] But see above, the introduction to List VI. Two names of donors occur in List VI, John Stokes †1466: **558** and **598**) and William Pykenham, †1497 (**604**).

[3] Given in Lay's lifetime. He is to be identified presumably with one of the two persons named Thomas Lee in *BRUO*: the first died in 1499 and the second in 1502. His gift may have been a good deal earlier than 1495, the approximate date of List XIII.

[4] In *BRUO* the gift of *594 is wrongly assigned to this William Elyot: see above at 1483.

1508–9. John Cole, †1536. List XXVII. Cf. *1332–4 (List XXI) which were joint gifts of John Cole and John Holt; also Vellum Inv. f. 25 (above, p. 82).

†1511. Stephen Barworth. List XXVIA.

1514 (or later). Michael Wogan. *1376–7 (additions to List XXI).

†1519. Walter Stone. *1415–18, *1425b (list XXII), *1436 (addition to List XXII). List XXVIA. These seven books probably came with Cockys's in 1545–6.

†1519. Richard Gaunt. List XXVIA. See also List XXVIA, Bisshop.

†c. 1520. John Alexander. List XXVIA.

†1522. William Hone. *1233 (List XVII).

†1523. Robert Honywood. List XXVIA.

1525 (or later). William Broke. List XXVIA.

†1525. William Derlyngton. List XXVIA.

†1528. Nicholas Halswell. *1097–8 (List XVI). List XXVIA.

c. 1530. John More. 700–14 (List VIII).

1533–4. William Warham, †1532. 609–99 (List VII). List XXVII.

1540–1. John Cockys. List XXVII. See also at 1545–6 below.

1540–1. Thomas Rich. List XXVII. Cf. 1119–25.

c. 1543(?). Edmund Shether. List XXVIA.

1544–5. Unspecified books to the value of £36. 12s. 4d. bought by the bursars, Bullyngham and Heryng: the price probably includes binding and chaining (List XXVII, at 1545–6). The books may be identified with most of 1126–80a (List XVI), many of 1380–1431f (List XXII), and List XXVIB. 11. Twenty-six of those that still survive have escaped rebinding and are in Oxford bindings by one binder (Gibson, rolls VII–X; Oldham, roll HM. a. 5).[1]

1545. William Latymer. Will 13 April 1545, proved 17 October 1545 (P.C.C. 38 Pynnyng): bequest to All Souls College or to Corpus Christi College of his books in Greek, if the children of his executors did not want them. It is unlikely that All Souls received any books from this bequest.

[1] Ker, *Pastedowns*.

301	1165		317	1155
302–3	1166		318	1151
304–5	1153		319	1398
306–7	1167		320	XXVIB.11
308–9	1135		322	1144
310	1150		323	1136
311–3	1407–9		327–8	1399, 1400
314	1400 e–g		329	1400 b–d
315	1154		330	1145
316	1152			

1545. Robert Weston. ***1391** (List XXII).

1545–6. John Cockys. List XXVII. Will, 14 April 1545, proved 19 April 1546 (P.C.C. 7 Alen): 'Item I will that all suche bookes that I haue which were doctoʳ Stones and by him after my decease bequethed to Allsoules colleage in Oxforde and also such bookes of Lawe that I shall leve at the tyme of my decease goo vnto the behove of the warden and felowes of the saide colleage theire to be chaynid in the lybrarye'. For the books which had been Stone's see above at 1519. Cockys's own books, received either in 1540–1 (see above) or now, are ***1413**, ***1414**, ***1414d**, ***1431f** (List XXII), ***1434**, ***1448**, ***1451–3** (additions to List XXII) and List XXVIA (3 books). Cf. also **1437**, footnote.

1547–8. ***1138 c–j**, ***1146–8** (List XVI) and **1410–12** (List XXII) bought for £9. 10s. 0d., chains excluded (List XXVII). ***1138 c–j**, ***1146–8** are in bindings like those noticed at 1544–5 above.[1]

1549–50. ***1202–4** (additions to List XVI) bought for £2. 12s. 0d (list XXVII).

1550–1. Richard Bartlatt. List XXVII: ***1227**, cf. ***1229–30** (List XVII) and List XXVIA.

1550–1. Richard Mugge. List XXVII: cf. ***1180a** (List XVI) and ***1458–9**, ***1463** (List XXIII) and List XXVIA.

1558–9. William Tucker. List XXVII: cf. ***1214–18** (List XVII) and List XXVIA.

c. 1560. William Dalby. ***1442–3** (additions to List XXII).

1560. John Weston. ***1432** (addition to List XXII). Cf. at 1565 below.

1565. John Weston. ***1456** (List XXIII). Cf. List XXVIA and at 1560 above.

†1565. John Warner. List XXVIA.

†1566. Sir John Mason. ***1183** (?), ***1184–9**, ***1194–7**, ***1199**, ***1200**, ***1205**, ***1237–8** (additions to List XVI). List XXVIA.

1572. Thomas Kaye. List XXVIA.

1574–5. David Pole, †1568. List XXVII. **715–964a** (List IX).

1575. William Pigot. ***1465** (List XXIII)

1575. Robert Mowsherst. ***1466** (List XXIII).

1576. Andrew Kingsmill. ***965–74** (List X).

---

[1] Ker, *Pastedowns.*
324–6.   1138 c–j
App. ciii.   1146–8.

LIST XXIX. TABLE SHOWING THE PROBABLE CHRONOLOGICAL ORDER AND DATES OF THE GENERAL LISTS II, VI, XIII–XXIV

1. List II. Before 12 April 1443.
2. List XVIII. *c.* 1460.
3. Additions to list XVIII.
4. List VI. *c.* 1494.
5. Lists XIII, XIX. *c.* 1495.
6. Additions to Lists XIII, XIX.
7. Lists XIV, XX. *c.* 1505.
8. Additions to Lists XIV, XX.
9. List XXIV. s. xvi in.
10. List XV.[1] *c.* 1513.
11. List XXI.[1] 1512–13 (?).
12. Additions to Lists XV, XXI.
13. Lists XVI, XXII. *c.* 1548.
14. Additions to Lists XVI, XXII.
15. Lists XVII, XXIII. 1576 and 1575.

[1] Lists XV and XXI are not, like the others, a pair, but they are nearly contemporary.

NOTES

LIST I

12. Perhaps an unknown work of Edmund Lacy (bishop of Hereford 1417 and Exeter 1420, †1455). But 'compilatus per M. E. Lacy' may be a misunderstanding of an inscription 'per M. E. Lacy', indicating probably a gift by him (to the king?). Not ascribed to Lacy in Lists XIII–XV. See more in Addenda.

*14. MS. 5. s. xiii in. A handsome copy of Job, Acts, Catholic Epistles, and Apocalypse, with gloss. 'Liber Collegii animarum omnium fidelium Oxonie ex dono Regis Henrici vi^{ti}. Oretis pro inclito statu eiusdem.' Binding of s. xv/xvi.

*19. MS. 28. s. xii ex. Inscribed as **14**. Medieval binding.

*20. MS. 46. s. xii. Inscribed as **14**. Binding as **77**.

26. Bale, *Scriptores* (ed. 1559, p. 495), says that Casterton, a Benedictine at Norwich in the late fourteenth century, wrote a commentary on the Apocalypse beginning 'Posuit castra in medio' (Judith 16. 4). No copy has been found.

28. The words *verba Dei* (or *Domini*) *cogitatione* are in Jerome's letter to Paulinus: ed. Rome, 1926, p. 16/4.

LIST II

*35. MS. 12. s. xiii in. The commentary is Stegmüller, no. 6124. The ascription here to Isidore is in a late medieval hand. 'Liber sancte marie de stanleia' (f. 180ᵛ). 'Liber Collegii animarum omnium fidelium defunctorum de Oxon'' in an early seventeenth-century hand which wrote the same eight words in many manuscripts and printed books. Medieval binding, rebacked.

*38. MS. 16. s. xiii/xiv. College *ex libris* as in **35**. Rebound in s. xviii.

*43. MS. 13. s. xiii in. 'Exposicio Radulfi Flauiacensis Monachi super leuiticum ex donacione Magistri Ricardi Andrew 2° fo loquente' on the fly-leaf. Sixteen leaves of this handsome book are in the bindings of **980–7** and two leaves are in a binding at Winchester College: cf. Ker, *Pastedowns*, p. xi. Medieval binding. It had once five bosses on each cover: cf. **54**.

48. Presumably on Pss. 80–150. Merton College MSS. 33, 34 are an early fourteenth century two-volume copy of Augustine on the Psalms, the second volume beginning at Ps. 77.

53. This probably contained both De civitate Dei and De Trinitate.

*54. MS. 30. s. xiii in. Script and decoration are like the script and decoration of **43** and the leaves are numbered at the foot of the first column on versos in the same hand as in **43**: probably therefore an inscription of gift from Andrew was on the now missing fly-leaf. College *ex libris* as in **35**. Medieval binding. It had once five bosses on each cover: cf. **43**.

57. The word *impietatis* occurs in Jerome's letter 84 (*PL* xxii, 744, near the foot of

the column). Probably therefore this was a copy of the letters of St. Jerome, beginning, like B. M. Royal 6 B. iv and other manuscripts, with Ep. 83 and Ep. 84.

*59. MS. 18. s. xii ex. 'Registrum sancti gregorii pape (*erased*) in xiii libris. datum collegio animarum fidelium per magistrum Thomam gascoigne sacre pagine professorem eboracensis diocesis et dator vult quod concathenetur in libraria communi prefati collegii. 1439' in Gascoigne's hand on f. iii^v. Rebound in s. xix.

*73. MS. 31. s. xv. Inscribed as **35**. Old boards, re-covered.

(*)74. Possibly the four leaves of a twelfth-century manuscript of the *Gesta regum* used to wrap the Bursars' Book for 1548–9 (cf. Ker, *Pastedowns*, p. 180) came from this copy. Cf. List XXVIc.

*75. MS. 19. s. xii ex. (ff. 1–84) and s. xiv (ff. 85–159). 'Liber collegii omnium fidelium defunctorum Oxon' datus per Henricum Penwortham' (f. 2). Medieval binding.

*77. MS. 37. s. xv in. Inscribed as **75** (f. 2). Rebound in s. xviii (?): white leather covers (cf. App. III).

78. The title in List XIII (cf. XV) suggests that this was not the common *Rosarium Theologie*, but the Wycliffite *Floretum*. Bodley 448 (*SC* 2395) is a copy of *Floretum* with the title 'Rosarium theologicum': cf. Bodley 55 (*SC* 1976).

*80. Probably MS. 89, which lacks the first quire. s. xv in. Written in France. Said in a seventeenth-century inscription on f. 2 in the same hand as the inscription in **35** to be the gift of Richard Andrew: cf. 'Cato Moralizatus' among Andrews's gifts in the Benefactors' Register, p. 1. Rebound in s. xix.

81. Perhaps the twelfth-century anthology of theological texts so called, of which Lincoln Cathedral 216 and Bodleian Lat. th. d. 30 are copies.

82. Miss H. E. Allen's *Writings ascribed to Richard Rolle*, pp. 231–45, shows that *De emendatione vitae* is the first item in a good many miscellanies.

83. The secundo folio in Lists II and XIII records the opening words of the text. The compilers of Lists XIIA (see Addenda), XIV chose better.

*86. MS. 27. s. xiii ex. Inscribed as **35**. Binding of s. xvi: in rebacking the covers have been placed upside down and back to front.

90. Probably not Aquinas, *De veritate*, but Hugo Ripelin, *Compendium theologicae veritatis*. In MS. Bodley 458 (*SC* 2414) the word Gregorius is eight lines down f. 2.

95. This copy of the *Catholicon* of John of Genoa is entered in two of the lists of chapel goods in the Vellum Inventory: f. 18, s. xv, 'Catholicon ex dono fundatoris cathenat' in choro secundo folio scribant[ur]'; f. 7, s. xv/xvi, 'Catholicon cathenatum in choro'.

97–8. Pontificals with secundo folios *ea* and *ordo* are recorded—as founder's relics?—in an inventory of the common chest in the tower (Archives, DD c 369) taken in 17 Henry VIII.[1] They and a 'Liber episcopalis 2° fo aut extendes' are listed again in inventories of 25, 35, 37, and 38 Henry VIII and 1 Edward VI,

---

[1] Misdated 8 Henry VIII.

but not in the inventory of 4 Edward VI nor in any later inventory. The same three books are also in the undated lists in Vellum Inventory, f. 18 and f. 19.

*109. Antwerp, Plantin–Moretus Museum, 26+341, ff. 15–22. s. xii. 'Liber Collegii animarum', f. 2, below an erasure. Numerous marginalia in the hand of James Goldwell. Rebound in s. xix. The erroneous title in Misc. 209 was reproduced in Misc. 210, but was corrected there by interlining 'trinitate' above 'ciuitate'.

*121. MS. 86. s. xiv in. The writer of the inscription in **35** (s. xvii) wrote his usual college *ex libris* on f. 2 followed by 'ex dono Iohannis Stokes 5ᵗⁱ Custodis huius collegii' (cf. **571**). Binding as **77**.

*124. MS. 85. Written by Albertus 'nacione Brabancie' in 1427–8. Inscribed as **35**. Binding as **77**.

*128. MS. 332. s. xiii in. Fragments dispersed as pastedowns in Oxford bindings, s. xvii in., and reassembled in 1948: cf. Ker, *Pastedowns*, pp. xi–xii.

129. Heremetis probably for Hermetis. It contained according to List XIII the *Summa astrologiae* of Cosmas of Alexandria: cf. Thorndike and Kibre, *Incipits*, ed. 2, col. 764.

133. Cf. Bodleian MSS. Digby 48, art. 10, and Digby 212, art. 5.

*135. MS. 95. s. xiii ex. 'Liber collegii animarum omnium fidelium defunctorum de Oxon' 1554' on the verso of the leaf formerly pasted down at the end. Binding of white skin over boards, s. xv/xvi?

*140. MS. 72. s. xiv. A pledge in the Rothbury chest in 1363 (?). Inscribed as **35**. Binding as **77**.

*142. MS. 79. s. xiv. 'Liber Elie Stoke quem emit de executoribus domini Iohannis Fodyngton', f. 166ᵛ. 'Liber Elie Stoke deliberatus Magistro Ricardo Mark' per manus magistri Iohannis [. . .]', f. 1ᵛ. College *ex libris* as in **35**. Medieval binding rebacked.

*145. Exeter Cathedral MS. 3506, by gift in 1659. s. xiv ex. Listed as an All Souls manuscript by T. James, *Ecloga Oxonio-Cantabrigiensis*, 1600, p. 46, no. 21. Acquired apparently by John Woolton (All Souls Coll. 1584–5, D.M. 1599, son of John Woolton, bishop of Exeter; cf. *DNB*), who wrote a note and twice his name on fly-leaves. Binding of s. xv/xvi.

*146. MS. 71. s. xiv in. Inscribed as **35**. Rebound in s. xix.

*147. MS. 69. s. xiii ex. Inscribed as **35**. Wooden boards covered with white skin, s. xv/xvi (?).

*182. MS. 82. s. xii. 'Liber Magistri Aluredi' in red, f. iiiᵛ. An *ex libris*, probably of Cirencester Abbey, f. iii, erased: cf. N. R. Ker, 'Sir John Prise', *The Library*, 5th ser. x (1955), 17. Inscribed as **75**, f. 2. Bound in Oxford, s. xv: Gibson, stamps 3, 4, 6, 13–15, 80, and another.

*197. MS. 62. s. xv. Paper. Written in Italy. This manuscript and New College MSS. 209, 210 are 'drei Bände (immer noch unvollständig) eines Exemplars', according to S. Kuttner, *Repertorium der Kanonistik*, 1937, p. 21 n. 2. No college *ex libris*. Rebound by Maltby in 1929, but the old white skin covers have been preserved.

208. No doubt the copy, 'secundo folio naturalis', which John Mottisfont (†1420) bequeathed to Chichele (*Registrum Chichele*, ii. 211).

223. Called 'Distincciones Iohannis Caldrini' in Lists II and XXI, 'Reportorium cum diuersis repeticionibus' in List XVIII, 'Liber de papiro' in List XIX, and 'Tabula auctoritatum' in List XX.

232. 'Io W G et Pau'. Probably Johannes Andreae, Willelmus de Monte Lauduno, Gescelinus de Cassanis, and Paulus de Lizariis: cf. Schulte, ii. 217, 197, 199, 313.

*240. MS. 59. Written at Orleans in 1406. 'Iohannes Faber doctor legum fuit iste quod Goldwell' is written in a sort of humanistic hand on the pastedown at the beginning. No college *ex libris*. Binding of white skin over boards, s. xv/xvi.

*242. MS. 56. s. xv. Paper. Written on the Continent. The secundo folio '5° nota' is given correctly in List XX, but misread as 'hoc nota' in Lists II, XXI. No college *ex libris*. Contemporary binding of white skin over boards.

*245. MS. 50. s. xiii. 'Istum librum dedit. Magister Iohannes Southam Archidiaconus Oxon' Rectori et consociis collegii Omnium Animarum in Vniuersitate Oxon' fundati et ordinati ad opus et vtilitatem collegiatorum eiusdem in libraria eorum cathenandum', f. 6ᵛ. Medieval binding, repaired. *mare* is the secundo folio in textu, *duodecimo* (cf. List XXII) the secundo folio in glosa.

*252. Almost certainly MS. 49, the secundo folio of which is *virum*. See the note to **1251**.

*259. MS. 51. s. xiv. Written in France. No college *ex libris*. Binding of white skin over wooden boards, s. xv/xvi (?). *ro eius* is the secundo folio in textu, *quod raro* (cf. List XXII) the secundo folio in glosa.

*264. MS. 52. s. xiv. College *ex libris* of s. xvii. Binding like **259**. *predii* is the secundo folio in textu, *in prouinciali* (cf. List XXII) the secundo folio in glosa.

*266. MS. 55. s. xiii ex. A fine Italian copy. 'Liber M Iohannis Lyndefeld archidiaconi Cic' titulo empcionis' on the pastedown, now raised. A pledge 'in cista Regine' in 13—. No college *ex libris*. Rebound in s. xviii.

*267. MS. 60. s. xv. Paper. Written in France. No college *ex libris*. Rebound in s. xix.

*308. MS. 53. s. xv. Paper. 'Liber domini simonis Northew Rectoris de Mechyng Cicestr' Dioc'' on the pastedown in front. College *ex libris* of s. xvii. Binding like **259**.

371. Commentaries by various authors on the New Digest: see the varying titles in Lists II, XVIII–XX.

*411. Antwerp, Plantin–Moretus Museum, 30. Decretum Gratiani, with the apparatus of Bartholomaeus Brixiensis (S. Kuttner, *Repertorium der Kanonistik*, p. 103). s. xiii/xiv. 'Liber Collegii Animarum omnium fidelium defunctorum in Oxonia', f. 1. Rebound in s. xix.

*415. Almost certainly Antwerp, Plantin–Moretus Museum, 12. Innocentius IV, Apparatus Decretalium. s. xiii ex. 'Liber Collegii Animarum omnium fidelium defunctorum', f. 2 and f. i^v. No name of donor, but Chichele was owner in 1400, as appears from a note on the fly-leaf, f. 282^v: 'Nota quot anni sunt ab origine mundi secundum hebraicam veritatem . . . istam computacionem annorum reperi ego Henricus Chichele in quodam antiquo libro in prioratu de Bradinstoke scriptam. Anno ab incarnacione domini Millesimo cccc^{mo}. ita quod additis ad predictos 'm' cccii annos computatos a passione domini xxxiii annis quibus vixit in mundo saluator noster. fuerunt anni domini tempore scripture predicte Mille cccxxxv. sic quod a tempore scripture prefate lapsi sunt lxv anni.' Bradenstoke lies a dozen miles from Sherston Magna, where Chichele was admitted as rector on 26 June 1400. Photographs of ff. 1–2^v and 282^v are at All Souls. Innocent's text is much annotated, but not, I think, by Chichele. Rebound in s. xix. Secundo folio *non poterant*.

416. J. de Athon: cf. *BRUO*, Acton. Copies are Gonville and Caius College, Cambridge, 282, Eton College, 30, and University College, Oxford, 71.

467. The opening words of the second leaf come in chapter 6 of Jerome's letter, *Biblia sacra*, ed. Rome, 1926, p. 19/10.

468. The opening word of the second leaf comes a few lines earlier than in **467**: ed. Rome, 1926, p. 19/7.

LIST IV

*522. MS. 57. s. xiv. Written in France. No college *ex libris*. Binding like **259**.

*525. Antwerp, Plantin–Moretus Museum, 144. s. xii in. Written probably in France. 'Liber Collegii animarum Oxon' ex dono Magistri Ricardi [Andrew pri]mi Custodis eiusdem quem qui abstulerit ana[the]ma Maranatha sit', f. 1. Rebound in s. xix. Title 'Canones generalium consiliorum', f. 1. Secundo folio *comitatum*.

LIST V

*530. MS. 75. s. xv. Paper. Inscribed as **35**. Rebound in s. xix.

*531. MS. 73. s. xv. Paper. Inscribed as **35**. Rebound in Oxford, s. xvi ex.: Gibson, rolls XII, XVIII.

*535. MS. 80. s. xv. Paper and parchment . 'Liber M. Wyllelmi Goldwyn' on the fly-leaf and 'Liber collegii omnium animarum in oxon'' in a good hand, s. xvi, on f. 2. Alienated before 26 August 1641, when Otho Polwheele gave it to some-one unnamed, and perhaps before 1600, since Thomas James does not list it in *Ecloga*.[1] Belonged to Narcissus Luttrell in 1693 and reacquired by gift of Luttrell Wynne in 1786. Rebound, s. xviii.

536. Ill catalogued in List XIV. The *Rosa Medicinae* begins with the word 'Galienus'.

*537. MS. 68. s. xiii ex. Pledged in the Lincoln chest in 1326 and 1327, in the latter year perhaps by J. de Middilton (cf. *BRUO*, p. 1276, for one of this name at this date). Inscribed as **35**. Binding as **77**.

*538. MS. 331. s. xv. Paper and parchment. 'Liber magistri Willelmi Goldwyn'

---

[1] This is not significant, since James omitted many manuscripts which were certainly at All Souls in 1600: cf. List XXVID.

inside the cover. 'Liber Collegii animarum omnium defunctorum in Oxon' ex dono Magistri Willelmi Goldewyn', f. 2. Alienated. Bought in 1938 from Mr. James Fairhurst. Original limp parchment cover, with '2° fo Oribasius' on it. No chainmark.

LIST VI

553. The secundo folio in Lists VI and XV coincides with words of Gen. 4: 5 in the later Wycliffite version. The secundo folio in Lists XIII and XIV is Gen. 1: 1.

554. The opening words of the second leaf are in chapter 7 of Jerome's letter to Paulinus: ed. Rome, 1926, p. 25/2.

*555, *556. MS. 4. A huge Bible, written in France (?), s. xii in., now bound in four volumes: the bindings are like those on 77. The secundo folio of 556 is Job 1: 1. MS. 4, vol. 3, now lacks the whole of Job and begins at the words 'perspexerit de hebreis uoluminibus' near the end of Jerome's preface, Psalterium dudum (Stegmüller, no. 430). The college ex libris is of s. xvii and in vols. 1 and 3 only.

*557, MS. 29. s. xiv/xv. 'Liber thome Wynterburn', f. 234ᵛ. Inscribed as 35. Binding as 77.

560. As ed. Cologne, 1480 (GKW 865). The copy now in the library was a gift from Richard Gaunt and has no chainmark: cf. the note to List XXVIA, Gaunt 1.

565. As ed. Oxford, 1482. The copy of this edition now in the library was a gift from Richard Gaunt: cf. the note to List XXVIA, Gaunt 5.

*567. LR 4. a. 7. Paris, sine anno (Hain 6428). No college ex libris. Rebound in s. xix.

*571. MS. 84. s. xiii ex. Inscribed as 121, but List II is right, no doubt, in saying that this book was bought by the college during Stokes's wardenship. It is listed on Desk 6 in all the inventories, XIII–XVII. Binding of s. xv/xvi (?), rebacked.

*572. MS. 90. s. xv. Paper. Given in 1457: 'Liber Collegii Animarum Oxon' ex dono M. Iohannis Dryelle xvii° die Aprilis Anno regni regis nunc xxxviᵗᵒ.' Binding as 77. Cf. List. XXVII at 1457–8.

573. Perhaps the Johannes Canonicus said to have been given by 'Thomas Harlow': cf. List XXVIA, Harlow.

*574. MS. 88. s. xv. 'Liber Collegii Animarum omnium fidelium defunctorum in Oxonia ex dono Magistri Walteri Hopton' quondam socii huius collegii. Anime cuius miseriatur deus Amen', f. 1ᵛ. A small book in contemporary binding.

584. Described in John Racour's will, Commissary Court of London, Reg. Lichfield, ff. 91ᵛ–2, as a book in parchment 'de operibus Ipocratis cum comento Galieni 2° fo hii uel quia plurium residet'.

*585. MS. 78. s. xv. 'Liber collegii omnium animarum fidelium defunctorum in Ox' Ex dono M' Iohannis Racour doctoris in medicinis nuper socii eiusdem. Cuius anime propicietur deus Amen', f. 2. Oxford stamped binding, s. xv²: cf. Gibson, p. 21, 'Rood and Hunt', stamps 44–7 and 51.

588. Cf. 1069.

*594. MS. 182. s. xv. 'Hunc librum Willelmus Elyot Clericus Magister Domus dei de port*i*smouth' Wynton' d*ioc*' in Com' Sutht' ol*im* Registrarius bone memorie Edmundi l*acy* Exon' Episcopi quartode*cimo* die mensis Iulii A*nno* Regni Regis Ricardi t*ercii* primo dedit legauit *ac* in vita sua natura*li* disposuit Collegio Animarum in Oxon' ad *vsum* Magistrorum Sociorum *et* eiusdem Collegii Sc*ol*arium quamdiu durau*erit* in libraria ibidem re*man*surum Cathenandum. Et *si* quis seu qui hunc librum a dicto Collegio contra predicti dan*tis* et disponentis volun*tatem* alienare remouere *seu* subtrahere presumpse*rit* ve(l) presumpserint se nouerit s*eu* nouerint indignacionem omnipotentis dei ac eius ma勒勒勒勒勒勒勒勒勒勒勒 ma勒ma勒 (italics show the missing letters). Elyot gave New College MS. 202 and Exeter College MS. 29 to New College on the same day, 14 July 1483. In *BRUO* the gift of MS. 182 is assigned to the wrong William Elyot. Binding of s. xv/xvi.

599–603. Perhaps gifts of Robert Est: cf. list XXVI A, Est 1–5.

LIST VII

609. Ludolph of Saxony. As ed. Paris, 1502 (Brasenose Coll.).

*613. LR 3. g. 5. Strasburg, 1496 (*GKW* 2192, pt. 1). 'Liber collegii animarum omnium fidelium defunctorum in Oxon' ex dono Reuerendissimi in cristo patris domini Willelmi Warham Cant' Archiepiscopi.' Rebound in s. xix.

614–15. As ed. Strasburg, 1496 (*GKW* 2192, pts. 2, 3).

*616. LR 3. g. 7. Strasburg, 1486 (*GKW* 2192, pt. 4). Inscribed and bound as **613**.

617. As ed. Lyons, 1500 (*GKW* 2193, pt. 1).

*618. LR 3. g. 6. Lyons, 1500 (*GKW* 2193, pt. 2). Inscribed and bound as **613**.

619. As ed. Lyons, 1500 (*GKW* 2193, pt. 3).

*620–1. LR 4. a. 13–4. Strasburg, 1494 (Hain 7625). Inscribed with the same words as **613**, but by another scribe who uses the spellings 'christo' and 'Warrham.' Rebound as **613**.

622. As ed. Strasburg, 1494: cf. **620–1**.

627–30. As ed. Nuremberg, 1497 (Bodleian).

*631. MS. 20. s. xv. Paper. Inscribed as **613**. Contemporary binding. Chainmark HS2.

*633. k. inf. 2. 10. Vincent of Beauvais. Venice, 1493 (Hain–Copinger 6241, vol. 3). Inscribed as **613**. Rebound in s. xix.

634. The words 'vir sanctus' begin sign. a. 4 in ed. Cologne, 1485 (Bodleian).

*635. t. inf. 4. Strasburg, 1495 (Hain 14919). Inscribed as **613**, and also 'Ex dono magistri thome wellys', so perhaps a gift to Warham from Thomas Wells. Other books so inscribed were of Wells's gift to New College. Contemporary binding by the 'Unicorn binder': Oldham, pl. xi, stamps 50, 61, 72. Chainmark FS1.

*636. SR 79. g. 8. Basel 1506. Inscribed as **613**. Contemporary stamped binding: Oldham, stamps 63, 81. Chainmarks FS1, HS1, HS2.

*637. LR 3. g. 12. Basel, 1492 (*GKW* 1599). Inscribed as **613**. Rebound in s. xix.

*639. LR 3. h. 12. R. de Sabunde. Strasburg, 1496 (Hain 14069). Inscribed as **613**. Contemporary stamped binding by 'W. G.': Oldham stamps 20–2, 24.

*640. LR 3. h. 8. J. de Turrecremata. sine anno et loco (Hain 15713). Inscribed as **613**. Contemporary stamped binding, rebacked. Chainmark HS1.

*648. SR 77. g. 11. Strasburg, 1518. Inscribed as **613**. Rebound in s. xix.

*650. f. 2. 11 (Strasburg, c. 1483–4: *GKW* 9533).[1] The first four leaves are missing. Rebound in s. xix.

*651. SR 81. a. 15. Lyons, 1528. 4°. Inscribed as **613** and also with an *ex dono* from Warham to New College. Contemporary binding: Oldham, roll HE. a. 1 and ornament C. 5.

656. As ed. Hagenau, 1498 and 1499 (Hain 9054 and 9055): cf. *Syon*, Q. 37.

665–6. As ed. Paris, 1519: cf. *Syon*, S 24–5.

667. J. Vivaldus. As ed. Hagenau, 1513 (Brasenose College).

*672. Glasgow, U. L., Bi. 4. g. 20. (1) Antonius de Rampegollis, *Aurea Biblia*. Paris, 1513. (2) *De contemptu mundi cum commento*. Paris, sine anno. (3) *Manuale sacerdotum*. Paris, sine anno. Inscribed as **613**. Contemporary parchment cover.

*677. SR 79. e. 1. Aretius Felinus (M. Bucer). Strasburg, 1529. 4°. Inscribed as **613**. Contemporary binding: Oldham, *Panels*, HM 15, AN 14.

*678. LR 4. b. 22. Pseudo-Bonaventura. Brussels, c. 1476–8 (*GKW* 4820). 4°. Inscribed as **613**. Contemporary stamped binding. Chainmarks HS1, HS2.

688. M. Bossus. Perhaps as ed. Bologna, 1492 (Bodleian).

*690. v. 2. 12. Sermones: (*a*) De tempore; (*b*) Quadragesimales; (*c*) De sanctis. Lyons, 1494 (Reichling 1112). 4°. Inscribed as **613**. Contemporary stamped binding by the 'Dragon binder': Oldham, pl. 15, stamps 146, 148. Chainmarks HS1, HS2.

698. As ed. Basel, 1505–6.

699. As ed. Oxford, 1482: cf. **564** and List XXVIA, Gaunt 5.

LIST VIII

701. Homiliarius Doctorum: cf. ***930** and Hain 8791–3.

702. Cf. ***672**.

*706. w. inf. 1. 9. M. Farinator. Strasburg, 1482 (Hain 10333). 'Hunc librum possidet Io[es] Moore' on the end-leaf. 'Liber Collegii animarum Oxon' Ex dono M' Ioannis Moore Artium magistri ac huius collegii quondam socii Com' Northamton.' An earlier owner wrote 'Lumen Anim[e]/Patricius Holy[. . . .]/ Arch*idiacon*us Totton'[2] in capitals on the back cover. Contemporary binding of brown leather over boards: the pastedowns are cut from accounts of a Devonshire household, s. xiv[2].

*711. LR 3. g. 11. Paris, 1495 (Hain 7932). 'Liber Collegii animarum omnium

---

[1] I owe thanks to Mr. Dennis Rhodes who identified the edition for me and to the Deputy Librarian of the University of St. Andrews who told me that the first words on a. 2 in the St. Andrews copy are *quod fit*.

[2] No person of this name is recorded in lists of archdeacons of Totnes.

fidelium defunctorum. ex dono Magistri Io. Moore, artium magistri ac huius collegii olim socii.' Rebound in s. xix.

LIST IX

*715–19. cc. 10. 5. 6, 12, ee. 1. 6. Lyons, 1517–18. One of the five volumes, Digestum Novum, is missing. 'Liber collegii omnium Animarum Oxon' ex Dono Reuerendi Dauidis Pole Episcopi Petriburg. huius collegii socii' in each volume.[1] 'Iste liber spectat ad Robertum Polum' in cc. 10. 5. cc. 10. 6 rebound in Oxford in s. xvi ex. (Gibson, rolls XII, XVIII), the rest in s. xix. Chainmark on cc. 10. 6 is FS1.

*720–4. z. 2. 2, 4–6, 8. Lyons, 1545 and (z. 2. 4) 1526. All rebound in s. xix.

*725–6. z. 1. 2, 3. Lyons, 1515. Rebound in s. xix.

*727. z. 1. 4. Venice, 1493 (*GKW* 7047). Rebound in s. xix.

*730–2. ee. 3. 5–7. Lyons, 1513–14, 1508, and sine anno. ee. 3. 5 in contemporary binding by John Reynes (Oldham, roll AN. b. 1 and ornament A. 1). ee. 3. 6, 7 rebound in s. xix. Chainmark on ee. 3. 5 is FS1.

*733–4. cc. 8. 1, 2. W. Durand. Lyons, 1521. 'Polus. precium tocius cursus xvs' on title-page of cc. 8. 1. Rebound in s. xix.

*735–6. cc. 9. 8, 9. Lyons, 1518–19. Rebound in s. xix.

*737. bb. 1. 3. Lyons, 1520. Rebound in s. xix.

*738. aa. 7. 1. Lyons, 1525. 'Polus precium viiis.' Rebound in Oxford in 1576–7: Gibson, rolls XII, XVIII.

*739. aa. 2. 3. *Collectarius Iuris*. Lyons, 1514. Contemporary Cambridge binding by N. Spierinck: Gray, rolls I, II, and ornament 5. Chainmarks FS1, HS1.

*742. cc. 9. 7. Lyons, 1517. Rebound in s. xix.

*743–5. z. 2. 12–14. J. de Imola. Lyons, 1517. Rebound in s. xix.

*746–7. aa. 7. 6, 7. Paris, 1512. 'Pole. precium tocius cursius xvis' on title-page of aa. 7. 6. Rebound in s. xix.

*748. aa. 7. 11. Paris, 1505. 'Pole precium iiiis.' Rebound in Oxford, s. xvi ex.: Gibson, rolls XII, XVIII.

*749–52. bb. 1. 6–9. Lyons, 1516–7. In bb. 1. 8 the usual inscription 'Liber . . . socii' (as in **715**) is followed in the same hand by the words 'Anno 1575° Mensis Aug. 2 repositus in communi libraria'. All rebound in s. xix.

*753. aa. 3. 5. Lyons, 1498 (*GKW* 4964). 'Io. Apharrius' on the title-page. Rebound in s. xix.

*754. aa. 3. 7. (1) Lyons, 1518. (2) *De officio delegati* (etc.). Pavia, 1488. (3) J. A. de Sancto Georgio (*et al.*). Lyons, 1519. (4) Philippus Francus. Trino, 1518. Contemporary binding by John Reynes, as **730**.

*755. bb. 5. 1. Lyons, 1522. Rebound in Oxford in s. xvi ex.: Gibson, rolls XII, XVIII. Cf. the note to List XXVIA, Mugge 1.

---

[1] This or nearly this is the form of inscription in all the books of Pole's gift, except **751, 826–30, 955**.

*756. aa. 7. 2. Milan, 1490 (*GKW* 3743), together with seven other law tracts printed between 1488 and 1496. Contemporary stamped binding: Oldham stamps 380–3 (Binder E).

*757. z. 2. 11. Lyons, 1522. 'Polus precium x*s*.' Rebound in Oxford in s. xvi ex.: Gibson, rolls XII, XVIII.

*758. bb. 1. 4. Lyons, 1511. Rebound in s. xix.

*759. bb. 5. 5. Lyons, 1516. Rebound in s. xix.

*760. bb. 1. 5. (1) Lyons, 1519. (2) Lanfrancus de Oriano, *Repetitiones*. sine anno et loco. Rebound in Oxford in s. xvi ex.: Gibson, rolls XII, XVIII.

*761. University College, Oxford, e. 1. Lyons, 1509. 4°. 'Ego sum liber M. thome byrd precium ii^s viiii^d', s. xvi in. Rebound in s. xix.

*762. aa. 11. 12. Paris, 1508. 4°. 'Liber Doctoris Pole precium xvi*d*.' Contemporary stamped binding: Oldham, stamp 1063 and another.

*768. bb. 1. 1. (1) J. A. de Sancto Georgio. Trino, 1515. (2) J. A. de. Sancto Georgio, *Super titulo de appellationibus*. Venice, 1497 (Hain 7595). Contemporary Cambridge binding by N. Spierinck: Gray, rolls II (variant, Oldham, roll DI. a. 3) and V. No chainmark.

*776. z. 2. 9. (1) Jason Maynus. Lyons, 1546. (2) *Repertorium in Jasonis praelectiones*. Lyons, 1545. Rebound in s. xix.

*787. SR 73. g. 4. (1) Epiphanius, *Contra octoginta haereses* (in Latin). Paris, 1544. (2) J. Damascenus, *Opera* (in Latin). Cologne, 1546. Rebound in s. xix.

*788. SR 73. g. 11. Paris, 1520. Rebound in s. xix. Cf. **821**.

*789. SR 72. d. 6. Paris, 1521. 'Liber D. Pole.' Rebound in s. xix.

*790. SR 80. g. 3. Erasmus, *Annotationes in Novum Testamentum*. Basel, 1540. 'Emptus a domino Radulpho Elcocke uicario chorali ecclesie Lich' precium vi*s*.' Contemporary binding: Oldham, roll FP. b. 2.

*791. SR 66. c. 17. Basel, 1527. Binding by Reynes. Chainmarks FS1, HS2.

*792. SR 79. g. 10. J. Brentius. Frankfurt, 1541. Contemporary London binding: Oldham, rolls FP. a. 6, RP. a. 5. Chainmark FS1.

*793. p. inf. 1. 5. *Concordantiae maiores sacrae Bibliae*. Basel, 1531. 'Liber D. Pole precium vi*s* viii*d*.' Rebound in s. xix.

794. (H. Petri ed.) Μικροπρεσβυτικον. Basel, 1550.

*795. ee. 4. 6. Cologne, 1530. Contemporary binding: Oldham, roll HM. a. 7. Chainmarks FS1, FS2.

*796. SR 73. g. 13. Cyprianus, *Opera*. Basel, 1540. 'Liber D. Pole precium v*s*.' There is no work of Cyril here (cf. **823**). Contemporary binding by John Reynes: Oldham, roll AN. b. 1. Chainmarks FS1, HS1.

797. The Ledger adds the title 'adversus haereses'.

*798. SR 73. a. 15. Theophylactus, *In quatuor evangelia* (in Latin). Cologne, 1536. 8°. Contemporary binding: Oldham, roll FL. a. 7. Chainmarks FS1, HS2.

*799. SR 73. a. 11. Theophylactus, *In Epistolas Pauli* (in Latin). Paris, 1537. 8°. Rebound in s. xix.

*800. SR 73. a. 8. Lactantius, *Opera*. Antwerp, 1539. 8°. Contemporary binding. Chainmarks FS1, HS1, HS2.

801. 'Polimarchus Theodoreti' (Ledger).

*802–4. v. inf. 2. 6–8. (1) T. Netter, *Doctrinale Fidei* (3 vols: bks. 1–4, Paris, 1532; bks. 5, 6, Paris, 1522–3). (2) in second place in v. inf. 2. 8, Jacobus Lopes, *Annotationes contra D. Erasmum Roterodamum* (etc.). Paris, 1522. 'Apharrius' on title-pages of v. inf. 2. 6, 7. All rebound, s. xix.

805–9. Three volumes of Erasmus's Paraphrases on the New Testament inscribed with Pole's *ex dono* remain. One is **807**. The other two, in spite of discrepancies in the contents, are presumably **806** and **808**.

> *806. SR 79. c. 11. *Tomus primus* . . . (Matthew, Mark only). Basel, 1534. 8°. 'liber D. Pole precium ii*s* viii*d*.' Contemporary binding: Oldham, roll FP. a. 1. Chainmark HS1.

> *807. SR 79. c. 12. *Tomus secundus continens paraphrasim in omneis epistolas apostolicas*. Basel, 1534. 8°. Binding and chainmark as **806**.

> *808. SR 79. f. 10. (1) *Tomus secundus* . . . (as **807**). Basel, 1532. (2) *In acta apostolorum paraphrasis*. Basel, 1535. Rebound in s. xix.

*810. Worcester College, Oxford, EE. u. 3. Dionysius Carthusianus, *Epistolarum ac Evangeliorum dominicalium . . . enarratio*. Cologne, 1537. Belonged to William Edys. Contemporary binding: Oldham, rolls HM. b. 1, HM. c. 1. No chainmark.

*811. SR 73. h. 6. Dionysius Carthusianus, *Epistolarum ac Evangeliorum de Sanctis . . . enarratio*. Cologne, 1537. Binding as **810**. No chainmark.

*820. SR 81. g. 9. Paris, 1502. Rebound in s. xix.

*821. SR 74. d. 6. Paris, 1527. 'D. Pole emptus a doctore Ramerige prec' viis.' Contemporary Oxford binding: Gibson, roll III, and Ker, orn. 14. Chainmarks FS1, HS2.

*822. SR 73. g. 6. Basel, 1523. Rebound in s. xix.

*823. SR 73. g. 5 and 74. b. 14 (in Latin, 2 vols). Cologne, 1546. 73. g. 5 rebound in s. xix. 74. b. 14 in contemporary binding: Oldham, roll FP. d. 1. Cf. **796**.

*824. SR 72. b. 10. (1) *Opera* (in Latin). Cologne, 1523. (2) Gregorius Nazianzenus, *De theologia* (in Latin). Basel, 1523. 'Sum Richardi Corren. testibus quatuor solidis.' Rebound in s. xix.

*826–30. SR 73. f. 2–5. (9 vols. in 4). Basel, 1537. Inscribed with the college *ex libris* and Pole's *ex dono* in the hand of the *ex libris* in **35**. Rebound in s. xix.

*831–2 and *833–4. (*a*) SR 74. a. 6, 7. Paris, 1519. 2 vols. 'Richardi Sortoni liber', cancelled. Rebound in s. xix. (*b*) SR 74. a. 8, 9. Paris, 1522. Rebound in s. xix.

*835–6. SR 72. b. 7, 8. *Opera* (2 vols., in Latin). Basel, 1517. Rebound in s. xix.

*837. SR 71. e. 10. Paris, 1508. Usual inscription, but written later (?). Contemporary stamped binding: Oldham's stamps 1042, 1044 and roll DI. c.1. No chainmark.

*838–9. SR 73. g. 9, 10. Basel, 1542. The editor is J. Gastius Brisacensis. Rebound in s. xix.

*840. LR 4. a. 8. Paris, c. 1499 (*GKW* 2921). Belonged to a monk of Rochester Cathedral Priory and to a monk of Winchester Cathedral Priory—the personal names are not legible—to 'Magister Chersey', and to Thomas Powell. Powell's renunciation of the Pope is on the title-page. Rebound in s. xix.

*841. SR 73. g. 12. Basel, 1515. Given by Margaret Pole, Countess of Salisbury, to John Rogers of Queen's College, Oxford. Contemporary Oxford binding: Gibson, roll I, and Ker, ornaments 8–10. No chainmark.

*842. SR 72. b. 19. Cologne, 1544. Contemporary Oxford binding: Gibson, roll XX, and Oldham, roll IN. 2. Chainmark HS1.

*844–5. LR 4. a. 15, 16. Strasburg, 1494 (Hain 7625) and Strasburg, 1502. 'Liber thome byrd emptus de executoribus Magistri Willelmi Wilton' in each vol. and in 4. a. 15 also, after 'Wilton', 'prec' tocius operis vs.' Rebound as **613**.

*846. SR 79. h. 6. Cologne, 1533. 'Codex Willelmi Edys decani.' Contemporary binding: Oldham, roll HE. h. 1 and orn. C. 4. Chainmark HS2.

*848. SR 79. h. 5. Jacobus Perez de Valentia. Paris, 1521. 'Liber D. Pole precium viis.' Contemporary binding: Oldham, roll SV. a. 6. Chainmark FS2.

*849. SR 79. g. 3. Cologne, 1536. 'Liber D. Pole precium iiiis.' Contemporary binding: Oldham, rolls CH. a. 2. and FL. a. 5. Chainmark FS1.

*850. SR 70. g. 9. Franciscus de Puteo, *Cathena aurea super Psalmos*. Paris, 1520. 4°. Rebound in s. xix.

*853. SR 81. h. 5. A. Osiander. Basel, 1537. 'Liber Ioannis Bulkeley.' Contemporary Cambridge binding: Oldham, roll DI. h. 3. Chainmark HS2.

*854–6. SR 13. g. 1/1–3. P. Berchorius. Lyons 1516–17 (3 vols.). Contemporary Oxford bindings: Gibson, roll I, and Ker, *Pastedowns*, orn. 5.

*857. SR 77. g. 13. Basel, 1502. Belonged to John Elkin, monk of Burton-on-Trent. Rebound in s. xix.

*858. SR 77. h. 17. Paris, 1516. Contemporary binding (Oxford?): Oldham, roll FL. a. 4 and Ker, *Pastedowns*, orn. 18. Chainmarks HS1, HS2.

*859. LR 3. h. 10. Strasburg, after 1496 (*GKW* 2034). Contemporary stamped binding, rebacked. Chainmarks FS1, HS1.

*860. Liverpool, Athenaeum. Nuremberg, 1519. Alienated. Belonged to 'Thomas Powell armig. ', to James West of Balliol College, and by his gift, 12 August 1722, to Thomas Hearne.

*861. SR 79. f. 8. Strasburg, 1519. Rebound in s. xix.

862. 'Speculum moralium I. Vitalis' (Ledger).

*863. SR 62. a. 5. Strasburg, 1513. Rebound in s. xix.

*864–72. Of these nine volumes of Pepin five, all octavos, are at All Souls.
   (i, ii) SR 79. c. 13, 14. *In Genesim*. Paris, 1528. 2 vols. (ii) belonged to

Alexander Barlow. Contemporary panel bindings: (i) Oldham, *Panels*, HE 32 and Quad. 3; (ii) Oldham, *Panels*, HE 34 and Quad. 4. Chainmark HS1.

(iii) v. 4.12. *Sermonum Dominicalium Pars secunda*. Paris, 1534. Bought by William Edys, abbot of Burton-on-Trent.[1] Rebound in s. xix, but the old panel-stamped covers (Oldham, *Panels*, HE 32 and Quad. 3) have been laid on, outside: cf. (iv).

(iv) v. 4. 16. *Sermones quadraginta de destructione Niniue*. Paris, 1527. Binding as (iii): 'restored 1884'.

(v) t. 8. 2. (1) *Expositio euangeliorum quadragesimalium*. Paris, 1532. (2) *Sermones quadragesimales*. Paris, 1532. Rebound in s. xix. The Ledger records also 'De aduentu domini', 'Super psalmos' (*Speculum aureum super septem psalmos penitentiales*), and 'Opusculum' (*Opusculum super confiteor*?).

*873 or 874. SR 77. c. 3. Louvain, 1544. 8°. Belonged to Philip Brade. 'emptus per me pro xvi*d* D. Pole.' Contemporary panel binding: Oldham, *Panels*, HM 27, 28 (Oxford?). Chainmark HS1.

*876. SR 77. h. 10. Lyons, 1544. 4°. Contemporary binding: Oldham, rolls FL. a. 8, DI. f. 1. Chainmarks FS2, HS1.

*879. t. 8. 7. M. Busingerus, *Ecclesia*. Dillingen, 1556. 8°. 'Liber D. Pole precium iiis emptus London 1557.' Contemporary binding. Chainmarks FS2, HS1.

*881. i. 12. 15. J. Wallensis. Lyons, 1511. 8°. Belonged to William Edys. Nearly contemporary Cambridge binding by Spierinck: Gray, roll VI. Chainmarks FS1, HS1.

*883. LR 4. e. 10. (1) Paris, 1498 (Hain 12046). 8°. (2) S. Brulefer, *Formalitates*. Paris, sine anno (variant of *GKW* 5582). 8°. Belonged to William Edys. Contemporary panel binding: Oldham, *Panels*, first state of VS 4.

*884. v. 4. 15. N. de Gorran, *Sermones Fundamenti aurei*. Paris, 1509. 8°. Rebound, but the old panel-stamped covers (Oldham, *Panels*, BIB 9 and REL 6) have been laid on, outside.

*885. SR 77. h. 16. Guillelmus Arvernus, *De claustro anime*; Hugo de Sancto Victore, *De claustro anime*. Paris, 1507. 4°. Rebound in s. xix.

*886. SR 77. d. 32. J. Wesselus. sine anno et loco. 4°. Sixteenth-century binding: a diaper roll. Chainmarks, FS2, HS1.

888. 'Anima fidelis Ioh. Royardi' (Ledger). For these Lenten sermons see *GKW* 1985–7. They were printed also in s. xvi.

890. 'Breve totius theologicae veritatis compendium' (Ledger).

893. 'Confessio fidei in Comitiis Augustae' (Ledger).

*901. v. 15. 17. Cologne, 1549. 8°. 'Glyn et amicorum.' '13° Iunii. anno domini 1549.' Contemporary binding (Cambridge?). Chain marks HS1, HS2.

*906. SR 62. a. 2. Paris, 1512. 4°. Belonged to William Edys. Rebound in s. xix.

---

[1] For the inscriptions in this and five other books belonging to Edys, **881, 883, 906, 932, 964,** see N. R. Ker, *Medieval libraries of Great Britain*, 2nd ed. (1964), p. 232, under Burton-on-Trent.

*908. v. 13. 3. Cologne, 1535. 8°. 'Liber D. Pole.' Contemporary (?) binding: Oldham, roll MW. d. 3. Chainmark HS1.

909. 'Lutheri enarratio in Psalmos' (Ledger).

911. Stephen Gardiner's *Confutatio cavillationum* printed at Paris in 1552.

915. 'Io. Ferii Examen' (Ledger).

916. 'Olivarius valentinus de sacramento altaris' (Ledger).

921. 'Pandectae scripturarum othonis' (Ledger).

*922. SR 79. h. 5. Jacobus Perez de Valentia. Paris, 1521. 'Liber D. Pole precium vii^s.' Contemporary binding: Oldham, roll SV. a. 6 and ornament B. 1. Chainmark FS2.

*927. v. 2. 8. Johannes Justus Lanspergius, *Sermones*. Cologne, 1539. 'Yf there be anything in this booke, or in any other booke of myne here or els where, contrarey vnto ye goodly laues, and statutes, made by ow^r moost sufferent lorde kinge h. ye viith I here vnterly refuse, forsake, and renoynce it, as a thing vtterly vnknoyne and contrarey vnto my mynde and wyll, wyttnes this writtyng, and protestation. writte and subscribde w^t this my one hand. anno eiusdem serenissimi regis nostri. h. 8^i. 31°. 6° die mensis iulii Per me Iohanen (*sic*) ramrige' on the fly-leaf. 'D. Pole emptus a doctore ramerige prec. iiis.' Rebound in s. xix.

*928. SR 80. f. 4. M. Luther, *Epistolarum et euangeliorum enarrationes*. Strasburg, 1535. Rebound in s. xix.

*929. w. 1. 2. (1) *Homiliarum centuria prima*. Cologne, 1541. (2) *Opera, Pars tertia*. Cologne, 1539. 'Liber D. Pole prec' viis.' Rebound in s. xix.

*930. SR 74. b. 7. Basel, 1513. Contemporary Oxford binding: Gibson, roll 1 and Ker, ornaments 5, 9, 10. No chainmark.

*931. v. 2. 6. Lyons, 1525. 4°. Contemporary binding: Oldham, roll AN. e. 1. and half-stamp ornament like, but not, Oldham, ornament B. 3. Chainmark HS1.

*932. v. 2. 13 *Sermones quadragesimales thesauri noui*. Paris, 1497 (Reichling, 177). 4°. Belonged to William Edys. 'Constat Monasterio de Burton super trent.' Contemporary panel binding (French?), St. George on one side, the other badly rubbed. Chainmark HS1.

*937. v. 2. 14. Antwerp, 1557. 8°. 'Liber D. Pole precii viis viii*d* emptus anno 1557.' Rebound in s. xvii in.

939-43. 'Roiardi homiliae in Eucarist. feriales quadragesimae, homiliarum Royardi pars hiemalis, Royardi homiliae hiemales' (Ledger).

944-7. Homilies in four volumes and 'loci communes' (*Encheiridion locorum communium*) (Ledger).

949. 'Bedae homiliae in Epist. Pauli' (Ledger).

*955. Probably v. 2. 15. P. Dorbellus, *Sermones hortuli conscientie super epistolas quadragesime*. Paris, 1518. 8°. The first two leaves are missing. Inscribed as **35**. Rebound in s. xix.

*958. v. 4. 14. G. Barelete, *Sermones quadragesimales et de sanctis*. Rouen, 1515. 8°.

Rebound in s. xix, but the old covers (Oldham, roll AN. c. 1 and ornament A. 3) have been laid on, outside.

960. Cf. **884**.

*963. SR 73 a. 9. N. Denyse. Rouen, 1507. 8°. Rebound in s. xix.

*964. v. 4. 13. N. Denyse. Paris, 1522. 8°. Belonged to William Edys. Rebound in s. xix, but the old panel-stamped covers (Oldham, *Panels*, HE 32 and Quad. 3) have been laid on, outside.

*964a. w. 2. 10. Basel, 1515. Rebound in s. xix.

LIST X

*965–74. 'Liber Collegii omnium Animarum fidelium defunctorum de Oxon' ex legatione M^{ri} Andree Kingsmill legum Baccalaurei nuper istius Collegii socii. 1576' beautifully written in each volume. All ten were rebound in s. xix.

*965. y. 4. 3. *Tractatus theologici omnes*. Geneva, 1573.

*966. SR 70. g. 1. Geneva, 1572.

*967. SR 70. g. 7. Geneva, 1572.

*968. SR 70. g. 8. (1) (Geneva) 1557. (2) Geneva, 1554.

*969. SR 70. g. 5. (1) Geneva, 1570. (2) Geneva, 1567.

*970. SR 70. g. 6. (1) (Lyons) 1571. (2) Geneva, 1567.

*971. SR 79. h. 9. (1) Zürich, 1571. (2) Zürich, 1575.

*972. SR 79. i. 2. Zürich, 1571.

*973. SR 79. i. 3. (1) Basel, 1568. (2) Zürich, 1572.

*974. w. 2. 9. P. Martyr, *Defensio doctrinae Eucharistiae*. (Zürich) 1562.

LIST XI

*975–9. dd. inf. 1. 12–15, dd. inf. 2. 1. *Concilia generalia*. Venice, 1585. Inscribed as **35**. Contemporary Oxford bindings (cf. List XXVII, 1586–7): Gibson, rolls XII, XVIII. Corner and centre metalpieces missing. Chainmarks FI, FS1, FS2.

LIST XII

*980–7. p. 1. 1–8. *Biblia Sacra*, ed. B. Arias Montanus. Antwerp, 1569–73. 'Liber Collegii Omnium Animarum fidelium defunctorum in Oxon'. Ex dono Francisci Milles, artium magistri, ac nuper ejusdem Collegii Socii. 1584' in each volume. Bound in Oxford by Pinart in 1584 (cf. List XXVII, 1583–4): Gibson, rolls XII, XVIII. Corner and centre metalpieces missing. Chainmark FS1. Cf. the note to **43**.

LIST XIII

*996. MS. 14. s. xv. 'Liber collegii Animarum omnium fidelium defunctorum in Ox' ex dono W. Folowys preceptoris quondam gramatice apud Euesham qui obiit 4 die Augusti Anno d' 1483. Oretis igitur pro anima eiusdem' (*the last five words lightly erased*). Contemporary binding of white skin over wooden boards.

997. **103** has the same secundo folio.

*1007. LR 5. i. 4. J. Duns Scotus, *Scriptum in quatuor libros sententiarum.* Nuremberg, 1481 (Hain 6417). 'Liber Collegii Animarum omnium fidelium in Oxon' ex dono Magistri Roberti Elyot Anno domini Millesimo CCCC^mo nonagesimo. Orate pro anima eius' on the fly-leaf. Rebound in Oxford in 1614–15: Gibson, roll XXVII. At this time, probably, two leaves of another copy were inserted to supply the beginning of the text: cf. List XXVIA, Gaunt 4.

*1010. MS. 97. s. xiii. 'Liber Willelmi Gruffyth bacularii' on the pastedown at the end. 'Liber collegii animarum omnium fidelium defunctorum in Oxon' datus per Magistrum Willelmum Griffyth', f. 1. Old binding of white skin over wooden boards, rebacked. Cf. List XXVII at 1452–3.

*1013. MS. 92. s. xv in. 'Liber Collegii animarum omnium fidelium defunctorum ex dono M. Thome lay. oretis pro bono statu eiusdem', f. 1ᵛ. Binding of s. xviii, rebacked.

*1015. MS. 98. s. xv. *Confessio amantis.* This copy now lacks the second leaf of the table of contents, from which the secundo folio was taken. The first leaf ends 'accusat' (bk. 2, ch. 1: ed. Macaulay, p. 6) and the second leaf began therefore 'Hic corripit'. Inscribed as **35**. Old binding, repaired. Cf. List XXVII at 1449–50.

*1016. Bodleian MS. Digby 44. s. xv. 'Liber collegii animarum omnium fidelium defunctorum in Ox'. Ex dono Magistri Iohannis Saundyr nuper socii eiusdem collegii cuius anime propicietur deus Amen', f. 3. In his will made in 1485 Saunder bequeaths this book, 'unum Questionistam super libros naturalis philosophie ex propria manu', which was lying in the Selton chest: it was to be redeemed thence and chained in the library, the expenses of redemption 'et alia omnia supportanda' to be secured by the sale of five hoods, 'volumina doctoris subtilis et volumina doctoris de lira'. Rebound in s. xvii. Cf. also List XXVIA, Saunder.

1022. Johannes de Spira (cf. Thorndike and Kibre, col. 204).

*1025. MS. 83. s. xv. Inscribed as **35**. Binding as **77**.

Additions to List XIII

1026. As ed. Strasburg, 1483 (Christ Church, Oxford).

*1028. LR 3. g. 10. sine anno et loco. 'Liber Collegii animarum etc' ex dono Reuerendi patris domini Iacobi goldwell nuper Norwicensis episcopi.' Rebound in s. xix. The secundo folio in tabula is *Brutorum.* 'sanctorum' was a mistake.

1029. As ed. Mainz, 1467 (Bodleian).

*1030. LR 5. k. 5. Mainz, 1471 (Hain 1447). 'Liber Collegii animarum etc' (*altered to* omnium fidelium, *s. xvii*) ex dono Reuerendi patris domini Iacobi Goldwell' nuper Norwicensis.' Rebound in s. xix.

*1032. LR 3. g. 9. Venice, sine anno (Hain 10984). Imperfect at the beginning. 'My lord of Norwych' at the end (cf. *1037), so of Goldwell's gift. Rebound in s. xix.

*1037. LR 4. a. 11. Leo Magnus, *Sermones et epistolae* (ed. J. Andreae). sine anno et loco (Hain 10010). 'My lorde of Norwych' at the end, so of Goldwell's gift:

his *ex dono* was probably at the foot of the second leaf, where a strip has been cut off. Rebound in s. xix.

1038–41. As ed. Nuremberg, 1481–2 (Bodleian).

*1042. w. i. i. *Sermones aurei de sanctis.* Nuremberg, 1478 (Hain 16134). 'Hunc librum legauit collegio omnium animarum Oxon' cathenand' in communi libraria ibidem M. Grafton. Orate pro anima M. Iohannis Grafton' quondam socii collegii predicti' and 'Liber collegii animarum in Oxonia ex dono magistri Grafton eiusdem collegii quondam socii'. Rebound in s. xix.

*1043. MS. 91. s. xv. 'Liber Collegii animarum omnium fidelium defunctorum in Oxon' ex dono reuerendi in cristo patris Iacobi Golldwell episcopi Norwic' et quondam socii huius Collegii.' Rebound as **77**.

1047. As ed. Nuremberg, 1478 (Bodleian).

LIST XIV

1055. Called 'Liber de humilitate' in List XV.

*1057. Bodleian, MS. Rawlinson G. 47. A.D. 1441, in a humanistic hand. Nine words of the inscription, 'ex dono Reuerendi patris iacobi Goldwell nuper Norwicensis episcopi' can still be read: the rest has been erased. 'Resarcitus per Gressup', f. 4, s. xvi (?): the present binding is of s. xviii.

*1067. a. 6. 7. Venice, 1472 (Hain 13074). 'Liber Collegii animarum omnium fidelium defunctorum in Oxon'. Ex dono Magistri Ricardi Toppliff quondam socii eiusdem cuius anime propicietur deus.' Contemporary Netherlandish (?) stamped binding, the clasps fastening from the lower to the upper cover.

1068. As ed. Venice, 1472 (Bodleian). *punctum* is the first word on sign. a 2, and *uirtus* (cf. List XVI) the first on sign. a 3.

1069. Perhaps the same as **588**. As ed. (Strasburg), sine anno (*GKW* 9531). The mistaken title in List XVII. 122 is derived from the first item in the table of contents.

1070. As ed. Rome, 1469 (Bodleian).

Additions to List XIV

1072. As ed. Rome, 1472 (Queen's College).

1073. As ed. Rome (1469) (Bodleian).

*1074. SR 11. s. Rome, 1470 (Hain 15116). 'Liber Collegii animarum omnium fidelium defunctorum de Oxon' ex dono Re^di patris iacobi Goldwell nuper Norwicensis episcopi et olim istius Collegii socii 'ac legum doctoris'.' Rebound in Oxford in s. xvi ex.: Gibson, rolls XII, XVIII.

*1075. LR 3. h. 2. Venice, 1472 (*GKW* 2293). 'Liber Collegii animarum omnium fidelium defunctorum de Oxon' ex dono Reuerendi patris iacobi Goldwell nuper Norwicensis episcopi et olim istius Collegii socii.' Rebound in s. xix.

*1076. MS. 93. A.D. 1465. Bought by Goldwell in Rome in 1467. 'Liber Collegii animarum omnium fidelium defunctorum de Oxon' ex dono Reuerendi patris iacobi Goldwell nuper Norwicensis episcopi et olim istius Collegii Socii.'

'Orate pro anima Iohannis Cole artium magistri' on the fly-leaf at the end. Binding of s. xv/xvi.

LIST XV

1077. Presumably this was a manuscript with the *ex libris* of the Cistercian abbey of Buildwas: cf. *MLGB*, 2nd ed., p. 14. Since it was on Desk I it is likely to have been a part of the Bible or a biblical commentary.

*1084, *1086, *1087. v. 1. 1–3. Rainerius de Pisis, *Pantheologia*. Nuremberg, 1477 (3 vols.: Hain 13018). 'Liber Collegii Animarum Omnium fidelium defunctorum in Oxon' Ex dono domini Iacobi Goldewell 'legum d' quondam Norwic' Episcopi et huius Collegii Socii' in vol. 2. Rebound in s. xix.

Additions to List XV

*1097–8. SR 58. f. 16/1, 2. Rasis, *Liber continens*. Brescia, 1486 (2 vols.: Hain 13901). 'Ex dono Nicholai Halswell quondam in medicina doctoris et socii huius Collegii.' Rebound in s. xix.

1100. Cf. Hain 15333–45.

*1103. i. 4. 4. Rome (1469) (*GKW* 4183). 'Ex dono Reuerendi patris ac domini domini Iacobi Goldwell quondam Norwycensis episcopi ad vsum sociorum Collegii animarum.' Platina's praise of this work is quoted in the margin of the first leaf, with this addition: 'Nos verò qui soli in hac Academia hunc authorem tam egregium nacti sumus, et habemus; legamus omnes quotquot sumus, integrum et ab ovo (quod aiunt), vsque ad mala; certè operae nostrae sic collocatae, non potest vnquam aliquem paenituisse. Scripsit Socius huius Collegii 29° die Mart[is] Anno Domini M°. D° lxxx et sexto.' The first thirty-one words of the quotation from Platina are in a fine hand. Rebound in s. xix.

*1104, *1104a, *1105. LR 3. g. 2–4. Parts 1–3. Basel, sine anno. Rebound in s. xix. **1105a**, pt. 4, is missing.

1106. Perhaps the name of a former owner.

*1107–12. SR 70. i. 1–5, 7. Textus Biblie cum glosa ordinaria . . . Basel, 1506–8. 6 vols. Inscribed as **35**. All rebound in s. xix.

1113. As ed. Basel, 1489 (Bodleian).

1115. As ed. Basel, 1489 (Bodleian) and other editions.

1116. As ed. Paris, 1499 (Bodleian).

1117. As ed. Basel, 1489 (Bodleian).

1118. As ed. Basel, 1489 (Bodleian).

*1119–25. SR 80. b. 2–8. Basel, 1502. 7 vols. 'Apud Thomam Ryche pertinet' in each volume. Inscribed as **35**. All rebound in s. xix.

LIST XVI

*1126. p. 5. 1, 2. Paris, 1538–40. No college *ex libris*. Originally one volume, but now two volumes in bindings of s. xix.

*1127–31. SR 72. d. 7–11. Basel, 1539. In Latin. 5 vols. 'Liber collegii omnium animarum fidelium defunctorum in Oxon', s. xvi, in vol. 1. The rest inscribed as **35**. All rebound in s. xix.

*1132. SR 74. c. 5. Paris, 1544. In Latin. 'Liber Collegii omnium Animarum fidelium defunctorum in Oxon', s. xvi/xvii. Rebound in s. xix.

*1133. SR 72. b. 9. Basel, 1539. Inscribed as **35**. Rebound in s. xix.

*1134. SR 73. h. 7. Basel, 1542. In Latin. Inscribed as **35**. Rebound in s. xix.

*1135. SR 73. g. 7. Basel, 1528. Inscribed as **35**. Nearly contemporary Oxford binding: Gibson, rolls VII, VIII, X.

*1136. SR 8. d. 5. Basel, 1540. Inscribed as **35**. Contemporary Oxford binding: Gibson, rolls VII, X.

*1137–8. SR 73. g. 2, 3. In Latin. Basel, 1536. 2 vols. Inscribed as **35**. Rebound in s. xix.

*1138a, b. SR 72. b. 4, 5. Basel, 1538. 2 vols. Inscribed as **35**. Rebound in s. xix.

*1138c–j. SR 71. d. 1–8. Basel, 1541–3. Bought in 1547–8 (cf. List XXVII, at 1547–8). Inscribed as **35**. Contemporary Oxford bindings, rebacked and repaired: Gibson, rolls IX, X, and Ker, *Pastedowns*, ornaments 25, 26.

1141d. Cf. List XXVIA, Polton, and List XXVIII, Polton.

1142. As ed. Basel, 1542.

*1143. SR 58. e. 9. Antonius Musa. Basel, 1541. Inscribed as **35**. Rebound in s. xix.

*1144. SR 58. g. 3. Basel, 1540. Inscribed as **35**. Contemporary Oxford binding: Gibson, rolls VII, VIII, X.

*1145. SR 58. c. 8. Basel, 1543. 'Liber collegii omnium animarum fidelium defunctorum . . .', s. xvi med. Contemporary Oxford binding: Gibson, roll VIII, Oldham, roll HM. a. 5, and Ker, *Pastedowns*, ornaments 25–7.

*1146–8. SR 58. e. 7/1–3. Basel, 1538. 3 vols. Inscribed as **35**. **1146** rebound in s. xix. **1147–8** in contemporary Oxford bindings: Gibson, roll VII. Cf. List XXVII at 1547–8.

*1149a. Gloucester Cathedral, H. 3. 6. Marburg, 1543. Inscribed as **35** and also, in two places, 'Liber Collegii omnium animarum'. Belonged to John Mower 'E coll. Merton. Oxon' in 1678. Contemporary Oxford binding: Gibson, roll X, and Oldham, roll HM. a. 5.

*1149b. Probably SR 59. a. 28. Basel, 1543. Inscribed as **35**. Rebound in s. xix. Chainmark F1 (?). See also List XXVIB. 10.

*1150. i. 5. 9. Venice, 1534. Inscribed as **35**. Contemporary Oxford binding: Gibson, rolls VII, X.

*1151. i. 5. 12. Venice, 1536. Inscribed as **35**. Contemporary Oxford binding: Gibson, rolls VII, X.

*1152. i. 5. 10. Venice, 1535. Inscribed as **35**. Contemporary Oxford binding: Gibson, rolls VII, X.

*1153. g. inf. 2, 3. (1) Alexander Aphrodisaeus, *Quaestiones naturales de anima* (etc.). Venice, 1536. (2) Joannes Philoponus, *Contra Proclum de mundi aeternitate.* Venice, 1535. Inscribed as **35**. Contemporary Oxford binding: Gibson, rolls VII, X.

*1154. g. inf. 2. 4. Venice, 1527. Inscribed as **35**. Contemporary Oxford binding: Gibson, rolls VII, X.

*1155. g. inf. 2. 5. Venice, 1535. Inscribed as **35**. Contemporary Oxford binding: Gibson, rolls VII, VIII, X.

*1156–7. i. 1. 6, 7. Basel, 1542. 2 vols. Inscribed as **35**. Rebound in s. xix.

*1158–63. Exeter College, 9. I. 1497. 6, 4, 1, 2, 3, 5. 6 vols. Venice, 1495–8 (*GKW* 2334). Inscribed as **35**. Bound in France, s. xvi (vol. 3 rebound).

1164. As ed. Basel 1537: cf. List XXVIA, Warner 4.

*1165. i. 7. 1. (1) A. Aphrodisaeus, *In Topica Aristotelis Commentarii.* Venice, 1513. (2) A. Aphrodisaeus, *In sophisticos Aristotelis elenchos commentaria.* Venice, 1520. Inscribed as **35**. Oxford binding, *c.* 1540: Gibson, rolls VII, X.

*1166. i. 6. 1. Venice, 1536. Inscribed as **35**. Oxford binding, *c.* 1540: Gibson, rolls VII, X.

*1167. i. 5. 11. Venice, 1527. Inscribed as **35**. Oxford binding, *c.* 1540: Gibson, rolls VII, X.

*1170. i. 5. 5 (1). P. Nicolettus, *Prima (. . . Sexta) pars summe naturalium.* Venice, 1476 (Hain 12515). Inscribed as **35**. Rebound in s. xvii in front of a copy of Aquinas given in 1619.

*1170a. i. 4. 5. Basel, 1539. College *ex libris*, s. xvii. Rebound in s. xix.

*1170c, d. SR 42. a. 1/1–2. M. Antonius Coccius Sabellicus, *Opera.* Basel, 1538. Rebound in s. xix.

*1171. a. 5. 6. Basel, 1532. Inscribed as **35**. Rebound in s. xix.

*1174. SR 13. h. 4. Cologne, 1540. 'Liber collegii omnium animarum.' Rebound in s. xix.

*1175–6. a. 1. 10, 11. Basel, 1540. 5 vols. in 2. 'Liber collegii omnium animarum' in both volumes. Inscribed also as **35**. Rebound in s. xix.

*1177. SR 11. l. 1. Basel, 1535. 'Liber collegii animarum' in front and 'Liber Collegii omnium animarum' at the end. Inscribed as **35**. Rebound in s. xix.

*1180a. SR 13. e. 3. Hagenau, 1526. Inscribed as **1458**. Rebound in s. xix.

Additions to List XVI

*1183. SR 73. h. 5. Paris, 1551. The *ex dono* of Sir John Mason is in a hand of s. xvii. Rebound in s. xix.

*1184–7. SR 79. h. 3, 4, and 70. h. 1, 2.

    79. h. 3. *In Psalmos.* Paris, 1547.

    70. h. 2. *In quinque Libros Sapientiales.* Paris, 1541.

    70. h. 1. *In Evangelia.* Paris, 1542.

79. h. 4. (1) *In Epistolas Pauli*. Paris, 1548. (2) *In Epistolas Catholicas et Actus Apostolorum*. Paris, 1548.

All inscribed in a fine hand, 'Ex dono Io. Masoni militis', and also as **35**. Bound in Oxford, s. xvi ex.: Gibson, rolls XII, XVIII.

*1188. SR 74. b. 12. Paris, 1550. In Latin. Inscribed as **1184**. Bound in Oxford, s. xvi ex.: Gibson, rolls XII, XVIII.

*1189. y. 2. 5. Paris, 1544. Inscribed as **1184**. Bound in Oxford, s. xvi ex.: Gibson, rolls XII, XVIII.

*1190–3. Bodleian, Antiq. b. G. S. 1549/1–4. Basel, 1549. Inscribed as **35**. All rebound in s. xix.

*1194. vv. inf. 2. 3. Lyons, 1554–5. Inscribed as **1184**. Rebound in s. xix.

*1195. vv. inf. 2. 9. Paris, 1552. Inscribed as **1184**. Rebound in s. xix.

*1196. g. inf. 2. 6. Venice, 1534. Inscribed as **1184**. Italian binding, s. xvi.

*1197. d. 2. 6. (1) Nicephorus Gregoras, *Historia Byzantina* (in Greek and Latin). Basel, 1562. (2) P. Paschalius, *Elogium Henrici II*. Paris, 1560. Inscribed as **1184**. Contemporary binding.

*1198. a. 7. 4. (1) Valerius Maximus. Venice, 1508. (2) P. de Castrovol, *Lectura super Ethica Aristotelis*. Ylerde, 1489 (Hain–Copinger, 1481). 'Tennand precium iiiis' on title-page of (1). 'Liber collegii animarum', s. xvi. on (1) and (2). (1) also inscribed as **35**. Rebound in s. xix.

*1199. SR 9. a. Basel, 1554. Inscribed as **1184**. Contemporary binding: gilt centre-piece.

*1200. SR 41. a. 8. Paulus Constantinus Phrygio. Basel 1534. Inscribed as **1184**. Contemporary binding by Reynes: Oldham, roll AN. b. 1 and ornament A. 1.

1201. Probably the edition of 1557, listed in the 1635 catalogue.

*1202–4. SR 13. d. 2/1–3. Paris, 1543. Bought in 1549–50: cf. List XXVII at 1549–50. Inscribed as **35**. Rebound in s. xviii.

*1205. a. 7. 13. Basel, 1555. Inscribed as **1184**. Contemporary binding: centre-piece.

LIST XVII

*1214–18. SR 73. f. 6–10. Basel, 1524–6. A long inscription in 73. f. 6 records the gift by William Tucker, vicar of Ermington, Devon, of this edition of Jerome and of the 1529 edition of Augustine (cf. List XXVIA, Tucker) 'regnante Elizabetha principe illustrissima, et Christianissima, præsidente tamen huic Collegio Doctore Ioanne Warnero . . . Quod fecit hic magister Gulielmus Tucker vt extaret hoc illius munus mnemosynon siue pignus perpetuum, suæ in matrem, quæ eum aluit et euexit, pietatis et obseruantiæ. Et vt posteris, qui ista lecturi sint, ad maiora incitamentum aliquod et inuitamentum foret.' All rebound in s. xix. Cf. List XXVII at 1558–9.

*1227. Pembroke College, Oxford, 2, included by my error in List XXVIA: see p. 160.

*1229–30. SR 58. f. 15/1, 2. Venice, 1509. 'Liber collegii animarum omnium fidelium defunctorum in oxonia ex dono venerabilis viri Ricardi bartlet in medicinis doctoris et quondam huius collegii socii.' Also inscribed as **35**. Contemporary bindings: Oldham, roll AN. b. 2 and ornament A. 1.

*1233. LR 3. h. 21. J. de Magistris, *Quaestiones super tota philosophia*. Venice, 1487 (Hain 10453). 4°. 'Liber Collegii Animarum Ex dono W. Hone quondam Eiusdem contubernii socii.' Rebound in s. xix.

*1235. i. 1. 5. Venice, 1483 (*GKW* 2337). 'Liber collegii animarum ex dono Iohannis Game in medicinis inceptoris et quondam socii huius collegii.' Rebound in s. xix.

*1237–8. MZ. 6. 15, 16. C. Gesner, *Bibliotheca universalis*. Zürich, 1545–8. Inscribed as **1184**. Vol. 1 rebound in s. xix. Vol. 2 in contemporary binding: Oldham, roll HM. c. 4, a centre-piece, and corner ornaments: chainmarks FS1, HS1.

LIST XVIII

*1251. MS. 49. s. xiv in. Written in Italy. Formerly 'L. 289' at the Benedictine abbey of Bury St. Edmunds. No College *ex libris*. *virum* is the secundo folio in textu, *de bonorum* (cf. List XXII) the secundo folio in glosa. Late medieval binding of white skin over boards. Almost certainly identical with **252**.

LIST XIX

1263. No doubt the now missing manuscript which Thomas James saw at All Souls (*Ecloga Oxonio-Cantabrigiensis*, 1600, no. 17) containing: (1) Aphorismi Damasceni; (2) P. Hispanus de oculis; (3) Flores diætarum; (4) Curæ Magistri Pontii de S. Ægidio, omnium ægritudinum quæ accidunt à summitate capitis, vsque ad Epilotum; (5) Tract. de medicinis simplicibus et compositis. Pr. Medicinarum quædam sunt; (6) Tract. de rebus Naturalibus et quæ contra naturam accidunt. Pr. Introducendis; (7) Tractatus Gerardi. Pr. Cum omne elementum. For arts. 2, 4, 5, 7 see Thorndike and Kibre, cols. 698, 254, 860 (W. Agilon), 324 (Geraldus Bituricensis).

*1266. SR 58. g. 1. *Consilia medica*. sine loco, 1476 (Hain 11551). Inscribed as **585** and, also, 'pro colegio omnium animarum Oxon'. Contemporary Oxford binding: Gibson, p. 21, 'Rood and Hunt', stamps 44–5, 49, 50.

Additions to List XIX

*1267. v. 1. 12. Arnoldus de Geilhoven. Brussels, 1476 (*GKW* 2512). 'Liber Collegii animarum in oxonia ex dono Reuerendi patris Iacobi golldwell Norwic' episcopi et quondam huius colleg' socii.' Rebound in s. xix.

*1272–3. LR 4. c. 8, 9. P. de Monte, *Repertorium iuris vtriusque*. Nuremberg, 1476 (Hain 11588). A–E and F–O only: for vol. 2 of another edition containing L–Z see **1429**. 'Liber Collegii animarum in Oxon Ex dono Iacobi Golldwell' Norwycensis episcopi et huius Collegii quondam socii' in vol. 2 (the inscription in vol. 1 is of s. xviii). Rebound in s. xviii. The secundo folio *athenas* (cf. Lists XX–XXII) is not an alternative to *nare*. I have not found it.

*1277. MS. 54. Paper. Written by John Elveden in 1417. No college *ex libris*. Rebound in s. xix.

1280. Perhaps for 'miles': cf. **1455**.

1287. As ed. Venice, sine anno (Glasgow, Hunterian Museum: *GKW* 3489).

*1289. cc. 4. 4. Antonius de Prato Veteri, *Repertorium aureum in toto iuris scripti.* (Milan) 1481 (*GKW* 2249). 'Liber Collegii omnium fidelium in Oxon' ex dono reuerendi patris Iacobi Gollwell' Norwicensis episcopi et quondam socii huius colleg' 'ac legum doctoris'.' Contemporary stamped binding.

*1290. MS. 64. s. xv. Paper. 'Liber Collegii omnium fidelium defunctorum de Oxon' ex dono Reuerendi patris Iacobi Goldwell nuper Norwicensis episcopi et olim istius Collegii socii 'ac legum doctoris'.' Bound in s. xv/xvi. The secundo folio is *tatorum* (*ta* lightly cancelled): f. 1ᵛ ends *attemp.*

1291. As ed. sine anno et loco (Bodleian: Proctor 2609).

1292–3. As ed. (Rome, 1470) (Bodleian, Auct. K. 1. 13, 14).

*1294. LR 4. c. 7. (Rome, 1469: Hain 15086). 'Liber Collegii animarum omnium fidelium defunctorum de oxon' ex dono Reuerendi patris Iacobi Goldwell 'legum doctoris' nuper Norwicensis episcopi et olim istius Collegii socii.' Rebound in s. xix.

1295. As ed. Venice, 1472 (Bodleian).

1296. As ed. Venice, 1469 (Bodleian).

1301. As ed. Venice, 1472 (Bodleian).

1303. As ed. Venice, 1478 (Bodleian).

LIST XX

1306–7. As ed. Speyer, sine anno (*GKW* 8648). For another copy of vol. 2 see List XXVIA, Broke. Cf. List XXVIA, Est 6, 7.

1311. Presumably an edition of Codex Justiniani printed by Baptista de Tortis. If so, it shares the secundo folio in glosa 'a. conferentibus' with the edition printed at Venice in 1491 by Georgius Arriuabene (Bodleian).

1313. As ed. Venice, 1491 (Bodleian).

*1319. dd. 4. 8. Baldus de Ubaldis. (Lyons) 1498 (Pellechet 1730). 'Liber collegii animarum ex dono Magistri Thome Mors nuper eiusdem collegii socii et licenciati in iure ciuili 'qui obiit vicesimo tercio die Iunii Anno domini mᵒ cccccᵒ primo'.' Rebound in s. xix. The secundo folio is *tia illi iuri.*

*1320. ee. 2. 3. (1) Baldus de Ubaldis, *Lectura super digesto nouo.* (Lyons) 1498. (2) Baldus de Ubaldis. *Lectura super prima et secunda parte infortiati.* (Lyons) sine anno (Hain–Copinger 815, 813). Inscribed as **1319**, without the addition. Rebound in s. xix.

*1321–2. ee. 2. 1, 2. Baldus de Ubaldis, *Consilia.* Venice, 1491 (Hain 2329). 2 vols. Inscribed as **1320**. Rebound in s. xix.

*1323. LR 5. k. 1. sine anno et loco (Hain 6985). 'Liber Ricardi Salter decr' doctoris'. Inscribed nearly as **1320**. Rebound in s. xix.

*1324, *1326. aa. 2. 5, 6. J. Calderinus, *Iuris Reportorium.* sine loco 1474 (*GKW* 5904). 2 vols.: 1326 is vol. 1 and 1324 vol. 2. 'Liber collegii animarum omnium fidelium defunctorum in Oxon' ex dono Reuerendi patris Iacobi golldwell' nuper Norwycensis episcopi et olim huius collegii socii 'ac legum doctoris" in aa. 2. 5. 'Liber Collegii Animarum oxonie Ex dono Reuerendi in cristo patris domini domini Iacobi Gowldewell' episcopi norwigencis legum doctoris et quondam socii huius collegii' in aa. 2. 6. The hands are not the same. Rebound in s. xix.

*1326. See *1324.

*1328. SR 14. b. 1. (Venice, 1474: Hain 15858. 1). 4°. 'Liber collegii animarum o. f. defunctorum Oxon Ex dono Reuerendissimi in cristo patris ac domini Domini Iacobi Goldwell Norwys' episcopi Legum doctoris ac quondam istius collegii Socii'. Rebound in s. xix.

LIST XXI

*1329. LR 5. l. 7. Venice 1481 (*GKW* 3747). No college *ex libris*. Rebound in s. xix.

1329a. As ed. Venice, 1492 (Bodleian).

1330. As ed. Venice, 1499 (Merton College).

*1332-4. LR 5. l. 3-5. W. Durand, *Speculum*. Padua, 1479 (*GKW* 9154). 3 vols. 'Liber collegii animarum omnium fidelium in oxonia ex dono magistrorum Iohannis holt et Iohannis Cole nuper sociorum huius collegii.' Rebound in s. xix. The alterations to the secundo folios and the cancellation of **1334** show that this 3-volume edition was replaced by a now missing 2-volume edition: see **1367, 1367a.**

1336. As ed. Venice, 1487 (Lincoln College).

1337. Ed. Venice, 1487 (Lincoln College) has *parti* as the first word of the second leaf.

1340. As ed. Venice, 1493 of J. A. de S. Georgio.

1345. The second part of the *Reportorium* of Bertachinus secundo folio *insti et* (as ed. Nuremberg, 1483: New College) was removed in favour of another *Reportorium*: see **1372a.**

1351. As ed. Venice, 1478 (Bodleian).

1353-4. As ed. Venice, 1478 (**1353**, New College; **1354**, Queen's College).

1356. As ed. Venice, 1477 (Bodleian) and other editions.

*1357. MS. 61. s. xv. Paper. 'Liber Collegii animarum omnium fidelium defunctorum de Oxon ex dono Reuerendi 'patris' Iacobi Goldwell' nuper Norwicensis episcopi 'legum doctoris' et olim istius Collegii socii.' Binding of s. xv/xvi.

*1359. a. 5. 5. Rome, 1470 (Hain 13645). 'Libri Institucionum quintiliani [. . . . .]dissimi domini domini Iacobi Goldewell' norwigenc' episcopi legum [. . . . .]us collegii.' Contemporary binding of white skin over wooden boards.

Additions to List XXI

1361. Not LR 5. k. 6.

1367, 1367a. As ed. Venice, 1501 (New College). Cf. **1332-4.**

1368. As ed. Basel, 1478 (Bodleian) and other editions.

1370. As ed. Venice, 1499 (New College).

1372a. Cf. **1345**.

*1376–7. cc. 10. 9, 10. Paris, 1504. 2 vols. 'Liber collegii Animarum Ex dono Michaelis Wogan utriusque Iuris baccalaurei quondam socii eiusdem collegii.' Rebound in s. xix.

LIST XXII

1380–5. As ed. Paris, 1540–2, in octavo (New College).

1386–90. As ed. Paris, 1515 (New College), and other editions.

*1391. Anson Room, 41. g. 3. (Paris) 1532. 'Ex dono Magistri Roberti Weston huius Collegii Sotii Anno domini Millesimo Quingentesimo Quadragesimo V^{to}.' Rebound in s. xvii.

*1393–7. dd. 8. 3, 2, 4, 5, 1. Lyons, 1544. 'Liber Collegii Omnium Animarum fidelium defunctorum de *Oxon*' in a hand of the later seventeenth century (?). All rebound in s. xix.

*1398. cc. 10. 7. Lyons, 1538. Inscribed as **1393**. Contemporary Oxford binding: Gibson, rolls VII, VIII, X.

*1399, 1400. l. inf. 2. 1, 2. London, 1543. 2 vols. College *ex libris*, s. xvii. Contemporary Oxford bindings: Gibson, rolls VII, VIII, X.

*1400a. dd. 2. 4, 5. Venice, 1492–3 (Consilia I–IV, Hain 15254), and Bologna 1490 (Consilia V, Hain 15263). No college *ex libris*. Bindings of s. xix. All five Consilia together are too big for one volume. Perhaps only I–IV (in one volume) were in the library in 1556 and V was added at the time of the nineteenth-century rebinding.

*1400b–d. ee. 1. 3–5. Lyons, 1543. Inscribed as **1393**. ee. 1. 4 in contemporary Oxford binding: Gibson, rolls VII, VIII, X. ee. 1. 3, 5 rebound in s. xix.

*1400e–i. ee. 2. 5–7. ee. 1. 1, 2. Lyons, 1534–5. Inscribed as **1393**. ee. 2. 7 bound as **1400c**; the rest rebound in s. xix.

1401. As ed. Basel, 1537 (New College).

1402. As. ed. Basel, 1539 (New College).

*1403. ee. 4. 7. Basel, 1540. No college *ex libris*. Rebound in s. xix. The secundo folio is *Hoc pactum* on sign. A. 2 or *Lecturæ* (cf. List XXIII) on sign. *a* 2.

1404. As ed. Basel, 1538 (New College).

1405. As ed. Basel, 1526 (St. John's College) and other editions.

*1406. z. 7. 9. Frankfurt, 1542. Inscribed as **1393**. Rebound in Oxford in rough calf, s. xvii in, without Zasius.

*1407–9. dd. 2. 2, 3, 1. Lyons, 1534. Inscribed as **1393**. dd. 2. 1, 3 in contemporary Oxford bindings: Gibson, rolls VII, VIII, X. dd. 2. 2 rebound in s. xix.

1410–12. Cf. List XXVII at 1547–8.

*1413. l. 2. 11 (1) Baldus de Ubaldis, *Super feudis*. Lyons, 1502. (2) Antonius de S. Georgio, *Super usibus feudorum*. Trino, 1511. (3) Martinus de Garatis, *In* *opere feudorum.* Trino, 1516. 'Ex dono Iohannis Cockys legum doctoris quondam huius collegii bonarum animarum in Oxon Socii.' Rebound in s. xix.

*1414. dd. 1. 11. (1) J. de Imola, *Consilia*. Bologna, 1495 (Hain 9152). (2) Baldus de Ubaldis, *Super feudis*. Pavia, 1495 (Hain 2323). No college *ex libris*. Contemporary binding by the 'Foliaged Staff Binder': Oldham, stamps 339, 340, 343, 345. The secundo folio is *prima ratio*.

1414a–c. Cf. **1318–20**.

*1414d, or 1414e. ee. 1. 7. (1) Baldus de Ubaldis, *Super Institutionibus commentum*. Venice, 1496 (Hain 2276). (2) Baldus de Ubaldis. *Super Feudis commentum*. Pavia, 1495 (Hain 2323). (3) Baldus de Ubaldis, *Circa materiam Statutorum*. Venice, 1486 (Hain 2332). Inscribed 'Liber collegii omnium animarum' and 'cox'. Rebound in s. xix.

*1415–18. z. 5. 1–4. Venice, 1494–5 (Hain 4614, 4625, 4632, 4600). 'Ex dono egregii viri Domini Gualteri Stone quondam Reuerendissimi cant' archipresulis Officialis principalis ac huius collegii bonarum animarum in Oxon' Socii optime meriti' in z. 5. 3. A shorter inscription to the same effect in z. 5. 1, 2, 4. Contemporary bindings, as on **1414**, but without stamp 345.

*1421–2. cc. 7. 8, 9. Lyons, 1540–1. 3 vols. in 2. No college *ex libris*. Rebound in s. xix.

*1425b. bb. 5. 10. Venice (B. Benalius), 1496 (*GKW* 8208). 'Ex dono Gualteri Stone legum doctoris quondam socii huius collegii bonarum animarum in Oxon.' Contemporary Oxford binding by the 'Fruit and Flower Binder': Oldham, mps 181, 182, 184, 189, 191.

1427. As ed. Paris, 1501.

*1429. LR 5. k. 4. Petrus de Monte, *Repertorium iuris utriusque* (pt. 2, L–Z). Padua, 1480 (Hain 11589). 'Liber collegii animarum', to which an *ex dono* of James Goldwell was added in s. xvii (probably without good reason: cf. **1272**). Rebound in s. xviii.

*1431a. dd. 2. 8. Angelus de Gambilionibus, *Super Institutionibus*. (Lyons) 1504. Inscribed as **1393**. Contemporary English binding: Oldham, roll AN. b. 2 and ornament K. 7.

*1431f. z. 9. 18. (1) Henricus Bruno de Piro, *Super Institutionibus*. Louvain, sine anno (Hain 4015). (2) F. Accursius, *Casus in terminis . . . super nouem libris Codicis*. sine anno et loco (*GKW* 188). 'Liber Collegii omnium animarum ex dono doctoris Cox.' Contemporary Oxford binding by the 'Floral Binder': Oldham, stamps 172, 174, 177, 178.

Additions to List XXII

*1432. dd. 2. 9. (1) Angelus de Gambilionibus, *Circa maleficia punienda*. Venice, 1497 (Hain–Copinger 600). (2) Albertus de Gandino (*et al.*), *In materia maleficiorum*. (Venice) 1497 (Hain–Copinger 2627). (3) Albericus de Rosate, *Super Statutis*. Venice, 1493 (*GKW* 529). (4) De fallaciis (MS., s. xvi in.: 164 leaves).

"1560 2 Elysabet' Tractatus Malefitiorum D. Angeli et D. Alberici 'repositi per Iohannem Weston", on the first leaf. Nearly contemporary English binding: Oldham, roll AN. b. 2 and ornament A.1.

*1433. z. 5. 8. Paulus de Castro, *Consilia*. Nuremberg, 1485 (Hain 4641). No college *ex libris*. Rebound in s. xix.

*1434. dd. 1. 3. Lucas de Penna, *Super tres libros Codicis*. Paris, 1509. 'Liber collegii animarum omnium ex dono M^{ri} Cox iuris cesarii doctoris.' Rebound in s. xix. *Tabula* is the first word on sign. Aa iii and *Tabella* the first word on sign. Aa ii.

*1435. LR 4. c. 11. (1) Johannes Baptista de Caccialupis, *Repetitio*. Siena, 1493 (*GKW* 5844). (2–17). Repetitiones on civil law printed at Siena, Pavia, Bologna, Milan, Brescia, Venice, and Pisa in 1475 and 1491–5. College *ex libris*, s. xvii. Nearly contemporary binding.

*1436. bb. 5. 11. (1) Venice (J. and G. de Gregoriis), 1496 (*GKW* 8207). (2) Baldus de Ubaldis, *Super tribus libris Codicis*, sine loco et anno (? Hain 2290). 'Liber collegii bonarum animarum in Oxon' ex Dono Gualteri Stone legum doctoris quondam huius collegii socii.' Contemporary binding: stag, fleur-de-lis, and rose stamps.

1438. The secundo folio given in the Vellum Inventory is the beginning of the table of contents in the edition, Paris, 1501, and other editions.

*1439. LR 4. c. 10. (1) Lanfrancus de Oriano, *Tractatus de arbitris*. Milan, 1493 (Hain 9889). (2–18) Tracts on civil law printed at Milan, Venice, Bologna, Pisa, Siena, and Pavia between 1477 and 1493. No college *ex libris*. Rebound in s. xviii.

*1442–3. bb. 5. 6, 7. Johannes Andreae, *Novella super primo* (. . . *quinto*) *Decretalium*. Pavia, 1504–5. 2 vols. 'Liber Collegii Animarum ex dono magistri Will(el)mi Dalby quondam socii huius Collegii' in bb. 5. 6 and 'Liber . . . Dalby Iuris bachalaurei quondam . . . Collegii' in bb. 5. 7. Contemporary stamped bindings by N. Spierinck of Cambridge: Gray, stamps 2, 4.

*1444. ee. 2. 4. (1) Baldus Novellus de Bartolinis de Perusio, *De dotibus*. Venice, 1496 (*GKW* 3468). (2) J. Petrus de Ferrariis, *Practica*. Venice, 1495 (Hain 6994). (3) *Margarita Nova Baldi* (etc.). Venice, 1499 (Hain 2342). No college *ex libris*. Contemporary binding, as **1414**.

*1445. ee. 5. 2. Andreas Barbatia, *Consilia*, pts. 3, 4. Venice, 1515. No college *ex libris*. Contemporary binding by John Reynes: Oldham, roll AN. b. 1 and ornament A. 1.

*1446. cc. 4. 3. (1) Oldradus de Ponte, *Consilia*. Venice, 1499 (Hain 9938). (2) Johannes de Anania, *Consilia*. Venice, 1496 (Hain 937). (3) Franciscus de Accoltis de Aretio, *Consilia*. Venice, 1499 (*GKW* 144). No college *ex libris*. Contemporary English binding by the 'Foliaged Staff Binder': Oldham, stamps 342, 345, 346, 379, and another.

*1448. cc. 4. 1. (1) Ludovicus Pontanus, *Super rubrica de arbitris*. Venice, sine anno (Hain 13280). L. Pontanus, *Super L. si vero* (*et al.*). Siena, 1494 (Hain 13284). (3) L. Pontanus, *Consilia*. Venice, 1493 (Hain 13277). 'Liber collegii omnium animarum ex dono Magistri Cox legum doctoris ac quondam huius collegii socii.' Contemporary Oxford binding by the 'Fruit and Flower Binder': Oldham, stamps 181, 182, 184, 189, 190, and Ker, *Pastedowns*, ornament 7.

*1449. As ed. sine anno et loco (All Souls aa. 4. 8) and ed. Venice, 1486 (All Souls aa. 4. 10). Perhaps to be identified with aa. 4. 10, which has been rebound and lacks the first leaf of the text.

*1451-3. bb. 2. 3-5. Johannes de Turrecremata, *Super Decreto*. Lyons, 1519-20. 6 parts in 3 vols. 'Liber I Cockys empt' 13 Iunii 1528' and 'Liber collegii omnium animarum in Oxonia ex dono dicti doctoris Cockys' in vol. 2 and similar inscriptions without the date in vols. 1, 3. The secundo folios given first begin the preface in each volume (sign. a ii): better chosen references were substituted for them. Rebound in s. xix.

*1455. aa. 10. 15. Lyons, 1510. 4°. 'Liber col' animarum Cox.' Rebound in s. xix.

LIST XXIII

*1456. bb. 4. 3. (1) Andreas Barbatia, *Aurea lectura super titulis de officio delegati* (*et al.*). Pavia, 1488 (*GKW* 3367). (2) P. Decius, *Consilia*. Lyons, 1519. 'Hic liber collocatus est in Libraria per Iohannem Westonum anno domini 1565 19 Octobris.' Rebound in s. xix.

*1458. aa. 4. 11. Dominicus de S. Geminiano, *Super sexto libro Decretalium*. Lyons, 1514. 'Liber Ricardi Mugge.' 'Ex dono magistri Richardi Mugge decretorum doctoris ac quondam huius collegii socii.' Rebound in s. xix.

*1459. cc. 9. 10. Petrus de Ancharano, *Super sexto Decretalium*. Lyons, 1517. Inscribed as **1458**. Rebound in s. xix.

*1461. aa 4. 12. Dominicus de S. Geminiano, *In Decretum*. Venice, 1504. No college *ex libris*. Rebound in s. xix.

*1463. bb. 2. 15. (1) Franciscus Zabarella, *Commentaria in Clementinarum volumen*. Lyons, 1511. (2) Johannes de Imola, *In Clementinas*. Venice, 1502. (3) Lapus de Castelnovo, *Allegationes*. Trino, 1509. Inscribed as **1458**. Rebound in s. xix.

*1464. LR 5. k. 8. (1) Azo de Ramenghis, *Repetitiones*. Venice, 1496 (*GKW* 3149). (2-8) Tracts on civil law printed at Venice between 1493 and 1499 Inscribed as **1435**. Rebound in s. xix.

*1465. cc. 5. 10. Joachim Mynsinger, *Apotelesma*. Basel, 1559. 'Liber collegii omnium animarum fidelium defunctorum in oxonia, ex dono Gulihelmi Pigot in legibus bac' ac quondam huius Collegii Socii: A° 1575' in a fine hand. Rebound in s. xix.

*1466. y. inf. 2. 6. J. Faber, *De Institutis*. Lyons 1523. 8°. 'Liber R. Mowshersti, omnium animarum in Oxon' iii*s*. iiii*d*.' 'Liber collegii omnium animarum fidelium defunctorum in oxonia ex dono Robarti Mowshersti in legibus Baccalaurei huius Collegii Socii. 1575. Aug. 3°' in the hand of the Pigot inscription in **1465**. Contemporary English binding: Oldham, roll HM. a. 17.

LIST XXIV

1468. As ed. Rome, 1470 (Bodleian).

*1469. On the second (*not* the first) book. LR 3. h. 11. (Venice, ed. T. Penketh) 1478 (Hain 6416). No college *ex libris*. Contemporary stamped binding (French ?). No chainmark. Cf. List XXVIA, Gaunt 2, for another copy.

*1470. LR 4. a. 5. (1) On the third (*not* the second) book. Venice 1477 (Hain 6416). (2) Johannes Duns Scotus, *Quodlibeta*. Venice, 1477 (Hain 6434). 'Liber collegii Animarum omnium fidelium defunctorum in Oxon ex dono Reuerendi in cristo domini domini Iacobi goldewell' Norwigencis episcopi et huius collegii socii.' Rebound in s. xix.

*1473. LR 4. b. 18. Venice, 1481 (Hain 6418). 4°. 'Ex dono Reuerendi patris et domini domini Iacobi Goldwell' quondam Norwycensis episcopi ad vsum sociorum Collegii animarum.' Rebound in Oxford by Pinart in 1614–15: Gibson, roll XX. No chainmark.

*1475. LR 4. b. 19. Venice, 1481 (Hain 6418). 4°. Inscribed and bound as **1473**. No chainmark.

*1476. LR 3. h. 22. Johannes Duns Scotus, *Questiones quodlibetales*. Venice, 1481 (Hain 6436). 4°. Inscribed as **1473**. 'My lord of Norwych' at the end. Contemporary binding of pink leather over wooden boards. No chainmark. Cf. List XXVIA, Gaunt 3, for another copy.

*1477. LR 3. h. 7. Johannes de Turrecremata, *Expositio super toto Psalterio*. Mainz, 1476 (Hain 15699). 'Liber Collegii animarum omnium fidelium defunctorum in Ox' ex dono Reuerendissimi in cristo patris et domini domini Norwycensis episcopi Iacobi Goldewell'.' 'My lord of Norwych' in front. Contemporary binding of white leather over wooden boards. Chainmark FS2.

1478. Philippus de Bronnerde. As ed. Cologne, sine anno (Bodleian).

*1479. LR 4. d. 23. Guibertus Tornacensis, *Sermones ad omnes status*. sine anno et loco (Hain–Copinger 2883). 'Liber collegii' at end, s. xv/xvi. 'Liber Collegii Omnium Animarum fidelium defunctorum de Oxon'', s. xvii. Rebound in s. xix.

*1480. w. 1. 7. *Sermones aurei de Sanctis*. sine loco, 1475 (Hain 16131). 'Liber Collegii Animarum ex dono Reuerendi in cristo domini domini Iacobi Goldewell nuper episcopi Norwic' et quondam socii huius collegii.' Rebound in s. xix.

*1485. LR 5. i. 2. Nicholaus de Lyra, *Postille in Bibliam*, vol. 3. Rome, 1472 (Hain 10363). 'Liber Collegii animarum In Oxonia ex dono reverendissimi In cristo patris et domini. Domini Iacobi Goldewell Norwycensis episcopi. Ac eiusdem collegii quondam Socii' in a humanistic hand. Rebound in Oxford in 1614–15: Gibson, roll XXVII. No chainmark.

1490. As ed. sine loco 1474 (Bodleian).

*1491. LR 5. i. 3. (Rome, 1472: Hain 10363). Inscribed as **1485**, without 'Ac' and with 'nuper' instead of 'quondam'. Bound as **1485**. No chainmark.

1492. As ed. Rome, 1470 (Bodleian).

*1496. LR 3. g. 8. (Paris, *c.* 1472: *GKW* 1609). 'Ex dono Reuerendi patris et domini domini Iacobi Goldwell' quondam Norwycensis episcopi ad vsum sociorum Collegii animarum.' Rebound in s. xviii.

*1498. SR 14. e. 1. Rome, 1471 (Hain 15801). 'Liber Collegii animarum etc' ex dono Reuerendi patris domini Iacobi Goldwell' nuper Norwicensis episcopi olim istius collegii socii.' Rebound in s. xix.

1521. Cf. List XXVIA, Lovelich 5.

*1532. a. 7. 1. (Padua, 1481/2: *GKW* 6948). 'Liber collegii animarum omnium fidelium defunctorum in Oxonia ex dono Reuerendissimi patris in cristo domini domini Iacobi Goldwell norwhichenc' episcopi doctoris legum et quondam socii huius collegii.' Rebound in s. xix.

1534. As ed. Venice, 1479 (Bodleian), and other editions.

1535. As ed. Rome, 1471 (Bodleian).

1537. Cf. List XXVIA, Est 8.

1543. As ed. Louvain, sine anno (Bodleian).

LIST XXV

1577, Carpenter.[1] The inventory of his goods, University Archives, Inventories, vol. 2 (BR–C), lists 98 books, including 'Tabula Wickeri viiis.' and 'Epithome Galeni viis.'.

　1. SR 58. g. 4. Basel, 1576. 'Liber collegii Omnium Animarum fidelium defunctorum de Oxon ex dono m^{ri} Thomæ Carpenteri, olim huius Collegii socii, nuper ex pestilenti contagione mortui, quæ accidit in prætorio Oxoniensi. 1577.' Contemporary Oxford binding: Gibson, roll XIX. Chainmark FS1.

　2. SR 58. e. 8. Basel, 1571. Inscribed as (1). Bound and chained as (1).

1586, Lucke.

　1. SR 74. b. 11. Basel, 1551. 'Liber Collegii omnium animarum ex dono M^{stri} Thomæ Lucke, in artibus Magistri, nuper eiusdem Collegii Socii; qui obiit Nouemb. xxvi°. Anno Domini M.D.LXXXVI°. Sandovici.' Contemporary binding. Chainmarks F1, HS2.

1587, Richard Master.

　1. SR 58. f. 9. Basel, 1556. 'Liber Collegii animarum omnium fidelium defunctorum de Oxon': ex dono Richardi Master Medici primarii Serenissimæ Dominæ Elizabethæ Reginæ et quondam huius Collegii Socii 1587.' Oxford binding, s. xvi/xvii: Gibson, roll XII. Chainmark HS2.

　2, 3. o. 4. 5, 6. Zürich, 1558. 2 vols. o. 4. 6 inscribed as (1). The same words in o. 4. 5 are in the hand of the inscription in **35**. Oxford bindings, s. xvi/xvii: Gibson, rolls XII and XVIII on o. 4. 5 and roll XII on o. 4. 6 (cf. Ker, *Pastedowns*, pp. 93, 212). Chainmarks HS2.

---

[1] A third book, not referred to in Carpenter's will, C. Galenus, Libri aliquot græci . . . per Ioannem Caium, Basel, 1544, 4°, now SR 58. e. 6, is inscribed 'Liber Collegii animarum omnium fidelium defunctorum de Oxon. ex dono Thomæ Carpenter socii' in the hand of the inscription in **35**. Contemporary Oxford binding: Gibson, roll VIII, and Ker, *Pastedowns*, ornaments 25, 27. Chainmark HS1.

1587–8. See List XXVII at 1587–8.

1. h. 3. 7. Arras, 1587. Inscribed as **35**. Contemporary Oxford binding: Gibson, roll XXI. Chainmarks F1, HS2.

2. r. 5. 5. Paris, 1582. Inscribed as **35**. Contemporary Oxford binding: Gibson, roll XXI. Chainmarks FI, HS2.

1588, Dow. The inventory of his goods, University Archives, Inventories, vol. 3, has a list of 282 books, priced at £28. 13s. 10d. The list is an interesting one.

1. Q. 4. 2. Antwerp, 1574. 'Liber Collegii omnium animarum fidelium defunctorum in Oxon' ex dono Roberti Dowi in legibus Baccalaurei, quondam socii huius Collegii, qui obiit 10° Nouembris anno domini 1588.' Rebound in s. xix.

1592, Jones.

1–9. cc. 3. 6–12, cc. 1. 1, 2. Lyons, 1553. 'Liber Collegii Animarum omnium fidelium defunctorum de Oxon', quem unà cum reliquis VIII voluminibus Mr Henricus Iones LL. Doctor Aduocat' Curiæ Cant. de Arcub. et quondam istius Coll. Socius legato dedit huic Collegio, reseruato usu eorundem M^{ro} Ioanni Lloid LL. Doctori, quem usum dictus Mr Ioan. Lloid istius etiam Collegii nuper Socius remisit, et hos libros in Coll. Bibliothecâ reponendos tradidit' in vol. 1. The other volumes have a shorter form of *ex dono*. Oxford bindings of 1591–2 (cf. Bursars' Roll, 1591–2): Gibson, roll XIX. Chainmarks FS1, FS2, HS1.

10, 11. cc. 9. 12, 13. Lyons, 1550–1. 'Liber Collegii omnium Animarum fidelium defunctorum, de Oxon' ex dono M^{ri} Henrici Jones, LL Doctoris, et Aduocati Curiæ de Arcub. quondam hujus Collegii Socii.' Bound as Jones 1–9. Chainmarks FS1, HS1.

1592, Boys.

1. z. 4. 5. Frankfurt, 1586. 'Liber Collegii omnium animarum Oxon', ex dono M^{ri} Thomæ Boys, LL Bacchalaurei, et ejusdem Collegii Socii. Anno Domini M.D.XCII Aprilis XII°.' Contemporary Oxford binding: Ker, centre-piece ii and ornament 55. Chainmark FS1.

1593, Lynch. The inventory of his goods, University Archives, Inventories, records unspecified books to the value of £12. 11s. 7d.

1. g. 3. 5. Basel, 1550. 'Liber Collegii Omnium Animarum fidelium defunctorum Oxon, ex legato Stephani Linch artium magistri, eiusdemque collegii Capellani, Haldenæ apud Cantios oriundi, qui obiit 12° die Ianuarii 1592.' Rebound in s. xviii.

1598, Robert Master.

1–4. SR 80. f. 6–9. Zürich, 1539. 'Liber Collegii Animarum omnium fidelium defunctorum de Oxon': ex dono Roberti Master Doctoris in Iure civili Vicecustodis istius Collegii et Principalis Aulæ Albanæ, 1598.' Rebound in s. xix.

1598, Porter.

1–4. 78. c. 6–9. Neustadt, 1589. 'Liber Collegii omnium Animarum fidelium defunctorum de Oxon', ex dono Roberti Porter, M^{ri} Artium, nuper Socii ejusdem Collegii. An. D. 1598.' Contemporary Oxford bindings: Ker, centre-piece ii and ornament 55. Chainmark FS2.

1598, Hovenden.

1–4. aa. 2. 9–12. Basel, 1573. 'Liber Collegii omnium Animarum fidelium defunctorum de Oxon'. ex dono venerabilis viri Rob. Houenden S. Theologiæ Professoris, et Custodis ejusdem Collegii. 1598 Nov. 30'. Rebound in s. xix.

1598–9, Richard Franklyn. Cf. list XXVII at 1598–9.

1–5. SR 72. c. 1–5. Paris, 1589. 'Liber Collegii animarum omnium fidelium defunctorum de Oxon'. Ex dono magistri Ricardi Francklin Armigeri' in the hand of the inscription in **35**. Contemporary calf, plain except for the college arms in gilt. Chainmark FS2.

6–14. SR 68. e. 1–9. Basel, 1564–74. Inscribed as 1–5. Contemporary bindings: gilt centre-piece. Chainmark HS2.

15. y. 1. 10. Lyons, 1592. Inscribed and bound as 1–5. Chain mark HS1.

1599, Hendley.

1. LR 4. b. 6. (*a*) sine anno et loco. (*b*) Paris, 1516. (*c*) Oppenheim, 1513. (*d*) Paris, 1515. 'Liber collegii omnium animarum fidelium defunctorum ex dono Gulihelmi Hendley artium magistri et socii huius collegii: March: 13: 1598.' Contemporary binding by John Reynes: Oldham, roll AN. b. 1 and ornament A.1. Chainmark HS1.

1599, Milles. Cf. Bursars' Roll 1598–9.

1–6. q. 1. 1–6. Lyons, 1590. 'Liber Collegii Animarum omnium fidelium defunct. de Oxon', ex dono Francisci Mylles Artium Mag^{ri} quondam Socii hujus Collegii. 1599.' Oxford bindings by D. Pinart, 1598–9: Gibson, rolls XII, XVIII. Chainmark HS2.

7, 8. w. 2. 7, 8. Basel, 1541. 'Liber . . . Mag^{ri}' (as 1–6) 'An. Domini MDXCIX. Octob.' Oxford bindings by D. Pinart, 1598–9: Gibson, roll XII, and gilt centre-piece of the college arms. Chainmark FS2.

9. aa. 3. 9. Lyons, 1591. Inscribed as **1–6**. Oxford binding by D. Pinart, 1598–9: Gibson, roll XII.

10–12. bb. 4. 4–6. Lyons, 1589. 3 vols. Inscribed as **1–6**. Rebound in s. xix.

1600, Francis James.

aa. 5. 1–14, aa. 3. 1–4. Lyons, 1549 (18 vols.). 'Liber Collegii Animarum omnium fidelium defunctorum de Oxon', ex dono Francisci James, LL. Doctoris, Advocati Curiæ Cant' de Arcubus, Cancellarii Episcopi Bathon, et Wellen. Custodis Spiritualitatis Sedis Episcopalis Bristoll, et nuper Socii huius Collegii. Anno Domini M.DC. Ian. VI' in vols. 1 and 18. A shorter form of inscription by another hand in vols. 2–17: the date is given as 6 Jan. 1599. Contemporary bindings of plain calf with the college arms in gilt: cf. List XXVII at 1599–1600. Some chainmarks HS1, others HS2.

LIST XXVIA

Alexander, 1. MS. 322. 'Liber collegii animarum ox' Ex domo (*sic*) Magistri Iohannis Alysaunder in artibus M''', f. 2^v. Colophon in main hand: 'Explicit sentenciosa atque studio digna exposicio venerabilis Alexandri super 3^m librum de anima. Scripta a I. Alexandro Anno necessarie regencie sue Anno domini

1477mo tunc temporis socio Collegii animarum omnium fidelium defunctorum in oxon'.' Contemporary and presumably Oxford binding: four stamps, two of them like Gibson 15—but facing left—and Oldham 1055. No chainmark. Secundo folio *anime proficit*. Long alienated. Bought from Messrs. Maggs in 1929.

Bartlatt, 1. Pembroke College, Oxford, MS. 2. s. xv. 'Liber collegii animarum omnium fidelium defunctorum in Oxon' ex dono venerabilis viri Ricardi Bartlett in medicinis doctoris et quondam huius collegii socii', f. 12, erased. Contemporary binding of white skin over wooden boards. Bosses. No chainmark. Secundo folio *sed quia* or (f. 12) *at de*. Cf. *1227 and List XXVII at 1550–1.

Barworth, 1. vv. inf. 2. 5. Rome, 1478 (*GKW* 587). 'Liber Collegii animarum omnium fidelium defunctorum in Ox' Ex dono doctoris Berewurth' on the second leaf and again at the end where a cancelled '1554' stands between *Oxon* and *ex dono*. Rebound in s. xix.

Betts. The relevant section of the will was printed by Plomer, 'Books mentioned in wills', *Trans. Bibl. Soc.* vii (1904), 119. The donor requested that his books should be inscribed with his name and chained in the library. This request may have been embarrassing, since the library had just received a three-volume Pantheologia from James Goldwell (**1084, 1086–7**). Cf. List XXVII at 1504–5.

Bisshop, 1. MS. 42. s. xv in. 'Liber collegii animarum omnium fidelium defunctorum in oxonia Ex dono Magistri thome Byshope iuris canonici bachalarii cathenandus in biblioteca.' 'The hewse off thys boke Mr Thomas beshype hath grant to Mayster Ric' Gawnt durying hiis lyffe and aftyr hiis dissese to be *delive*red on to the colege off Allsolne to be chanyd in the lybrari off the colege', f. 315. Binding as **77**. A chainmark HS2 can be seen on the endleaves. Secundo folio (f. 2) *Clerici* or (f. 10) *sicut per inuidiam*.

Broke, 1. aa. 4. 9. Speyer, sine anno (*GKW* 8648). 'Liber Magistri Willelmi Broke decretorum doctoris ac custodis collegii animarum omnium fidelium defunctorum in Oxon' ad vsum Magistri Simonis Bynde dum stetit in eodem Collegio et post eius recessum a collegio predicto ad collegium animarum ex dono antedicti Magistri Willelmi Broke orate pro eo.' Rebound in s. xix. Secundo folio *inhonestis*. For a copy of both parts of this edition see **1306–7**, which may be identical with List XXVIA, Est 6, 7 (cf. below).

Byconyll. The will is printed in *Proceedings of the Somerset Archaeological Society*, xl. 191. The donor's gifts to All Souls were 'in aliqualem recompensam beneficiorum per felicis memorie dominum Henricum nuper Cantuariensis archiepiscopum dicti collegii fundatorem michi collatorum'.

1, 2. Bodleian, MSS. Bodley 741–2. A.D. 1444. 'Liber Collegii animarum omnium fidelium defunctorum in Oxon' ex dono magistri Willelmi Bygonell' post mortem magistri Byrkhed' in each volume, erased. A gift to the Bodleian from the Dean and Canons of Windsor in 1612; probably never at All Souls.

11. Cf. **1241**.

12. Cf. **83, 94–5, 471**.

13. Cf. **220, 234**.

16. Cf. **470**.

Caunton. These books should have come to All Souls after Lloyd's death in 1478 and may have done so. Lloyd was a considerable benefactor of Hereford Cathedral and his bequest included four out of the five volumes of a 'course of civil' (Hereford Cathedral MSS. P. vii. 2 and 5, P. viii. 8 and 11: cf. *MLGB*, 2nd ed., pp. 99, 268). The first three of these manuscripts have been pledged in university chests, but there is no evidence that they ever belonged to Caunton.

Cockys. Cf. List XXVII at 1540-1 and 1545-6.

1. aa. 3. 8. Venice, 1491 (Hain 9193). 'Liber Collegii animarum in Oxonia ex dono M^ri Coxe legum doctoris ac eiusdem collegii quondam socii.' Contemporary Oxford binding, as **1448**. No chainmark.

2. bb. 1. 2. Venice, 1493 (Hain 7588). Inscribed 'Liber collegii omnium animarum' and 'cox' (cf. **1414d**). Contemporary binding by the 'Foliaged Staff Binder': Oldham, stamps 339, 340, 343. Chainmark H1.

3. bb. 5. 9. (1) Trino, 1508. (2) Pavia, 1509. 'Ex dono Io. Cockys legum doctoris quondam huius collegii bonorum animarum in Oxon socii.' Contemporary Oxford binding by the 'Fruit and Flower Binder': Oldham, stamps 182, 187. Chainmark FS1.

Derlington, 1. MS. 2. 'Liber Collegii animarum in Oxonia ex dono Magistri Derlyngton. quondam Collegii Noui in oxonia Socius. Cuius anime propicietur deus. Intercessione M. Iohannis Cole huius Collegii Custodis.' Binding as **77**. Chainmark F1 shows on the pastedown. Secundo folio *dabor pelle*.

Est. These eight books arrived in 1494 or 1495 (cf. List XXVII at 1494-5).

1-5. Cf. **599-603**.

6, 7. Cf. **1306-7**.

8. Cf. **1286, 1310, 1314**.

Gaunt. Cf. List XXVIA, Bisshop, 1.

1. LR 5. i. 5. Cologne, 1480. 'Liber collegii omnium animarum fidelium in oxonia ex dono Magistri gawnte nuper socii eiusdem.' Old binding. Bosses once. No chainmark. Cf. **560**.

2. LR 4. a. 4. Venice, 1478 (Hain 6416). 'Liber collegii animarum in oxonia ex dono Ric' gaunt artium Magistri sociique quondam eiusdem collegii.' Rebound in s. xviii. A duplicate of **1469**.

3. LR 4. b. 17. Venice, 1481 (Hain 6436). 'Liber collegii animarum in oxonia ex dono Magistri Richardi Gawnt eiusdem collegii olim socii': hand as in Gaunt 2. Rebound in Oxford in 1614-15: Gibson, roll XX. No chainmark. A duplicate of **1476**.

4. LR 5. i. 4 (2 leaves). 'Liber collegii animarum in oxonia ex dono Magistri Richardi Gawnt quondam eiusdem collegii socii.' Cf. **1007**.

5. LR 3. g. 15. Oxford, 1482. 'Liber collegii animarum in oxonia ex dono Magistri Richardi Gaunt quondam eiusdem collegii socii.' Contemporary Oxford 'Rood and Hunt' binding: Gibson, stamps 45, 49-51 (p. 20, pl. IX, and pl. XXIX, no. 3). Chainmark FS1. Cf. **565**.

Goldwell.

1. MS. 38. s. xv. Paper. 'Liber Collegii animarum omnium fidelium defunctorum in oxonia ex (dono) Reuerendissimi domini domini Iacobi Golwell nuper episcopi Norwichienc' et huius collegii quondam socii.' Binding of white skin over boards, s. xv/xvi, much repaired. Marks of chaining by a six-nail staple at the foot of the lower cover and FS2. Secundo folio *fice est.*

2. MS. 67. s. xv. Paper. 'Ex dono magistri Iacobi Goldwele legum doctoris et Norwicensis episcopi Anno a natali Christiano millesimo vndequingentesimo' in a humanistic hand. Rebound in s. xix. Secundo folio *Abrogare.*

3. Tokyo, University, A. 100. 1300. s. xv. For the contents, letters of Barzizza and Guarino, and of Petworth and other Englishmen, copied as specimens of epistolary style, see R. Weiss in *Italian Studies*, ii (1939), 110–17. An erased inscription in four lines at the foot of the second leaf of the text (f. 4): 'Liber Collegii animarum omnium fidelium defunctorum Ex (dono) reuerendissimi patris Iacobi Goldwell norwicensis episcopi et legum doctoris ac quondam huius collegii socii': cf. *BQR* v. 134.[1] Contemporary Canterbury binding, repaired in Oxford in 1930: Oldham, stamps 210, 214, 215, 224, 225, 226, and two others, rosette and dog. No chainmark. Secundo folio *ad antonium.*

Alienated at some time. Given to the University of Tokyo by B. H. Streeter between 1930 and 1939, together with the relevant copy of *BQR*, on which he wrote a note saying that 'The MS came to me from the books of the elder brother of my grandfather, a London Physician born in 1790'.

4. LR 5. l. 1. (Mainz) 1459 (*GKW* 9101). Parchment. 'Liber collegii omnium animarum Oxon quem Reuerendus pater Iacobus Goldwell Episcopus norwicen' emit in Ciuitate Hamburgensis dum erat missus in ambaciatam a Cristianissimo principe Edwardo Rege Anglie etc' ad illustrissimum Principem Regem Dacie voluitque dictus Reuerendus pater vt cathenetur in Choro dicti Collegii ad vtilitatem studencium. Et si quis eum alienauerit vel contra hanc disposicionem fecerit anathema sit. Et hec disposicio erat per prefatum Reuerendum patrem Anno domini millesimo cccc lxxxx viii°.' Old boards re-covered in s. xviii (?). Chainmark F1. Secundo folio *aut orationis.*

5. LR 3. g. 13. Utrecht, 1473. Inscribed as **1491**. Contemporary binding. Chainmark HS1. Secundo folio *voluit eam.*

6. LR 4. a. 6. sine anno et loco (Hain 6428). 'Liber collegii animarum ex dono domini goldwell' 2° fo ad ens.' Rebound in s. xix.

7. LR 5. i. 1. Rome, 1471 (Hain 10363). Inscribed and bound as **1485, 1491**, with which it forms a set. No chainmark. Secundo folio *est: huic.*

8. a. 8. 5. (1) Rome, by 1472 (*GKW* 7872). (2) *Defensorium fidei* (Utrecht, 1473). 'Liber collegii animarum in Oxon' ex dono venerabilis in Christo patris domini Domini Iacobi Goldwel nuper Norwycensis episcopi legum doctoris olimque socii dicti collegii' in a humanistic hand. Rebound in s. xix. Secundo folio *ut a tergo.* Goldwell annotated (2).

---

[1] Professor Fumio Kuriyagawa kindly sent me photographs of this manuscript and its binding. The Bodleian Library now has a microfilm of it, MS. Film 782.

9. Bodleian, Auct. 1 Q. 3. 1. (Rome, 1483: Hain 14796). 'Liber collegii ani-marum (*these two words cancelled*) ex dono domini Goldwell Norwisenc' archipi-scopi.' Rebound in s. xix. Secundo folio *quid nominis*. Goldwell wrote many annotations in the margins of this book by the pope who made him bishop of Norwich.

Halswell, 1. MS. 70. s. xiv. 'Liber Iohannis Racour titulo empcionis', f. iᵛ. 'Liber Collegii omnium animarum in Oxon' ex dono Magistri Doctoris halswell quondam socii eiusdem.' Medieval binding of pink skin over boards. Chainmark HS2. Secundo folio *et sine nocumento*.

Harlow, 1. Cf. note to **573**.

Honywood, 1. MS. 15. s. xv ex. 'Pertinet hic liber Collegio animarum in Oxonia. Ex dono venerabilis Roberti honywood legum doctoris' inside the cover. Medieval binding of white skin over boards. Chainmark HS1. Secundo folio *de diuinis*.

Lovelich, 1–5. No doubt among the law-books in List II.

Mason.

1. FFF. 4. 1. Basel, 1556. Inscribed as **1184**. Contemporary binding: Oldham, roll HE. g. 2. Chainmarks FS1, HS1.

2. g. inf. 1. 12. Venice, 1499 (Hain 14757). Inscribed as **1184**. Contemporary Italian binding. Chainmarks FS1, FS2. Secundo folio στολελουσ.

3. cc. 1. 4. Basel, 1551. Inscribed as **1184**. Contemporary binding. Chainmarks FS1, FS2.

4, 5. SR 41. d. 2. Cologne, 1564. Inscribed as **1184**. Rebound in s. xvii. Chain-marks FS1, HS1.

6. SR 79. f. 9. Basel, 1555. Inscribed as **1184**. Rebound in s. xix. Secundo folio *Inuictissimo*.

7. Printed in 1557.

Mugge. Cf. List XXVII at 1550–1.

1. bb. 5. 2. Lyons, 1513. Inscribed as **1458**. Rebound in s. xix. Secundo folio *Clarissimi*. This copy may have been put in the library when first received and then taken out when the later edition came among Pole's books: cf. **755** and List XXIII, no. 75, which may be Mugge's copy and not Pole's.

Polton, 1. MS. 47. s. xv. Paper. 'Liber Collegii animarum omnium fidelium de-functorum in Oxon'. Ex dono M. Philippi Polton Archidiaconi Glocestr' Anno domini mᵒ ccccᵒ lxiiᵒ.' Rebound in s. xviii. Chainmark HS2 shows on the paste-down. Secundo folio *solum a voluntate*.

Racour, 1. MS. 76. s. xv. 'Liber collegii omnium animarum in Oxon' ex dono Magistri doctoris Rachar' quondam ocii eiusdem.' Medieval binding of white skin over boards. Chainmark FS1. Secundo folio *et sanguis*.[1]

Shether.

1. SR 59. b. 6. (a) Venice, 1518. (b) Venice, 1515. 'Codex E. Sthetheri sotii sodalitii animarum omnium Oxn' p' viis.' 'Liber collegii animarum ex dono

---

[1] MS. Sloane 280 has the same secundo folio: see below, note to List XXVIB. 2.

edmundi shether quondam socii ibidem.' Contemporary English binding: Oldham, roll AN. g. 1 and ornament B. 3. Chainmarks FS1, HS1.

Stone.

1. MS. 63. s. xv ex. Paper. 'Galteri Stone' on the fly-leaf at the end. 'Liber Collegii omnium animarum 'fidelium Defunct. de Oxon Ex dono Gualteri Stone' (the addition, s. xvii). Contemporary Oxford binding by the 'Floral Binder': Oldham, stamps 172, 174, 177. Chainmarks HS1, HS2. Secundo folio in g. et ita.

Topclyffe.

1. b. 5. 4. (1) sine loco, 1478 (Hain 14207). (2) Treviso, 1482 (Hain 13076). 'Liber Collegii animarum omnium fidelium defunctorum De Oxon' ex dono Magistri Ricardi Topclyff quondam Socii eiusdem.' Rebound in s. xix.

Tucker. Cf. note to 1214.

Warham.

1. Antwerp, Plantin–Moretus Museum, 107. s. xiii. Inscribed as 613. Rebound in s. xix. Secundo folio ibi uoluntas.

2. t. inf. 2. sine anno et loco (Hain 3240). Inscribed as 613. Rebound in s. xix. Secundo folio in tabula. Et quantum. Secundo folio in textu inuoluerat.

Warner.

1. SR 58. f. 11. Lyons, 1525. 'Ex dono Io Warneri quondam custodis' in a fine hand. Inscribed also as 35. Contemporary English binding: Oldham, roll HM. d. 2. No chainmark.

2. SR 58. f. 13. (1) Hagenau, 1533. (2) Venice, 1508. Inscribed as Warner 1. Rebound in s. xix.

3. SR 59. a. 46. Basel, 1542. 'Ioannes Warnerus' and 'Liber collegii animarum' on the title-page. Contemporary Oxford binding: Gibson, roll VII. Chainmarks F1 and HS2.

4. SR 59. c. 25. Basel, 1537. Inscribed as Warner 1. Rebound in s. xix.

Weston. These books may have come at the same time as 1432 or 1456.

1. Probably z. 1. 6. Albertus Brunus, De statutis feminas . . . excludentibus, Milan, 1501, and four other law tracts printed at Milan between 1498 and 1503. No inscription. Rebound in s. xix.

2. z. 3. 2. Paris, 1507. 'Ioannis Westoni liber ex legato M^{ri} Nithingall De Croundall in Cantia.' Contemporary Oxford Binding: Oldham, stamp 1028 and ornament B. 6. Chainmarks F1 and FS1.

3. z. 1. 11. Lyons, 1528. 'Liber Walteri Wryght (†1561)'Liber Iohannis Westoni ex permuta[tione] 1562 17 Ianuarii 3° E[lyzabetis]" on the title-page of the Sext and similar inscriptions on the title-pages of the Clementines and the Extravagantes. Rebound in s. xix.

4. z. 3. 3. sine anno et loco. 'Ioannis Westoni liber ex bibliotheca patris dono datus anno domini 1557: Phil. et Marie 2/3 mensis Maii 10'; also a merchant's mark (?) between large I and W in pencil. Rebound in s. xix.

LIST XXVIB

1. Robinson Trust, London, MS. Phillipps 3119, ff. 176–205. s. xv. Probably the Rudborne here, thirty leaves in a miscellany of bits of books formed by and belonging to John Bale, is the Rudborne which Bale records having seen at All Souls: cf. N. R. Ker in *BLR* vi (1959), 492. Brian Twyne notes in Corpus Christi College, Oxford, MS. 255, f. 136, that 'Mr William Whitlock of Lichefeld prebendary 'of Curbarrow' told me that parson Darrell of Kent had Thomas Rudborn his historie ab initio mundi ad sua tempora. which was somtyme Mr Bales boke'. It is no. 27 in the list of Bale's books.[1]

2. British Museum, MS. Sloane 280. s. xv. 'Liber Willelmi Romesey (†1501 : *Reg. Mert.*, p. 259) quem fecit scribi.' 'Liber collegii omnium fidelium defunctorum in Oxon' ', f. 10, s. xv/xvi: cf. ff. 2^v, 4. Rebound in s. xix. Secundo folio *et sanguis*.[2]

3. Antwerp, Plantin–Moretus Museum, MS. 110. s. xiii. 'Liber collegii animarum', f. 133^v. Rebound in s. xix. Secundo folio *perueniat*.

4. MS. 74. s. xiii ex. Inscribed as **35**. No. 16 in Thomas James's list of All Souls manuscripts in *Ecloga* (1600). Oxford binding, s. xvi ex., with Gibson, roll XXII : Ker, *Pastedowns*, no. 1211. Chainmarks HS1 and HS2. Secundo folio *tanta generatur*.

5. College Archives (dep. in Bodleian Library, DD. c. 241). s. xv. Forty-one leaves used as wrappers of 'Abstracta Chartarum', including leaf 2 of the manuscript as it originally was, on which is 'Liber collegii animarum'. Secundo folio *de mandato*.

6. bb. 5. 4. Twenty-seven civil-law tracts printed between 1486 and 1499 and sine anno. No college *ex libris*. Rebound in s. xix, but a four-nail mark, like that on **1432**, **1435–6**, **1444–6**, and **1448**, is to be seen on the leaves at the beginning. Secundo folio *De pena*.

7. LR 3. h. 20. sine loco 1474: *GKW* 9434. 'Liber Collegii Omnium Animarum Oxon. 1580 R Houendeno Custode' in pencil in Hovenden's hand. Rebound in s. xviii. Secundo folio *Gennadius* or *que gens*.

8. b. 4. 1. Venice, 1513. 'Liber Collegii Omnium Animarum Fidelium Defunctorum de Oxon' ', s. xvi². 'boeceus / G B (or W B) /P' in three lines at beginning and end. Oxford binding, s. xvi/xvii: Gibson, rolls XII, XVIII. Chainmark HS2.

9. g. 3. 18. Cologne, 1530. 'Liber collegii Animarum omnium 'fidelium' defunctorum in Oxon' ex sumptibus collegii', s. xvi². Rebound in s. xviii.

10. SR 59. a. 27. Basel, 1537. 'Liber Collegii animarum omnium fidelium defunctorum in Oxon' ', s. xvi². Rebound in s. xix. Cf. **1149a**.

11. SR 73. f. 11. Basel, 1538. Inscribed as **826–30**: probably a bad guess. The Oxford binding with Gibson, rolls VII, X, the pastedowns (cf. Ker, *Pastedowns*, no. 320), and the chainmark F1 (cf. below, Appendix III) suggest that this was one of the books bought in 1544–5. Cf. List XVII. **34**.

---

[1] McCusker, p. 151.
[2] All Souls College, MS. 76 (List XXVIA, Racour 1), has the same secundo folio.

LIST XXVIc

Tollite iugum meum . . . Sermons on the common of saints.

Chronicon 'Stephani Eyton' . . . Leland records that Stephen de Edon, canon of Warter, wrote a chronicle of the time of Edward II 'indocto et barbaro stilo' (*Collectanea*, iv. 45, immediately after a list of seven books seen at Fountains Abbey). He does not give the opening words. Not improbably Bale saw at All Souls an anonymous chronicle which he later decided was Eyton's: perhaps it was in the same volume as 'Mattheus Florilegus'. This copy or another is in the list of Bale's books, no. 59.[1] The incipit given by Bale is almost the same as that of the chronicle in Bodleian MS., Rawlinson B. 152.

LIST XXVII

1449–50. Liber phisicorum Alberti. Probably **123**: cf. List XIII, 94.

Questionista. Cf. List XIII, 91 sqq., and especially 95 (**1019**).

Gower. Cf. ***1015**.

Willelmus in speculo. Cf. **313–14**.

1452–3. Baldus in utroque volumine. Cf. **250–1**.

Griffith. Cf ***1010**.

1459–60. Probably books distributed on loan to Robert Est and Nicholas Goldwell.

(1463–4). Kept with the undated rolls in c. 275 (no. 3).

(1464–5). Kept with the undated rolls in c. 275 (no. 11).

1465–6. The 'Repairs within College' section is headless and kept among undated rolls in c. 275 (no. 1). It is in the same hand as the roll for 1465–6, which ends imperfectly in the section 'Varie Expense', but may not be part of it. The same hand occurs in other years.

(1466–7). Kept with the undated rolls in c. 275 (no. 12). John Norfolk died by September 1467.

Petrus de Ankarano. Probably **595**.

'Liber M. Eliot.' Perhaps a book which had been in circulation among the fellows and last to William Eliot (admitted 1465) and which was now transferred to the library.

1467–8. Hugo de Vienna. Probably ***557**.

(1468–9). Kept with the undated rolls in c. 275 (no. 13). The date seems certain because of a payment under 'Varie expense' of 7*d*. 'in die sepulture doctoris hyll in nouo collegio'; Hill died on 31 Jan. 1469 (Emden, *BRUO*).

1470–1. A book bought from Robert Badcock (fellow 1461–72).

(1472–3). I have been unable to find the roll from which I made this excerpt twenty years ago.

1480–1. Six volumes of Antonius. Cf. **593, 597, 605–8**.

'Pro Lathbury . . . imprimendo. et emendo pargamenum.' Cf. N. R. Ker, in *BLR* ii. 185–8.

1481–2. Three volumes of Augustine. Cf. **561–4**.

[1] McCusker, p. 152.

1494–5. Dominicus, vol. 2, was no. 7 of Est's eight volumes; cf. list XXVIA, Est. (1498–9). Mors. Cf. *1319–22.

1502–3. Mors. Cf. *1319–22.

1512–13. Cf. Ker in *BLR* vi (1959), 477–9.

1533–4. Expenses in fetching **609–99**.

1540–1. Ryche. Cf. *1119–25.

Cockys. Cf. List XXVIII.

1544–5. Garbrand. The entry suggests that the books which bear Gibson's rolls VII–X and Oldham's roll HM. a. 5 were bound by the binder whom Garbrand Herks employed, if he was not actually Herks himself: cf. Ker, *Pastedowns*, p. xiii.

1545–6. John Hering and Nicholas Bullingham were bursars in 1544–5.

1547–8. Augustine, Jason: cf. *1138c–j, *1410–12. Galen: this can hardly be *1190–3, which was published in 1549.

1549–50. Stephanus: *1202–4.

Books sold to Garbrand (Herks). These may have been chapel books. Sir Edmund Craster drew attention in *BLR* iii. 120 to the All Souls Missal, now MS. 302,[1] which was sold by Garbrand[2] in the sixteenth century perhaps to one of the Fermor family, since it was found in the chapel at Tusmore in 1841.

1558–9. Cf *1214–18.

1571–2. Expenses over the college ledger, 1572–1606, now deposited in the Bodleian Library, DD b. 119. Cf. Appendix II.

1574–5. Payments for the fetching and chaining of the books given by David Pole.

Panormitan. *749–52.

1575–6. *965–74 were bought with this money.

1576–7. Innocentius. *738.

1580–1. Three volumes of the Civil Course. Three of *715–19, one of them *716.

1583–4. The Bible given by Francis Milles in 1584, *980–7.

1586–7. General Councils. *975–9.

1587–8. Cf. List XXV at 1587–8.

1591–2. Books from 'doctor Johns'. See List XXV at 1592, Jones 1–9.

---

[1] It is the sixth of nine missals listed in the chapel inventory in Vellum Inv., f. 18; Sextum 2 fo teriori.

[2] The reference may be to Herks senior, but the script of the inscription would suit *c.* 1600 better than *c.* 1550: Gibson's extreme dates for the family as Oxford stationers are 1519 and 1617 (*Wills and Testamentary Documents*, pp. 44–5). The history of MS. 302 give a little substance to Robert Plot's story of finding books with 'ex dono Henrici Chichele fundatoris' on them in the Fermors' house at Somerton (cf. R. T. Gunther, *Early Science in Oxford* (1949), 400). In 1697 Bernard listed (*CMA* ii. 9151–61) eleven medieval manuscripts belonging to Henry Fermor of Tusmore. None of them have been traced, apart from the well-known manuscript from the Hereford Franciscan convent, now British Museum, Add. 46919.

1593–4. Book of accounts. Now LR 5. b. 3. Cf. Ker, *Pastedowns*, no. 1010.

1595–6. Cynus and Lanfranc. Cf. **727** and **1439**, both rebound.

1597–8, 1598–9. Payments to Pinart, partly no doubt for rechaining books (cf. Appendix III) and partly for chaining books which had not been chained before, there being now much more room for books.

1598–9. Cf. List XXV at 1598–9, Franklyn, and 1599, Milles. The entries show why Milles's books are in Oxford bindings and Franklyn's books are not.

1599–1600. The arms were used on Franklyn's fifteen volumes, on Milles's Melancthon, and on the eighteen volumes from Francis James: cf. List XXV at 1598–9, 1599, and 1600. Not more than three or four volumes of the *Tractatus* can be covered by the charge of 15*s*.

Zanchius. Cf. List XXV at 1598, Porter.

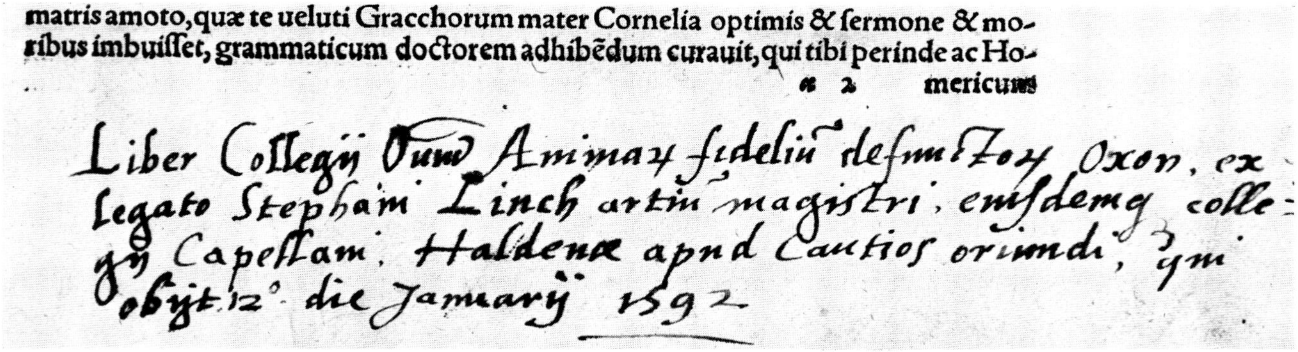

Liber Collegij omniũ aĩaꝝ Oxon, ex dono
Mri Thome Boys, LL. Bacchalaurei, &
ejusdem Collegij Socij. A. D. M.D.XCII.
Aprilis XII.

matris amoto, quæ te ueluti Gracchorum mater Cornelia optimis & sermone & mo-
ribus imbuisset, grammaticum doctorem adhibẽdum curauit, qui tibi perinde ac Ho-
mericus

Liber Collegij Oĩũ Aĩaꝝ fideliũ defũtoꝝ Oxon, ex
legato Stephani Linch artiũ magistri; eiuſdemꝗ colle=
gij Capellani. Habẽdæ apũd Cautios oriũda, ꝗm
obijt 12° die January 1592 -

PLATE III. *Ex libris* inscriptions in books given in 1592 and 1593
See pp. 104, 158

APPENDIX I

THE COLLEGE *EX LIBRIS*

Probably over half the books belonging to All Souls College before 1600 bore no college *ex libris*. King Henry's books were inscribed (List I) and so were Henry Penwortham's in List II and the three books in List II which were not chained in the library (**109, 411, 415**): other books in List II have at most an *ex dono*. The inscription when it occurs varies in form. The extremes are the eight-word 'Liber collegii animarum omnium (*or* omnium animarum) fidelium defunctorum in Oxonia (*or* de Oxonia)' and the three-word 'Liber collegii animarum'. In all I have noticed sixteen variants, some of them freaks. Only nos. 1, 2, 8, 11, 13, and 15 are common. Nos. 1 and 2 are the forms used from the late fifteenth century onwards by scribes who took the trouble to write so many words. In Warden Hovenden's time these full inscriptions were *de rigueur* and it was decided that 'de Oxon' ', not 'in Oxon' ' was the right way to end.[1] Earlier 'de' is rare, but one of the scribes who wrote in Goldwell's books used it (**1074–6, 1290, 1294, 1357**). Nos. 5 and 7 are the earliest forms (Henry VI and Penwortham). Nos. 8, 11, 13, 15 are the ordinary forms of the late fifteenth century and of the sixteenth century before Hovenden: 8 and 11 reflect common speech, in which from the first the college of the souls of all the faithful departed was the college of all souls.[2]

1. Liber collegii animarum omnium fidelium defunctorum in Oxonia (*or* de Oxonia *or* Oxonie).[3] **135** (inscription written in 1554), **574, 613** and all other books given by Warham, **996, 1010, 1016, 1043** and eleven other books given by Goldwell, **1067, 1132, 1229–30, 1332–4**; List XXV, Richard Master 3, Jones 1–9, Robert Master 1–4, Franklyn 1–15, Milles 1–12; List XXVIA, Bartlatt 1, Barworth 1, Bisshop 1, Byconill 1, 2, Polton 1, Topclyffe 1; List XXVIB. 9.

2. As no. 1, but 'omnium' precedes 'animarum'. **585, 965–74, 980–7, 1127, 1266, 1465–6**; List XXV, Carpenter 1, Dow 1, Jones 10, 11, Boys 1, Lynch 1, Porter 1–4, Hovenden 1–4, Hendley 1; List XXVIB. 8.

3. As no. 1, but omitting 'in Oxonia'. **415, 711, 1013**; List XXV, Hendley 1.

4. Liber collegii animarum o. f. defunctorum Oxon. **1328.**

5. Liber collegii animarum omnium fidelium Oxonie. **14, 19, 20, 1007** (in Oxonia).

6. Liber collegii omnium animarum fidelium in Oxonia. List XXVIA, Gaunt 1.

7. Liber collegii omnium fidelium defunctorum Oxon'. **75, 77, 182, 1290** (de Oxon'); List XXVIB. 2.

---

[1] See the heading to List IX for the English form of the name of the College given in Ledger A.   [2] See List I.

[3] The place-name is usually abbreviated.

8. Liber collegii omnium animarum Oxon' (*or* in Oxon'). **535, 715,** and nearly all the books given by David Pole, **1451–3**; List XXVIA, Goldwell 4, Halswell 1.

9. Liber collegii bonarum animarum in Oxon'. **1436.** Cf. **1413, 1417,** and List XXVIA, Cockys 3.

10. Liber collegii omnium fidelium in Oxonia. **1289.**

11. Liber collegii omnium animarum. **1149a, 1174–7, 1414d, 1431f, 1448**; List XXV, Lucke 1; List XXVIA, Cockys 2, Stone 1.

12. Liber collegii animarum omnium. **1434.**

13. Liber collegii animarum Oxon' (*or* in Oxon'). **525, 572, 706, 1042, 1267,** and seven other books given by Goldwell; List XXVIA, Alexander 1, Cockys 1, Darlington 1, Gaunt 2–5.

14. Liber collegii animarum, etc. **1028, 1030, 1498.**

15. Liber collegii animarum. **109, 1177, 1198, 1233, 1235, 1319–23, 1376–9, 1429, 1442–3, 1455, 1480**; List XXVIA, Goldwell 6, 9, Shether 1, Warner 3; List XXVIB. 3.

16. Liber collegii. **1479.**

In all but eighteen books in the preceding list the *ex libris* is followed by an *ex dono*. The exceptions may be exceptions to the general rule that a bought book was not inscribed. Two of them, **135** and **535**, were given an *ex libris* a considerable time after they came to All Souls, no doubt for special reasons.

Many books have *ex dono* inscriptions only, sometimes with and sometimes without mention of the recipient. These inscriptions differ much in their wording and were often written probably by the donor or on his behalf. The *ex dono* in **59** (MS. 18) is in Gascoigne's hand. As late as 1566 a simple 'Ex dono Io. Masoni militis'—beautifully written—was thought to be a sufficient form of words. Hovenden did not think it sufficient. The books given when he was warden have splendidly full inscriptions, 'Ex libris . . . ex dono . . .', often with the date of gift and some details about the donor, all in the monumental humanistica which he himself wrote. Some of the writing is certainly his. But he was not the only good writer in college at the end of the century. The hands of Richard Master, Robert Dow, and Christopher Hovenden have the same quality: cf. also the note to *1103.

In the first half of the seventeenth century someone was set to writing the now standard form of words, 'Liber Collegii animarum omnium fidelium defunctorum de Oxon'' in the manuscripts (**35**, etc.) and printed books which lacked them. He worked through most of the theology, but not through law. Many law books (**1393**, etc.) were inscribed later in the century, or *c.* 1700, by a scribe whose work is distinctive because he underlined the word 'Oxon''.

The foot of the second leaf is the usual position for the *ex libris*. It is here in the three books bequeathed in 1438, **75, 77,** and **182**, and in the books given by Francis James in 1600.

APPENDIX II
BINDERS AND BINDINGS

I am concerned here with (1) the bindings of Oxford bookbinders working for the college and (2) what may be called booksellers' stock bindings.

1. The college accounts are our only source of information. For the first 130 years they are almost no help. They name a few binders and give the titles of a few books which were bound. Since these books are no longer at All Souls such details are of little value. It is likely, however, that some of the manuscripts still in fifteenth-century or early sixteenth-century bindings are books for which the college paid money to a binder for new binding or repairs and that the entries concerning them in the accounts came on now missing rolls or are concealed in entries like 'pro ligacione librorum' in 1465–6. One binding with good claims to have been done for the college is on MS. 82 (**182**). It is decorated with stamps which an Oxford binder was using in the 1460s and 1470s. Even if it is earlier than this it is not likely to be a binding commissioned by the donor, Henry Penwortham, who died in 1438. When the manuscript first came to Oxford, or, more probably, when it was transferred from the collection of 'libri distribuendi' to the chained collection are likely times for rebinding. Chained books had to be strongly bound. Twelve other manuscripts form a group.[1] They are in boards, bevelled on the inside and covered with rather shabby white leather, which looks green where it is pasted to the inside of the boards. The boards project a good deal beyond the edges of the leaves. The clasps, except on one book, are of one pattern. A small variation in the pattern links MS. 51 and MS. 69. MSS. 51, 59, and 61 have pastedowns from the same early printed canon-law book. I am inclined to think that these manuscripts were rebound in Oxford at the beginning of the sixteenth century.

An entry in the accounts can be related to an existing binding first, it seems, in 1571–2. The college paid then for the binding of what is now called 'the first Ledger'.[2] The binder is not named. The covers bear a centre-piece and corner-pieces. A few years later some of the more important law books from David Pole's collection were rebound. Again the binder is not named, but since the books bear Gibson's rolls XII and XVIII we can be almost certain that he was Dominick Pinart.[3] Pinart was the leading Oxford binder in the seventies and eighties and until he was surpassed by Roger Barnes. He is first named in the account for

---

[1] MS. 5 (**14**), from Henry VI; MS. 57 (**522**), from Richard Andrew in 1471; MS. 84 (**571**), bought in the time of Warden Stokes; MSS. 93, 64, 61 (**1076, 1290, 1357**), from Goldwell; MSS. 95, 69, 59, 51, 52, 53 (**135, 147, 240, 259, 264, 308**).

[2] Ker, *Pastedowns*, no. 1541. The centre-piece is hidden by later leather. It is almost certainly centre-piece i, since the pastedowns are from the same manuscript as Ker, no. 1280.

[3] Rolls XII and XVIII (or XII alone) are on **531, 716, 738, 748, 755, 757, 760, 975-87, 1074, 1184-9**; List XXV at 1587, Ric. Master 1–3; List XXV at 1599, Francis Milles 1–9; List XXVIIB. 8.

1583–4, when he bound the great Antwerp Bible given by Francis Milles, and last in 1614–15, when he bound four volumes of Scotus.[1] Between 1575 and 1615 the college seems to have deserted Pinart only in 1591–2, when eleven volumes, given by Henry Jones and brought from London, were bound in Oxford. The bindings bear Gibson's roll XIX, which was then almost certainly being used by Thomas Middleton.[2]

I have not searched the accounts after 1620 for evidence of the rebinding and repair of the books listed in the Vellum Inventory. A great deal of rebinding was done, especially in the nineteenth century. This is less obvious among the manuscripts than in other sections of the library. Some of the covers there are not as old as they look. Sixteen form a clear group: admirably strong bindings of wooden boards covered with good-quality white skin, done probably in the eighteenth century.[3]

2. In the middle and end of the sixteenth century books came from the printers to the Oxford booksellers in sheets. Institutions and private persons buying new books did not as a rule have the sheets bound up by a binder of their own choosing.[4] The binding was done by or for the bookseller, before sale or on sale. Books bought in Oxford from Herman Evans and Garbrand Herks in the middle of the century and from Richard Garbrand and Joseph Barnes at the end of the century are, therefore, usually in 'Evans', 'Herks', 'Garbrand', and 'Barnes' bindings. In the case of Barnes we know that he employed his brother Roger as a binder. All Souls does not have 'Evans' or 'Roger Barnes' bindings because its suppliers were Garbrand Herks and his son Richard Garbrand, not that they used them much, save only in 1544–5. The big purchase then came in nearly uniform bindings, the larger books in covers bearing three rolls, Gibson's VII, VIII, and X, the smaller in covers bearing two rolls, Gibson's VII and X: the only exception is the Vesalius (**1145**).[5] The college thought that they were not shiny enough, and had Herks's servants in to polish them up. A few years later the binder had given up roll VIII in favour of roll IX: the popular combination IX and X is on the Augustine bought in 1547–8. The purchase of books from Richard Garbrand is only mentioned twice in the accounts. The two books bought in 1587–8 can be identified.[6] Both bear Gibson's roll XXI. The absence from the accounts of a binding charge shows that it was included in the sum the college paid to Garbrand.[7]

---

[1] Three of them are now LR 4. b. 17–19 (List XXVIA, Gaunt 3; **1473, 1475**).

[2] Cf. Ker, *Pastedowns*, p. 211.

[3] MSS. 46, 37, 86, 85, 72, 68, 4 (bound in 4 vols.), 29, 90, 83, 91, 42, 2 (**20, 77, 121, 124, 140, 537, 555–6, 557, 572, 1025, 1043**; List XXVIA, Bisshop 1, Darlington 1).

[4] **975–9** are exceptions to this rule. They were bought new and bound by Pinart.

[5] Cf. the note to List XXVIII at 1544–5.   [6] List XXV at 1587–8, 1, 2.

[7] The charge for binding can be calculated if the price before binding is written on the title-page, as it often is, and the price actually paid is recorded in college accounts. Examples are: Corpus Christi College, ST. i. 269, A. Rubius, 1610, which cost 5s. 6d. in 1611 ('4. 6' is written on the title page); Corpus Christi College, HH/ST. 3. 2, C. Gillius, 1611, which cost 19s. 6d. in 1611 ('17. 6' is written on the title-page); Magdalen College, c. 8. 14, F. Toletus, *In Johannem*, Cologne 1589, which cost 11s. in 1593 ('9' is written on the title-page). The first of these books is a quarto. The other two are folios.

APPENDIX III
CHAINING

Our knowledge of the history of a chained collection of books depends largely on the preservation of the old bindings. At All Souls enough medieval and sixteenth-century bindings remain to show the different ways in which the books were chained at different periods.

Position 1. Chaining from a staple on the back cover. The chain was fastened to a staple, a strip of metal some inches long, arched in the centre and lying horizontally across the cover a short distance from the foot. The staple was fixed to the cover by nails, usually six in number. No example survives, but it probably looked like the staple still *in situ* on New College MS. 49.[1]

The marks of the nails are to be seen on:

(6 nails) **14**,[2] **19, 20, 35, 38, 43, 54, 59, 73, 75, 77, 124, 140**.
(4 nails) **142, 245, 1251**.
(2 nails) **147, 1010** (?).

Of these eighteen books, twelve, **14, 20, 35, 38, 59, 73, 77, 124, 140, 147, 245, 1251**, have been rebound or repaired so that the chainmark is not visible on the outside of the binding, but only on a leaf or on leaves at the end, or (**245, 1251**) on the wood of the board, if looked at from the inside.

Position 2. Chaining from a strip of metal placed vertically at the foot of the front cover, usually about the middle. The strip ended in a loop to which the chain was attached. This position (F1) is to be seen on some fifty books: **585, 594, 677, 975–9, 1135, 1136, 1138c–j, 1144, 1145, 1147–8, 1149a, 1150–5, 1159–62, 1165–7, 1229–30, 1266, 1289, 1398–1400, 1400b–i, 1408–9, 1415–18, 1431f, 1442–3**. Variants are on **574** (F2) and on **1158, 1163, 1414, 1431a** (H1). These books are entered in Lists VI, VII, XI, XVI, XVII, XIX, XXII, and as additions to List XXII.

Position 3. Chaining from a staple on the front cover. The chainmark is like that of Position 1, but on the front cover near the foot. The marks of 6 or 4 nails are to be seen now in this position on seven large law books, all of them entered among additions to the mid-sixteenth-century catalogue in the Vellum Inventory (additions to List XXII, **1432, 1435–6, 1444–6, 1448**).[3] These books are in fact

---

[1] Cf. N. R. Ker, 'Chaining from a staple on the back cover', *BLR* iii (1950), 104–7. New College 49 is not likely to be from the medieval New College library: no other book was chained like this there. It may be the copy of Petrus Johannis Olivi on St. Matthew—a rare text in England—which William Duffield left to Merton College in 1453 'ad incathenandum in communi libraria' (*Test. Ebor.* iii. 128).

[2] In repairs the pastedown has been replaced upside down; wormholes testify to its original position.

[3] Ker, loc. cit., p. 105. I said there wrongly that only one of these books was an addition to this inventory.

all that survive from this section of the Inventory in their original bindings, apart from **1442–3**.

The chronological development is evident. Position 1 is that found on the books which have been chained for the longest time at All Souls. It shows that the books lay on the desks with their back covers uppermost. Position 2 came into use before 1500 (**574, 585, 594**) and was still being used in 1586–7 (**975–9**). It shows that the books had their front covers uppermost. Position 3 was used for a short time early in the second half of s. xvi, perhaps because the books on which it occurs required an unusually strong chain attachment.

Positions 4–7. Chaining from a strip of metal placed horizontally on the side of either the front or the back cover and either near the head or near the foot (FS1, FS2, HS1, HS2). Positions 1–3 became untenable in 1597–8 when the old desks were taken away and shelving was substituted on which the books stood on their tails, cover to cover, with the fore-edge outwards. All books already chained in these positions were re-chained at this time by Pinart, who spent many months in the library. Unfortunately for historians of libraries the positions in which books now had to be chained were positions in which they had sometimes been chained at an earlier date. In particular the side near the foot of the front cover (FS1) was not only the commonest position for the chain attachment for a decade or two after 1597–8 but also for three or four decades before it. All Mason's books and all Pole's seem to have been chained in this way. So too, at a much earlier date, was **182**. On **259** and **264** the mark is FS2.

The position on the side near the head of one of the covers (HS1 or HS2) is the normal position after the early years of s. xvii[1] and was used already on books which came into the library in 1598 and 1599. Before this it is very unusual, but it seems to be on **242, 308, 1189,** and **1425b**.

---

[1] h. 3. 3, 4 given in 1607 have FS1.

APPENDIX IV
SECUNDO FOLIO REFERENCES

In the later Middle Ages listers of books found that the best way to distinguish one book from another in a catalogue or inventory or will was by the opening words of the second leaf. 'Biblia secundo folio lingua volueret' may not distinguish from all other Bibles the Bible which in 1508 was kept chained in the library of Christ Church, Canterbury, but for practical purposes it is a satisfactory entry.[1] In a medieval manuscript there is not usually any doubt as to what the secundo folio is. The actual second leaf, not counting fly-leaves, and the second leaf of the text are the same thing. In case of doubt the cataloguer might write 'in libro', 'in prohemio', 'in textu', 'in glosa', or 'in tabula' after 'secundo folio' and he might enter the secundo folio on the book itself, on the outside of the cover, or on a fly-leaf, or after the *ex libris*. When this useful device was taken over by cataloguers of printed books there was, however, confusion over the status of preliminary matter, especially the newly invented title-page. Is the title-page the first leaf? If so, the secundo folio is the first word of the preface. In the Vellum Inventory, books recorded in List XVI as well as in List XVII and in List XXII as well as in List XXIII often have different secundo folios in the earlier and the later lists. The opening words of the second leaf of the text were chosen by the earlier cataloguers and the opening words of the preface by the later cataloguers: see, for example, **1402**. Confusion is apparent in the additions to List XXII: see the notes to **1434** and **1451–3**.

Applied to a printed book the secundo folio can at best only distinguish one edition from another and it may not do even that. It is still, however, a valuable reference. There is a world of difference between the Vellum Inventory, which records secundo folios, and the Benefactors' Register, which does not. Miss Bateson showed in her edition of the Syon Abbey catalogue how much can be done to bring a lost collection to life by finding what edition has the same secundo folio as is recorded in the Syon catalogue.[2] So did Dr. Pantin in his *Canterbury College Oxford*.[3] I have made a certain number of identifications—expressed by the formula 'As ed. . . .'—and should like to have made more. Secundo folio hunting is fun, but it takes time and can be strenuous.

[1] *Ancient Libraries of Canterbury and Dover*, ed. M. R. James, Cambridge, 1903, p. 152.
[2] *Catalogue of Syon Monastery, Isleworth*, ed. Mary Bateson, Cambridge, 1898.
[3] Oxford Historical Society, new series, vi, vol. i, Oxford, 1947.

CONCORDANCE OF SHELFMARKS AND RUNNING NUMBERS

MANUSCRIPTS

Oxford, All Souls College	
2	XXVIA, Derlyngton 1
4	555–6
5	14
12	35
13	43
14	996
15	XXVIA, Honywood 1
16	38
18	59
19	75
20	631
27	86
28	19
29	557
30	54
31	73
37	77
38	XXVIA, Goldwell 1
42	XXVIA, Bisshop 1
46	20
47	XXVIA, Polton 1
49	252, 1251
50	245
51	259
52	264
53	308
54	1277
55	266
56	242
57	522
59	240
60	267
61	1357
62	197
63	XXVIA, Stone 1
64	1290
67	XXVIA, Goldwell 2
68	537
69	147
70	XXVIA, Halswell 1
71	146
72	140
73	531
74	XXVIB, 4
75	530
76	XXVIA, Racour 1
78	585
79	142
80	535
82	182
83	1025
84	571
85	124
86	121
87	Addenda (XXXIB. 4a)
88	574
89	80
90	572
91	1043
92	1013
93	1076
95	135
97	1010
98	1015
182	594
322	XXVIA, Alexander 1
331	538
332	128
DD All Souls College b. 32[1]	74 (?)
DD All Souls College c. 241[1]	XXVIB. 5

Antwerp, Plantin–Moretus Museum	
12	415
26+341, ff. 15–22	109
30	411
107	XXVIA, Warham 1
110	XXVIB. 3
144	525
Exeter, Cathedral, 3506.	145

London, British Museum
Sloane 280 — XXVIB. 2

London, Messrs Robinson
(Phillipps 3119) — XXVIB. 1

Oxford:
Bodleian Library
Bodley 741–2 XXVIA, Byconyll 1, 2

[1] Wrappers of archives deposited in the Bodleian Library.

PRINTED BOOKS

[1] Numbers in italics are those in Ker, *Pastedowns*.

Store Room (*cont.*):

74. b. 14	823
74. c. 5	1132
74. d. 6	821 (*97*)
77. c. 3	873 or 874
77. d. 32	886
77. g. 11	648
77. g. 13	857
77. h. 10	876
77. h. 16	885
77. h. 17	858
78. c. 6–9	XXV. 1598, Porter 1–4
79. c. 11	806
79. c. 12	807
79. c. 13	864
79. c. 14	865
79. e. 1	677
79. f. 8	861
79. f. 9	XXVIA, Mason 6
79. f. 10	808
79. g. 3	849
79. g. 8	636
79. g. 10	792
79. h. 3	1184 (*990*)
79. h. 4	1187 (*991*)

79. h. 5	848
79. h. 6	846
79. h. 9	971
79. i. 2	972
79. i. 3	973
80. b. 2–8	1119–25
80. f. 4	928
80. f. 6–9	XXV. 1598, Robert Master 1–4
80. g. 3	790
81. a. 15	651
81. g. 9	820
81. h. 5	853

Glasgow, Univ. Libr., Bi. 4. g. 20   672
Gloucester, Cathedral   1149a (*503*)
Liverpool, Athenaeum   860
Oxford
  Bodleian Libr.
    Antiq. b. G.S. 1549/1–4   1190–3
    Auct. 1 Q. 3. 1   XXVIA, Goldwell 9
  Exeter College, 9. I. 1497   1158–63
  University College, e. 1   761
  Worcester College, EE. u. 3   810

CONCORDANCE OF RUNNING NUMBERS
AND LIST NUMBERS

154 II, 143
155 II, 144
156 II, 145
157 II, 146
158 II, 147
159 II, 148
160 II, 149
161 II, 150
162 II, 151
163 II, 152. XIII, 105. XIV, 149.
     XV, 126
164 II, 153
165 II, 154
166 II, 155
167 II, 156
168 II, 157
169 II, 158. Cf. **1060**
170 II, 159
171 II, 160. XIV, 131
172 II, 161. XV, 122
173 II, 162
174 II, 163
175 II, 164
176 II, 165
177 II, 166
178 II, 167
179 II, 168
180 II, 169
181 II, 170
*182 II, 171. XIII, 119. XIV, 176.
     XXI, 187. XVI, 153b
183 II, 172. VI, 31. XIV, 147
184 II, 173
185 II, 174. XIII, 106. XIV, 148.
     XV, 136
186 II, 175
187 II, 176. XIV, 162. XV, 148
188 II, 177
189 II, 178. XIV, 146. XV, 120
190 II, 179
191 II, 180
192 II, 181. XVIII, 1. XIX, 3.
     XX, 5. XXI, 7
193 II, 182
194 II, 183. XVIII, 6. XIX, 7.
     XX, 9. XXI, 18
195 II, 184. XVIII, 29. XX, 40.
     XXI, 8
196 II, 185. XX, 39. XXI, 104
*197 II, 186. XVIII, 4. XIX, 1. XX,
     3. XXI, 16. XXII, 119.
     XXIII, 104
198 II, 187. XVIII, 2. XIX, 2.
     XX, 4. XXI, 17. XXII,
     120

199 II, 188. XVIII, 25. XX, 41.
     XXI, 11
200 II, 189. XVIII, 5. XIX, 8.
     XX, 10
201 II, 190
202 II, 191. XIX, 45. XXI, 46
203 II, 192. XVIII, 43. XIX, 42.
     XXI, 57
204 II, 193. XIX, 86. XXI, 162
205 II, 194. XIX, 55. XX, 69. XXI,
     68. XXII, 83
206 II, 195
207 II, 196
208 II, 197. XVIII, 50. XX, 70.
     XXI, 101
209 II, 198. XVIII, 11. XIX, 12.
     XX, 17
210 II, 199. XVIII, 12. XIX, 13.
     XX, 18. XXII, 127
211 II, 202. XVIII, 18. XIX, 24.
     XX, 22. XXI, 64
212 II, 203. XVIII, 19. XIX, 26.
     XX, 20. XXI, 65
213 II, 204. XVIII, 21. XIX, 17.
     XX, 32. XXI, 66
214 II, 205. XVIII, 45. XIX, 58.
     XXI, 62. XXII, 92
215 II, 206. XVIII, 46. XIX, 57.
     XXI, 63. XXII, 93
216 II, 207. XVIII, 15. XIX, 16.
     XX, 33. XXI, 48. XXII, 68
217 II, 208. XVIII, 16. XIX, 18.
     XX, 35. XXI, 49. XXII, 69
218 II, 209. XIX, 59. XXI, 58
219 II, 210. XVIII, 13. XIX, 9.
     XX, 13. XXII, 75
220 II, 211. XIX, 44. XXI, 52.
     XXII, 82
221 II, 212. XVIII, 8. XIX, 14.
     XX, 31. XXI, 89
222 II, 213. XVIII, 39. XIX, 43.
     XXI, 101
223 II, 214. XVIII, 48. XIX, 29.
     XX, 59. XXI, 10
224 II, 215. XVIII, 7. XIX, 6.
     XX, 8. XXI, 91
225 II, 216. XIX, 34. XX, 55. XXI,
     90. XXII, 137d (?)
226 II, 218. XIX, 40. XX, 58. XXI,
     78. XXII, 109
227 II, 219
228 II, 220. XVIII, 41. XIX, 31.
     XX, 62. XXI, 81
229 II, 221. XVIII, 27. XIX, 38.
     XX, 56. XXI, 73

230 II, 222. XVIII, 32
231 II, 223. XVIII, 37. XIX, 50.
 XX, 68. XXI, 84
232 II, 224. XIX, 49. XX, 72.
 XXI, 86
233 II, 225. XX, 42. XXI, 82
234 II, 226. XIX, 26a. XX, 24.
 XXI, 76
235 II, 227. XVIII, 40. XIX, 52.
 XX, 74. XXI, 93
236 II, 228. XVIII, 17. XIX, 23.
 XX, 19. XXI, 20
237 II, 229. XVIII, 33. XIX, 37.
 XX, 52. XXI, 19
238 II, 230. XXI, 154
239 II, 231. XVIII, 83. XIX, 84.
 XX, 125. XXI, 123
*240 II, 232. XIX, 80. XX, 116.
 XXI, 151. XXII, 105d.
 XXIII, 98
241 II, 233
*242 II, 234. XX, 127. XXI, 152.
 XXII, 136
243 II, 235. XXI, 153. XXII, 125
244 II, 237. XVIII, 64a. XIX. 64
*245 II, 238. XVIII, 53. XX, 84.
 XXI, 142. XXII, 17. XXIII,
 17
246 II, 239. XVIII, 55. XX, 81
247 II, 240. XVIII, 54. XX, 80
248 II, 241
249 II, 242. XVIII, 57. XX, 85
250 II, 243
251 II, 244. XVIII, 51
*252 II, 245. Cf. **1251**
253 II, 246.
254 II, 247. XVIII, 61. XIX, 65.
 XX, 91. XXI, 114
255 II, 248. XVIII, 70
256 II, 249. XVIII, 71. XIX, 67.
 XX, 137. XXI, 149
257 II, 250. XVIII, 68, 85. XIX,
 66. XX, 138. XXI, 148.
 XXII, 56
258 II, 251. XX, 123. XXII, 57
*259 II, 252. XVIII, 67. XIX, 79.
 XXI, 145. XXII, 15. XXIII,
 15
260 II, 253. XVIII, 76. XIX, 76,
 78. XX, 106. XXI, 132
261 II, 254. XVIII, 75. XX, 104.
 XXI, 133
262 II, 255. Cf. **1254**
263 II, 256. XVIII, 82. XIX, 85.
 XXI, 159

*264 II, 257. XVIII, 74. XIX, 75.
 XX, 103. XXI, 144. XXII,
 16. XXIII, 16
265 II, 258. XIX, 69
*266 II, 259. XIX, 81. XX, 117.
 XXI, 157
*267 II, 260. XX, 122. XXI, 161.
 XXII, 100. XXIII, 100
268 II, 261. XVIII, 63. XX, 79.
 XXI, 138
269 II, 262. XVIII, 79. XIX, 71.
 XX, 139. XXII, 67
270 II, 263. XVIII, 66
271 II, 264. XVIII, 77. XIX, 70
272 II, 265. XVIII, 73. XIX, 73
273 II, 266. XVIII, 62
274 II, 267. XVIII, 44. XIX, 35.
 XX, 54. XXI, 59. XXII,
 95
275 II, 268
276 II, 269
277 II, 270
278 II, 271
279 II, 272
280 II, 273
281 II, 274
282 II, 275
283 II, 276. XXIV, 64
284 II, 277
285 II, 278
286 II, 279
287 II, 280. XXIV, 73
288 II, 281
289 II, 282
290 II, 283
291 II, 284
292 II, 285. XXIV, 94
293 II, 286
294 II, 287. XXIV, 95
295 II, 288
296 II, 289
297 II, 290
298 II, 291
299 II, 292
300 II, 293. XXIV, 53
301 II, 294
302 II, 295
303 II, 296
304 II, 297
305 II, 298
306 II, 299
307 II, 300
*308 II, 301. VI, 52. XIX, 36. XX,
 53. XXI, 85
309 II, 302

310	II, 303		365	II, 359
311	II, 304		366	II, 360
312	II, 305		367	II, 361
313	II, 306		368	II, 362
314	II, 307		369	II, 363
315	II, 309		370	II, 364
316	II, 310		371	II, 365. XVIII, 84. XIX, 68. XXI, 134
317	II, 311		372	II, 366
318	II, 312		373	II, 367
319	II, 313		374	II, 368
320	II, 314		375	II, 369. XVIII, 78. XIX, 74. XX, 136
321	II, 315		376	II, 395
322	II, 316		377	II, 396
323	II, 317		378	II, 397
324	II, 318		379	II, 398. XIII, 102. XIV, 141
325	II, 319		380	II, 399. XV, 69
326	II, 320. XXIV, 77		381	II, 400. XXIV, 43
327	II, 321		382	II, 401
328	II, 322		383	II, 402
329	II, 323		384	II, 403. XIII, 75. XIV, 112. XV, 94
330	II, 324		385	II, 404
331	II, 325. XXIV, 91		386	II, 405
332	II, 326		387	II, 406
333	II, 327		388	II, 407
334	II, 328		389	II, 408
335	II, 329		390	II, 409
336	II, 330		391	II, 410
337	II, 331		392	II, 411
338	II, 332		393	II, 412
339	II, 333		394	II, 413
340	II, 334		395	II, 414
341	II, 335		396	II, 415
342	II, 336		397	II, 416. Cf. **147**
343	II, 337		398	II, 417
344	II, 338		399	II, 418
345	II, 339		400	II, 419. XIII, 32. XIV, 47. XVI, 48
346	II, 340		401	II, 420
347	II, 341		402	II, 421
348	II, 342		403	II, 422
349	II, 343		404	II, 423
350	II, 344. XXIV, 40		405	II, 424
351	II, 345		406	II, 425
352	II, 346		407	II, 426
353	II, 347. XXIV, 68		408	II, 427
354	II, 348		409	II, 428
355	II, 349		410	II, 429. Cf. **1003**
356	II, 350		*411	II, 430. XXIV, 96
357	II, 351. XXIV, 88		412	II, 431
358	II, 352		413	II, 432. Cf. **570**
359	II, 353		414	II, 433. XVIII, 22. XIX, 15. XX, 34. XXI, 67
360	II, 354			
361	II, 355			
362	II, 356			
363	II, 357			
364	II, 358			

*415　II, 434
416　II, 435
417　II, 436
418　II, 437. VI, 19. XIII, 84. XIV,
　　　122. XV, 115
419　II, 438
420　II, 439
421　II, 440
422　II, 441
423　II, 442
424　II, 443
425　II, 444
426　II, 445
427　II, 446
428　II, 447
429　II, 448
430　II, 449
431　II, 450
432　II, 451. XVIII, 26. XIX, 25.
　　　XX, 21. XXI, 103
433　II, 452
434　II, 453
435　II, 454
436　II, 455. XXIV, 42
437　II, 456
438　II, 457. XVIII, 56. XIX, 62.
　　　XX, 88
439　II, 458
440　II, 459
441　II, 460. XXIV, 69
442　II, 461
443　II, 462
444　II, 463. XVIII, 47. XIX,
　　　41
445　II, 464
446　II, 465
447　II, 466
448　II, 467
449　II, 468
450　II, 469
451　II, 470
452　II, 471
453　II, 472
454　II, 473
455　II, 475
456　II, 476
457　II, 477
458　II, 478
459　II, 479
460　II, 480
461　II, 481
462　II, 90
463　II, 93
464　II, 94
465　II, 99. Cf. **995**

466　II, 295
467　II, 391
468　II, 392
469　II, 394
470　II, 482. XIII, 89. XIV, 125.
　　　XV, 116
471　II, 483
472　III, 1
473　III, 2
474　III, 3
475　III, 4
476　III, 5. Cf. **1484**
477　III, 6
478　III, 7
479　III, 8
480　III, 9
481　III, 10
482　III, 11
483　III, 12
484　III, 13
485　III, 14
486　III, 15
487　III, 16
488　III, 17
489　III, 18
490　III, 19
491　III, 20
492　III, 21
493　III, 22
494　III, 23
495　III, 24
496　III, 25
497　IV, 1. XXIV, 87
498　IV, 2
499　IV, 3
500　IV, 4. XXIV, 72
501　IV, 5
502　IV, 6
503　IV, 7
504　IV, 8
505　IV, 9
506　IV, 10
507　IV, 11. XXIV, 41
508　IV, 12
509　IV, 13
510　IV, 14. XXIV, 97
511　IV, 15
512　IV. 16
513　IV, 17
514　IV, 18. XXIV, 52
515　IV, 19
516　IV, 20. XXIV, 83
517　IV, 21
518　IV, 22. VI, 50. XIX, 54. XX,
　　　76

519 IV, 23
520 IV, 24. VI, 51. XIX, 46. XX, 71. XXI, 37
521 IV, 25
*522 IV, 26. XXII, 60
523 IV, 27. XVIII, 64. XX, 87. XXI, 115
524 IV, 28
*525 IV, 29
526 IV, 30
527 IV, 31
528 IV, 32
529 IV, 33
*530 Va, 1. XIX, 101. XX, 142. XV, 163. XVI, 92. XVII, 72
*531 Va, 2. XIX, 99. XX, 128. XV, 155. XVI, 82
532 Va, 3. XIX, 95. XX, 131. XV, 129. XVI, 93b
533 Va, 4
534 Va, 5. XIX, 96. XX, 135. XV, 165. XVI, 93a
*535 Va, 6. XIX, 98. XX, 141. XV, 160
536 Va, 7. XX, 140. XV, 164
*537 Va, 8. XX, 144. XV, 162. XVI, 93. XVII, 74
*538 Va, 9. XXIV, 3
539 Va, 10
540 Va, 11. XXIV, 2
541 Vb, 1
542 Vb, 2. XXIV, 4
543 Vb, 3
544 Vb, 4
545 Vb, 5
546 Vb, 6
547 Vb, 7
548 Vb, 8
549 Vb, 9
550 Vb, 10
551 Vb, 11
552 Vc, 1
553 VI, 1. XIII, 11. XIV, 12. XV, 16
554 VI, 2. XIII, 1. XIV, 1. XV, 3
*555 VI, 3. XIII, 16. XIV, 16. XV, 20. XVI, 1. XVII, 1
*556 VI, 4. XIII, 18. XIV, 17. XV, 21. XVI, 2. XVII, 2
*557 VI, 5. XIII, 17. XIV, 24. XV, 22
558 VI, 6. XIV, 23. XV, 28
559 VI, 7. XIV, 41

560 VI, 8. XIII, 33. XIV, 46. XV, 42
561 VI, 9. XIV, 37
562 VI, 10. XIII, 24. XIV, 33
563 VI, 11. XIII, 22. XIV, 40. XV, 37
564 VI, 12
565 VI, 13. XIII, 35. XIV, 50. XV, 43. XVI, 45. XVII, 41
566 VI, 14. XIII, 53a. XIV, 79
*567 VI, 15. XIII, 65. XIV, 89. XV, 79
568 VI, 16. XIII, 78. XIV, 116. XV, 91
569 VI, 17. XIII, 70. XIV, 108. XV, 92
570 VI, 18. XIII, 71. XIV, 107. XV, 93
*571 VI, 21. XIII, 82. XIV, 120. XV, 112. XVI, 111. XVII, 91
*572 VI, 22. XIII, 85. XIV, 142. XVI, 112. XVII, 92
573 VI, 23. Cf. **1061**
*574 VI, 24. XIII, 81. XIV, 123. XV, 111. XVI, 110
575 VI, 25. XIV, 130. XV, 121. XVI, 122a
576 VI, 26. XIV, 135. XV, 119
577 VI, 27. XIV, 145
578 VI, 28. XIV, 161. XV, 147
579 VI, 29. XIII, 113. XIV, 164. XV, 144
580 VI, 30
581 VI, 32. XIII, 112. XIV, 155. XV, 133. XVI, 123e
582 VI, 33
583 VI, 34. XIII, 108. XIV, 153. XV, 127
584 VI, 35. XIX, 105. XX, 146. XV, 141
*585 VI, 36. XIX, 102. XX, 150. XV, 166. XVI, 83. XVII, 95
586 VI, 37. Cf. **1265**
587 VI, 38
588 VI, 39. Cf. **1069**
589 VI, 40
590 VI, 41
591 VI, 42
592 VI, 43
593 VI, 44. XVIII, 14. XIX, 10. XX, 14. XXII, 74
*594 VI, 45. XVIII, 23. XIX, 28. XX, 60. XXII, 97. XXIII, 106

595	VI, 46. XVIII, 30. XIX, 39. XX, 57. XXI, 71		641	VII, 33
596	VI, 47. XVIII, 31. XX, 45		642	VII, 34
597	VI, 48. XVIII, 35. XX, 36		643	VII, 35
598	VI, 49. XVIII, 42. XIX, 32. XX, 63. XXI, 74		644	VII, 36
			645	VII, 37
599	VI, 53. XIX, 47. XXI, 40		646	VII, 38
600	VI, 54. XIX, 20. XX, 29. XXI, 42		647	VII, 39
			*648	VII, 40
601	VI, 55. XIX, 19. XX, 28. XXI, 41		649	VII, 41
			*650	VII, 42
602	VI, 56. XIX, 53. XX, 66. XXI, 43		*651	VII, 43. XV, 186. XVI, 18. XVII, 9
603	VI, 57. XIX, 48. XX, 67. XXI, 25, 44		652	VII, 44
			653	VII, 45
604	VI, 58. XX, 44. XXI, 92		654	VII, 46
605	VI, 59. XVIII, 89. XIX, 11. XX, 16. XXII, 73		655	VII, 47
			656	VII, 48
606	VI, 60. XVIII, 86. XIX, 22. XX, 30. XXII, 72		657	VII, 49
			658	VII, 50
607	VI, 61. XVIII, 88. XIX, 33. XX, 51		659	VII, 51
			660	VII, 52
608	VI, 62. XVIII, 87. XX, 48		661	VII, 53
609	VII, 1		662	VII, 54
610	VII, 2		663	VII, 55
611	VII, 3		664	VII, 56
612	VII, 4		665	VII, 57
*613	VII, 5		666	VII, 58
614	VII, 6		667	VII, 59
615	VII, 7		668	VII, 60
*616	VII, 8		669	VII, 61
617	VII, 9		670	VII, 62
*618	VII, 10		671	VII, 63
619	VII, 11		*672	VII, 64
*620	VII, 12		673	VII, 65
*621	VII, 13		674	VII, 66
622	VII, 14		675	VII, 67
623	VII, 15		676	VII, 68
624	VII, 16		*677	VII, 69. XV, 185. XVI, 11. XVII, 36
625	VII, 17		678	VII, 70
626	VII, 18		*678	VII, 70
627	VII, 19		679	VII, 71
628	VII, 20		680	VII, 72
629	VII, 21		681	VII, 73
630	VII, 22		682	VII, 74
*631	VII, 23		683	VII, 75
632	VII, 24		684	VII, 76
*633	VII, 25		685	VII, 77
634	VII, 26		686	VII, 78
*635	VII, 27		687	VII, 79
*636	VII, 28		688	VII, 80
*637	VII, 29		689	VII, 81
638	VII, 30		*690	VII, 82
*639	VII, 31		691	VII, 83
*640	VII, 32		692	VII, 84
			693	VII, 85

694	VII, 86	
695	VII, 87	
696	VII, 88	
697	VII, 89	
698	VII, 90. XV, 193. XVI, 39	
699	VII, 91	
700	VIII, 1	
701	VIII, 2	
702	VIII, 3	
703	VIII, 4	
704	VIII, 5	
705	VIII, 6	
*706	VIII, 7	
707	VIII, 8	
708	VIII, 9	
709	VIII, 10	
710	VIII, 11	
*711	VIII, 12	
712	VIII, 13	
713	VIII, 14	
714	VIII, 15	
*715	IX, 1	
*716	IX, 2	
717	IX, 3	
*718	IX. 4	
*719	IX, 5	
*720	IX, 6. XXIII, 37	
*721	IX, 7. XXIII, 41	
*722	IX, 8. XXIII, 42	
*723	IX, 9. XXIII, 43	
*724	IX, 10. XXIII, 44	
*725	IX, 11. XXIII, 39	
*726	IX, 12. XXIII, 40	
*727	IX, 13. XXIII, 38	
728	IX, 14	
729	IX, 15	
*730	IX, 16	
*731	IX, 17	
*732	IX, 18	
*733	IX, 19. XXIII, 50	
*734	IX, 20. XXIII, 51	
735	IX, 21. XXIII, 60	
736	IX, 22. XXIII, 61	
*737	IX, 23. XXIII, 59	
*738	IX, 24. XXIII, 58	
*739	IX, 25	
740	IX, 26	
741	IX, 27	
*742	IX, 28	
*743	IX, 29	
*744	IX, 30. XXIII, 63	
*745	IX, 31. XXIII, 64	
*746	IX, 32	
*747	IX, 33	
*748	IX, 34. XXIII, 69	

*749	IX, 35. XXIII, 65	
*750	IX, 36. XXIII, 66	
*751	IX, 37. XXIII, 67	
*752	IX, 38. XXIII, 68	
*753	IX, 39. XXIII, 72	
*754	IX, 40. XXIII, 73	
*755	IX, 41. XXIII, 75	
*756	IX, 42. XXIII, 86	
*757	IX, 43. XXIII, 84	
*758	IX, 44. XXIII, 81	
*759	IX, 45. XXIII, 80	
*760	IX, 46. XXIII, 79	
*761	IX, 47. XXIII, 90	
*762	IX, 48. XXIII, 96	
763	IX, 49	
764	IX, 50	
765	IX, 51	
716	IX, 52	
767	IX, 53	
*768	IX, 54	
769	IX, 55	
770	IX, 56	
771	IX, 57	
772	IX, 58	
773	IX, 59	
774	IX, 60	
775	IX, 61	
*776	IX, 62. XXIII, 103	
777	IX, 63	
778	IX, 64	
779	IX, 65	
780	IX, 66	
781	IX, 67	
782	IX, 68	
783	IX, 69	
784	IX, 70	
785	IX, 71	
786	IX, 72	
*787	IX, 73	
*788	IX, 74	
*789	IX, 75	
*790	IX, 76. XVII, 56	
*791	IX, 77. XVII, 11	
*792	IX, 78	
*793	IX, 79. XVII, 12	
794	IX, 80. XVII, 55	
*795	IX, 81	
*796	IX, 82	
797	IX, 83	
*798	IX, 84	
*799	IX, 85	
*800	IX, 86	
801	IX, 87	
*802	IX, 88. XVII, 42	
*803	IX, 89. XVII, 43	

*804	IX, 90. XVII, 44		*859	IX, 145	
805	IX, 91		*860	IX, 146	
*806	IX, 92		*861	IX, 147. XVII, 35	
*807	IX, 93		862	IX, 148	
*808	IX, 94		*863	IX, 149	
809	IX, 95		*864	IX, 150	
*810	IX, 96		*865	IX, 151	
*811	IX, 97		*866	IX, 152	
812	IX, 98		*867	IX, 153	
813	IX, 99		*868	IX, 154	
814	IX, 100		869	IX, 155	
815	IX, 101		870	IX, 156	
816	IX, 102		871	IX, 157	
817	IX, 103		872	IX, 158	
818	IX, 104		*873	IX, 159	
819	IX, 105		874	IX, 160	
*820	IX, 106		875	IX, 161	
*821	IX, 107		*876	IX, 162	
*822	IX, 108		877	IX, 163	
*823	IX, 109. XVII, 25		878	IX, 164	
*824	IX, 110		*879	IX, 165	
825	IX, 111		880	IX, 166	
*826	IX, 112		*881	IX, 167	
*827	IX, 113		882	IX, 168	
*828	IX, 114		*883	IX, 169	
*829	IX, 115		*884	IX, 170	
*830	IX, 116		*885	IX, 171	
*831	IX, 117		*886	IX, 172	
*832	IX, 118		887	IX, 173	
*833	IX, 119		888	IX, 174	
*834	IX, 120		889	IX, 175	
*835	IX, 121		890	IX, 176	
*836	IX, 122		891	IX, 177	
*837	IX, 123		892	IX, 178	
*838	IX, 124		893	IX, 179	
*839	IX, 125		894	IX, 180	
*840	IX, 126		895	IX, 181	
*841	IX, 127		896	IX, 182	
*842	IX, 128		897	IX, 183	
843	IX, 129		898	IX, 184	
*844	IX, 130		899	IX, 185	
*845	IX, 131		900	IX, 186	
*846	IX, 132		*901	IX, 187	
847	IX, 133		902	IX, 188	
*848	IX, 134		903	IX, 189	
*849	IX, 135		904	IX, 190	
*850	IX, 136		905	IX, 191	
851	IX, 137		*906	IX, 192	
852	IX, 138		907	IX, 193	
*853	IX, 139		*908	IX, 194	
*854	IX, 140. XVII, 37		909	IX, 195	
*855	IX, 141. XVII, 38		910	IX, 196	
*856	IX, 142. XVII, 39		911	IX, 197	
*857	IX, 143		912	IX, 198	
*858	IX, 144		913	IX, 199	

914	IX, 200	*968	X, 4
915	IX, 201	*969	X, 5
916	IX, 202	*970	X, 6
917	IX, 203	*971	X, 7
918	IX, 204	*972	X, 8
919	IX, 205	*973	X, 9
920	IX, 206	*974	X, 10
921	IX, 207	*975	XI, 1
*922	IX, 208	*976	XI, 2
923	IX, 209	*977	XI, 3
924	IX, 210	*978	XI, 4
925	IX, 211	*979	XI, 5
926	IX, 212	*980	XII, 1
*927	IX, 213	*981	XII, 2
*928	IX, 214	*982	XII, 3
*929	IX, 215	*983	XII, 4
*930	IX, 216	*984	XII, 5
*931	IX, 217	*985	XII, 6
*932	IX, 218	*986	XII, 7
933	IX, 219	*987	XII, 8
934	IX, 220	988	XIII, 2. XIV, 2. XV, 18
935	IX, 221	989	XIII, 5. XIV, 10. XV, 13
936	IX, 222	990	XIII, 8. XIV, 5. XV, 15
*937	IX, 223	991	XIII, 9. XIV, 8. XV, 8
938	IX, 224	992	XIII, 10. XIV, 11. XV, 7
939	IX, 225	993	Vacant
940	IX, 226	994	XIII, 12. XIV, 14. XV, 17
941	IX, 227	995	XIII, 14. XIV, 18. XV, 27
942	IX, 228	*996	XIII, 15. XIV, 19. XV, 26.
943	IX, 229		XVI, 37
944	IX, 230	997	XIII, 20. XIV, 21. XV, 30
945	IX, 231	998	XIII, 27. XIV, 45. XVI, 54
946	IX, 232	999	XIII, 30. XIV, 49. XVI, 55
947	IX, 233	1000	XIII, 31. XIV, 48. XVI, 53
948	IX, 234	1001	XIII, 36. XIV, 53
949	IX, 235	1002	XIII, 38. XIV, 55. XV, 49
950	IX, 236	1003	XIII, 46
951	IX, 237	1004	XIII, 48. XIV, 61
952	IX, 238	1005	XIII, 50. XIV, 66. XVI, 62
953	IX, 239	1006	XIII, 54. XIV, 81. XVI, 69
954	IX, 240	*1007	XIII, 55. XIV, 80. XVI, 70
*955	IX, 241	1008	XIII, 57. XIV, 84
956	IX, 242	1009	XIII, 59. XIV, 82
957	IX, 243	*1010	XIII, 63. XIV, 103. XXI, 176
*958	IX, 244	1011	XIII, 72. XIV, 115. XV, 89
959	IX, 245	1012	XIII, 77. XV, 97. Cf. **65**
960	IX, 246	*1013	XIII, 80. XV, 106. XVI, 109.
961	IX, 247		XVII, 90
962	IX, 248	1014	XIII, 83. XIV, 121. XV, 114
*963	IX, 249	*1015	XIII, 90. XIV, 125a. XV, 118
*964	IX, 250	*1016	XIII, 91. XIV, 136
*964a	IX, 251	1017	XIII, 92
*965	X, 1	1018	XIII, 93. XIV, 137
*966	X, 2	1019	XIII, 95. XIV, 143
*967	X, 3	1020	XIII, 96. XIV, 139

1021 XIII, 101. XIV, 144
1022 XIII, 110. XV, 130. Cf. **127**
1023 XIII, 117. XIV, 158. XV, 143. XVI, 126
1024 XIII, 118. XIV, 178. XXI, 174
*1025 XIII, 120. XIV, 177. XXI, 181. XVI, 153c
1026 XIII, 124. XIV, 6. XV, 5
1027 XIII, 125. XIV, 13
*1028 XIII, 126. XIV, 62
1029 XIII, 127. XIV, 65. XV, 72. Cf. **1141a, b**
*1030 XIII, 128. XIV, 72. XV, 71. Cf. **1141a, b**
1031 XIII, 129. XIV, 75
*1032 XIII, 130. XIV, 88
1033 XIII, 131. XIV, 90. XV, 75
1034 XIII, 132. XIV, 91. XV, 76
1035 XIII, 133. XIV, 92. XV, 77
1036 XIII, 134. XV, 82
*1037 XIII, 135. XIV, 111. XV, 110
1038 XIII, 136. XIV, 125b. XV, 102
1039 XIII, 137. XV, 107
1040 XIII, 138. XV, 103
1041 XIII, 139. XV, 100
*1042 XIII, 140. XIV, 110. XV, 101. XVI, 65
*1043 XIII, 141. XIV, 118. XV, 108. XVI, 123c.
1043a XIII, 33a. XIV, 42
1044 XIII, 97. Cf. **1059**
1045 XIII, 99
1046 XIII, 100. XIV, 126. XVI, 126
1047 XIII, 123. XV, 6
1048 XIV, 26. XV, 36. XVI, 42
1049 XIV, 27
1050 XIV, 29
1051 XIV, 31
1052 Vacant
1053 XIV, 63
1054 XIV, 96
1055 XIV, 102. XV, 88
1056 XIV, 104. XV, 86
*1057 XIV, 117. XV, 117
1058 XIV, 127
1059 XIV, 128. Cf. **1044**
1060 XIV, 129. Cf. after XIII, 90
1061 XIV, 132
1062 XIV, 159. XV, 145. XVI, 123b
1063 XIV, 160. XV, 146
1064 XIV, 163. XV, 149. XVI, 123i
1065 XIV, 167. XXI, 194
1066 XIV, 168. XXI, 173

*1067 XIV, 171
1068 XIV, 172. XXI, 178. XVI, 151. XVII, 123
1069 XIV, 174. XXI, 169. XVI, 148. XVII, 122. Cf. **588**
1070 XIV, 175. XXI, 167
1071 XIV, 78
1072 XIV, 169. XXI, 165
1073 XIV, 170. XXI, 166
*1074 XIV, 179. XXI, 175. XVI, 153e
*1075 XIV, 180. XXI, 180. XVI, 128
*1076 XIV, 181. XXI, 188. XVI, 153f
1077 XV, 10
1078 XV, 31. Cf. **52**
1079 XV, 32
1080 XV, 34
1081 Vacant
1082 XV, 39
1083 XV, 41
*1084 XV, 48. XVI, 67
1085 XV, 50. XVI, 25
*1086 XV, 52. XVI, 66
*1087 XV, 53. XVI, 68
1088 XV, 70
1089 XV, 81
1090 XV, 84
1091 XV, 87. Cf. **87**
1092 XV, 123
1093 XV, 128
1094 XV, 150
1095 XV, 151
1096 XV, 95
*1097 XV, 167. XVI, 93c. XVII, 78
*1098 XV, 168. XVI, 93d. XVII, 79
1099 XV, 169
1100 XV, 170
1101 XV, 171
1102 XV, 172
*1103 XV, 173. XVII, 96
*1104 XV, 174. XVI, 56
*1104a XV, 175. XVI, 57
*1105 XV, 176. XVI, 58
1105a XV, 177
1106 XV, 178
*1107 XV, 179. XVI, 4. XVII, 3
*1108 XV, 180. XVI, 5. XVII, 4
*1109 XV, 181. XVI, 6. XVII, 5
*1110 XV, 182. XVI, 7. XVII, 6
*1111 XV, 183. XVI, 8. XVII, 7
*1112 XV, 184. XVI, 9. XVII, 8
1113 XV, 187
1114 XV, 188
1115 XV, 189
1116 XV, 190

1117 XV, 191
1118 XV, 192
*1119 XV, 194. XVI, 61. XVII, 48
*1120 XV, 195. XVI, 61a. XVII, 49
*1121 XV, 196. XVI, 61b. XVII, 50
*1122 XV, 197. XVI, 61c. XVII, 51
*1123 XV, 198. XVI, 61d. XVII, 52
*1124 XV, 199. XVI, 61e. XVII, 53
*1125 XV, 200. XVI, 61f. XVII, 54
*1126 XVI, 3. XVII, 10
*1127 XVI, 12. XVII, 15
*1128 XVI, 13. XVII, 16
*1129 XVI, 14. XVII, 17
*1130 XVI, 15
*1131 XVI, 16
*1132 XVI, 17
*1133 XVI, 19
*1134 XVI, 20. XVII, 23
*1135 XVI, 21. XVII, 26
*1136 XVI, 22. XVII, 24
*1137 XVI, 23. XVII, 13
*1138 XVI, 24. XVII, 14
*1138a XVI, 24a. XVII, 27
*1138b XVI, 24b. XVII, 28
*1138c XVI, 24c.
*1138d XVI, 24d
*1138e XVI, 24e
*1138f XVI, 24f
*1138g XVI, 24g. XVII, 18
*1138h XVI, 24h. XVII, 19
*1138i XVI, 24i. XVII, 20
*1138j XVI, 24j. XVII, 21
1139 XVI, 35
1140 XVI, 41
1141 XVI, 47
1141a XVI, 61g
1141b XVI, 61h
1141c XVI, 61j
1141d XVI, 61l
1142 XVI, 71. XVII, 63
*1143 XVI, 72. XVII, 68
*1144 XVI, 73. XVII, 62
*1145 XVI, 74
*1146 XVI, 75. XVII, 58
*1147 XVI, 76. XVII, 59
*1148 XVI, 77. XVII, 60
1149 XVI, 85
*1149a XVI, 93e
*1149b XVI, 93f. XVII, 77
*1150 XVI, 94
*1151 XVI, 95
*1152 XVI, 96
*1153 XVI, 97
*1154 XVI, 98
*1155 XVI, 99

*1156 XVI, 100. XVII, 83
*1157 XVI, 101. XVII, 82
*1158 XVI, 102, 114. XVII, 84
*1159 XVI, 103. XVII, 85
*1160 XVI, 104. XVII, 88
*1161 XVI, 105. XVII, 87
*1162 XVI, 106, 115. XVII, 86
*1163 XVI, 108, 115a. XVII, 105
*1164 XVI, 113, 116. XVII, 97
*1165 XVI, 117. XVII, 98
*1166 XVI, 118. XVII, 101
*1167 XVI, 119. XVII, 100
1168 XVI, 120. XVII, 106
1169 XVI, 121. XVII, 107
*1170 XVI, 122. XVII, 103
*1170a XVI, 123a. XVII, 108
1170b XVI, 123d
*1170c XVI, 123f
*1170d XVI, 123g
*1171 XVI, 130. XVII, 113
1172 XVI, 131. XVII, 114
1173 XVI, 132. XVII, 115
*1174 XVI, 133. XVII, 116
*1175 XVI, 134. XVII, 117
*1176 XVI, 135. XVII, 118
*1177 XVI, 136. XVII, 120
1178 Vacant
1179 XVI, 149
1180 XVI, 150
*1180a XVI, 153a. XVII, 125
1181 XVI, 10
1182 XVI, 26
*1183 XVI, 27
*1184 XVI, 29
*1185 XVI, 30
*1186 XVI, 31
*1187 XVI, 32
*1188 XVI, 33. XVII, 22
*1189 XVI, 34
*1190 XVI, 78. XVII, 64
*1191 XVI, 79. XVII, 65
*1192 XVI, 80. XVII, 66
*1193 XVI, 81. XVII, 67
*1194 XVI, 88. XVII, 69
*1195 XVI, 89. XVII, 61
*1196 XVI, 107
*1197 XVI, 123
*1198 XVI, 137. XVII, 119
*1199 XVI, 138. XVII, 111
*1200 XVI, 139. XVII, 112
1201 XVI, 140. XVII, 121
*1202 XVI, 141. XVII, 129
*1203 XVI, 142. XVII, 130
*1204 XVI, 143. XVII, 131
*1205 XVI, 153. XVII, 128

1206 Vacant
1207 Vacant
1208 Vacant
1209 Vacant
1210 Vacant
1211 Vacant
1212 Vacant
1213 Vacant
*1214 XVII, 29
*1215 XVII, 30
*1216 XVII, 31
*1217 XVII, 32
*1218 XVII, 33
1219 XVII, 40
1220 XVII, 45
1221 XVII, 46
1222 XVII, 47
1223 Vacant
1224 XVII, 57
1225 XVII, 70
1226 XVII, 75
*1227 XVII, 76
1228 Vacant
*1229 XVII, 80
*1230 XVII, 81
1231 XVII, 89
1232 XVII, 99
*1233 XVII, 102
1234 Vacant
*1235 XVII, 104
1236 Vacant
*1237 XVII, 109
*1238 XVII, 110
1239 Vacant
1240 Vacant
1241 XVIII, 3. XIX, 5. XX, 7. XXI, 45
1242 XVIII, 9. XIX, 4. XX, 6
1243 XVIII, 10. XIX, 21. XX, 25. XXI, 53
1244 XVIII, 20. XIX, 27. XX, 23. XXI, 61. XXII, 85
1245 XVIII, 24. Cf. **1259**
1246 XVIII, 28
1247 XVIII, 34. XX, 64. XXI, 50. XXII, 110
1248 XVIII, 36
1249 XVIII, 38
1250 XVIII, 52. XX, 93. XXI, 146.
*1251 XVIII, 60. XX, 95. XXI, 143. XXII, 14. XXIII, 14. Cf. **252**
1252 XVIII, 65. XIX, 72. XXI, 113
1253 XVIII, 66. Cf. 270
1254 XVIII, 80. XIX, 83. XX, 119. XXI, 128

1255 XVIII, 58. XX, 83. XXI, 137. XXII, 62
1256 XVIII, 59. XIX, 63. XX, 89. XXI, 139
1257 XVIII, 69. XIX, 77. XX, 107. XXI, 141
1258 XVIII, 72
1259 XIX, 30. XX, 61. Cf. **1245**
1260 XIX, 82. XX, 118. XXI, 140
1261 XIX, 87
1262 XIX, 89. XX, 130. XV, 137. XVI, 86
1263 XIX, 90. XX, 148. XV, 158. XVI, 84. XVII, 71
1264 XIX, 94. XV, 139. XVI, 90
1265 XIX, 97. XX, 134. XV, 157
*1266 XIX, 100. XX, 133. XV, 156
*1267 XIX, 106. XX, 1. XXI, 88
1268 XIX, 107. XX, 11. XXI, 9
1269 XIX, 108. XX, 2. XXI, 15
1270 XIX, 109. XX, 12. XXI, 51. XXII, 70. XXIII, 105
1271 XIX, 110. XX, 15. XXI, 38. XXII, 71. XXIII, 88
*1272 XIX, 111. XX, 26. XXIII, 92
*1273 XIX, 112. XX, 27. XXI, 56. XXII, 131. XXIII, 93
1274 XIX, 113. XX, 38. XXI, 70
1275 XIX, 114. XX, 49. XXI, 36
1276 XIX, 115. XX, 50. XXI, 60
*1277 XIX, 116. XX, 37. XXI, 75
1278 Vacant
1279 XIX, 117
1280 XIX, 118
1281 XIX, 119. XXI, 22
1282 XIX, 120. XX, 65. XXI, 23
1283 XIX, 121. XX, 75. XXII, 105a
1284 XIX, 122. XX, 94. XXII, 38
1285 XIX, 123. XX, 82. XXII, 39
1286 XIX, 124. XX, 78, 97. XXI, 147
1287 XIX, 125. XX, 86
1288 XIX, 126. XX, 90
*1289 XIX, 127. XX, 92
*1290 XIX, 128. XX, 96. XXI, 21. XXII, 99. XXIII, 107
1291 XIX, 129. XX, 153. XXI, 191
1292 XIX, 130. XX, 154. XXI, 197
1293 XIX, 131. XX, 155. XXI, 198
*1294 XIX, 132. XX, 156. XXI, 168. XVI, 152
1295 XIX, 133. XX, 151. XXI, 179. XVI, 146

1296 XIX, 134. XX, 152. XXI, 196.
     XVI, 93g
1297 XIX, 135. XX, 162. XXI, 171
1298 XIX, 136. XX, 161. XXI, 183
1299 XIX, 137. XX, 160. XXI, 186
1300 XIX, 138. XX, 159. XXI, 195
1301 XIX, 139. XX, 158. XXI, 184
1302 XIX, 140
1303 XIX, 141. XX, 163. XXI, 185.
     XVI, 129
1304 XIX, 142. XX, 157. XXI, 182
1305 XX, 43
1306 XX, 46. XXI, 80. XXII, 106
1307 XX, 47. XXI, 79. XXII, 107
1308 Vacant
1309 XX, 77
1310 XX, 98. XXI, 105
1311 XX, 99
1312 XX, 100
1313 XX, 101. XXI, 118
1314 XX, 102. XXI, 106
1315 XX, 105. XXI, 160
1316 XX, 108. XXII, 59. XXIII,
     57
1317 XX, 109
1318 XX, 110. XXI, 120 ⎫
*1319 XX, 111. XXI, 119 ⎬ cf. **1414**
*1320 XX, 112. XXI, 131 ⎭ **a–b**
*1321 XX, 113. XXI, 116. XXII, 44
*1322 XX, 114. XXI, 117. XXII, 45
*1323 XX, 115. XXI, 163. XXII, 113
*1324 XX, 120. XXI, 100. XXII,
     129. XXIII, 95
1325 XX, 121. XXI, 102
*1326 XX, 124. XXI, 99. XXII, 128,
     XXIII, 94
1327 XX, 126. XXI, 158
*1328 XX, 164. XXI, 172. XVI, 145
1329 XXI, 6. XXII, 123
1329a XXI, 13, 83
1330 XXI, 14. XXII, 124
1331 XXI, 26
*1332 XXI, 27
*1333 XXI, 28
*1334 XXI, 29
1335 XXI, 30
1336 XXI, 31
1337 XXI, 32
1338 XXI, 33
1339 XXI, 34
1340 XXI, 35
1341 XXI, 55. XXII, 132
1342 Vacant
1343 Vacant
1344 XXI, 97

1345 XXI, 98
1346 XXI, 107
1347 XXI, 108
1348 XXI, 109
1349 XXI, 121
1350 XXI, 122
1351 XXI, 124
1352 XXI, 125
1353 XXI, 126
1354 XXI, 127
1355 XXI, 129
1356 XXI, 130
*1357 XXI, 156. XXII, 117. XXIII,
     89
1358 XXI, 164
*1359 XXI, 170. XVI, 123h. XVII,
     124
1360 XXI, 189. XVI, 153d
1361 XXI, 1
1362 XXI, 2
1363 XXI, 3
1364 XXI, 4
1365 XXI, 5
1366 XXI, 12
1367 XXI, 27a. XXII, 52
1367a XXI, 28a. XXII, 53
1368 XXI, 39, 47
1369 XXI, 69
1370 XXI, 72. XXII, 105c
1371 XXI, 77. XXIII, 99
1372 XXI, 24, 87
1372a XXI, 94
1372b XXI, 95
1372c XXI, 96
1373 XXI, 110
1374 XXI, 111
1375 XXI, 112
*1376 XXI, 135. XXII, 37, 54a.
     XXIII, 55
*1377 XXI, 136. XXII, 36, 54.
     XXIII, 54
1378 XXI, 150. XXII, 134
1379 XXI, 177. XVI, 147. XVII, 126
1380 XXII, 1. XXIII, 2
1381 XXII, 2. XXIII, 3
1382 XXII, 3. XXIII, 4
1383 XXII, 4. XXIII, 5
1384 XXII, 5. XXIII, 6
1385 XXII, 6. XXIII, 7
1386 XXII, 7. XXIII, 9
1387 XXII, 8. XXIII, 10
1388 XXII, 9. XXIII, 11
1389 XXII, 10. XXIII, 12
1390 XXII, 11. XXIII, 13
*1391 XXII, 12. XXIII, 8

1392 XXII, 13. XXIII, 1
*1393 XXII, 18. XXIII, 26
*1394 XXII, 19. XXIII, 25
*1395 XXII, 20. XXIII, 24
*1396 XXII, 21. XXIII, 23
*1397 XXII, 22. XXIII, 18
*1398 XXII, 23. XXIII, 20
*1399 XXII, 24. XXIII, 21
*1400 XXII, 25. XXIII, 22
*1400a XXII, 25a
*1400b XXII, 25b
*1400c XXII, 25c
*1400d XXII, 25d
*1400e XXII, 25e
*1400f XXII, 25f
*1400g XXII, 25g
*1400h XXII, 25h
*1400i XXII, 25i
1401 XXII, 26. XXIII, 27
1402 XXII, 27. XXIII, 30
*1403 XXII, 28. XXIII, 36
1404 XXII, 29. XXIII, 31
1405 XXII, 30. XXIII, 29
*1406 XXII, 31. XXIII, 28
*1407 XXII, 32. XXIII, 32
*1408 XXII, 33. XXIII, 33
*1409 XXII, 34. XXIII, 34
1410 XXII, 40
1411 XXII, 41
1412 XXII, 42
*1413 XXII, 43
*1414 XXII, 46
1414a XXII, 46a ⎫
1414b XXII, 46b ⎬ cf. 1318–20
1414c XXII, 46c ⎭
*1414d XXII, 46d
1414e XXII, 46e
*1415 XXII, 47
*1416 XXII, 48. XXIII, 47
*1417 XXII, 49. XXIII, 48
*1418 XXII, 50. XXIII, 49
1419 XXII, 58
1420 XXII, 64
*1421 XXII, 65
*1422 XXII, 66
1422a XXII, 69a
1422b XXII, 69b
1422c XXII, 69c
1422d XXII, 69d
1422e XXII, 69e
1422f XXII, 69f
1422g XXII, 69g
1423 XXII, 76
1424 XXII, 94
1425 XXII, 102

1425a XXII, 105b
*1425b XXII, 105e
1425c XXII, 105f. Cf. 1459
1426 XXII, 111
1427 XXII, 118
1428 XXII, 126
*1429 XXII, 130. XXIII, 91
1430 XXII, 133
1431 XXII, 135
*1431a XXII, 137
1431b XXII, 137a
1431c XXII, 137b
1431d XXII, 137c
1431e XXII, 137d
*1431f XXII, 137e
*1432 XXII, 35
*1433 XXII, 51
*1434 XXII, 55. XXII, 53
*1435 XXII, 61. XXIII, 52
*1436 XXII, 63
1437 XXII, 77
1438 XXII, 78
*1439 XXII, 79, 81. XXII, 87
1440 XXII, 80
1441 XXII, 84
*1442 XXII, 87. XXIII, 70
*1443 XXII, 88. XXIII, 71
*1444 XXII, 91. XXIII, 56
*1445 XXII, 96
*1446 XXII, 98
1447 XXII, 101
*1448 XXII, 103
*1449 XXII, 108
1450 XXII, 112
*1451 XXII, 114
*1452 XXII, 115
*1453 XXII, 116
1454 XXII, 121
*1455 XXII, 122. XXIII, 97
*1456 XXIII, 19
1457 Vacant
*1458 XXIII, 74
*1459 XXIII, 76
1460 XXIII, 77
*1461 XXIII, 78
1462 XXIII, 82
*1463 XXIII, 83
*1464 XXIII, 85
*1465 XXIII, 101
*1466 XXIII, 102
1467 Vacant
1468 XXIV, 1
*1469 XXIV, 5
*1470 XXIV, 6
1471 XXIV, 7

1472	XXIV, 8		1508	XXIV, 49
*1473	XXIV, 9		1509	XXIV, 50
1474	XXIV, 10		1510	XXIV, 51
*1475	XXIV, 11		1511	XXIV, 54
*1476	XXIV, 12		1512	XXIV, 55
*1477	XXIV, 13		1513	XXIV, 56
1478	XXIV, 14		1514	XXIV, 57
*1479	XXIV, 15		1515	XXIV, 58
*1480	XXIV, 16		1516	XXIV, 59
1481	XXIV, 17		1517	XXIV, 60
1482	XXIV, 18		1518	XXIV, 61
1483	XXIV, 19		1519	XXIV, 62
1484	XXIV, 21. Cf. **476**		1520	XXIV, 63
*1485	XXIV, 22		1521	XXIV, 65
1486	XXIV, 23		1522	XXIV, 66
1487	XXIV, 24		1523	XXIV, 67
1488	XXIV, 25		1524	XXIV, 70
1489	XXIV, 26		1525	XXIV, 71
1490	XXIV, 27		1526	XXIV, 74
*1491	XXIV, 28		1527	XXIV, 75
1492	XXIV, 29		1528	XXIV, 76
1493	XXIV, 30		1529	XXIV, 78
1494	XXIV, 31		1530	XXIV, 79
1495	XXIV, 32		1531	XXIV, 80
*1496	XXIV, 33		*1532	XXIV, 81
1497	XXIV, 34		1533	XXIV, 82
*1498	XXIV, 35		1534	XXIV, 84
1499	XXIV, 36		1535	XXIV, 85
1500	XXIV, 37		1536	XXIV, 86
1501	XXIV, 38		1537	XXIV, 89
1502	XXIV, 39		1538	XXIV, 90
1503	XXIV, 44		1539	XXIV, 92
1504	XXIV, 45		1540	XXIV, 93
1505	XXIV, 46		1541	XXIV, 98
1506	XXIV, 47		1542	XXIV, 99
1507	XXIV, 48		1543	XXIV, 100

INDEX OF AUTHORS

In Lists I–XXIV authors are referred to by both Christian name and surname, by surname only—so, mainly, for sixteenth-century authors and English authors of any date—and by Christian name only: for example Antonius de Butrio super primo Decretalium, Burley super libros Ethicorum, Angelus in tribus voluminibus. Some books are given titles only, for example Horologium sapientiae. To avoid too many cross-references I have kept the index entries as near to the list entries as possible, placing Antonius de Butrio under A, (Walterus de) Burley under B, Angelus (de Ubaldis) under A and Horologium sapientiae (Henrici Susonis) under H. Cross-references are used only for personal nicknames, for example Lincolniensis, *see* Robertus Grosseteste, and for a few book-titles, for example Liber aurorae, *see* Petrus Riga. Inverted commas show my ignorance of what an entry means: thus, 'Lima vitiorum', 'Boleus super Inst''. Vague titles like Meditacio scripturarum and Liber spissus have not been indexed. Inadequate titles are left as they are, for example Gesta passionis Christi. All Souls College MS. 20, in which this is the first of three items listed in Coxe's catalogue, is a good example of what is sufficiently obvious, that the lists here printed are no guide to the contents of miscellanies.

References are to numbers, unless 'page' is specified.

* shows that the book in question is still in existence and *ipso facto* identified in the Notes on pp. 128–57.

Abbas, *see* Nicholaus de Tudeschis.
Abraham Avenesre, 133.
Aegidius (Corboliensis), *585.
Aegidius (Romanus), 1044.
  De anima, 577.
  De caelo et mundo, 171.
  De regimine principum, *1013.
  Super primum librum Sententiarum Petri Lombardi, 478.
Aetius (Amidenus), 1142.
Alacen, 379, 409.
Albericus (de Rosate), *1400e–i.
Albertus (Brunus), p. *110.
Albertus (Geleottus: Savigny, v. 527), 371.
Albertus (Magnus), 123, 1021; p. 113.
  De animalibus, 189; p. *105.
  De origine animae, 576.
Alchemia, 407.
(Andreas) Alciatus, 779, 1392.
Alexander de Ancilla, 269, 444.
Alexander Aphrodisaeus, *1153 (in Greek), *1165 (in Greek).
Alexander de Hales:
  Expositio librorum de anima Aristotelis, p. *105.
  Summa theologica, 1038–41.
Alexander (Tartagni) de Imola.
  Consilia, 728–9, *1400a.
  In Digestum, *1400b–d.
Algerus (Cluniacensis), *908.
Algorismus, 130, 1093.
(Robertus) Alington, 179.
Almansor, 141; p. 105; cf. Rasis.
Alphonsus de Castro, 797.

Ambrosius:
  Opera, *1138a, b.
  De officiis, 1496.
  Epistolae, *637.
Anathomia, *535; p. 106.
Angelus (de Gambilionibus):
  In Instituta, 785, 1327, *1431a.
  De maleficiis, *1432.
Angelus (de Ubaldis de Perusio), *1407–9.
Anima fidelis, 888.
Anselmus:
  Opera quaedam, 18, 649, 703, *859, 1141c.
  Monologion, 18.
Antididagma capituli ecclesiae Coloniensis, *873, 874.
Antoninus (archiepiscopus Florentiae), Summa theologiae, *613–14–15–*16 (4 parts), 617–*18–19 (3 parts), 1220–2 (3 parts), *1104–*4a–*5–5a (4 parts).
Antonius de Butrio, In Decretales, 219 (bk. 2), 458 (bk. 4), 552, 593 (bk. 2), 597 (bk. 4), 605–6 (bk. 1), 607 (bk. 3), 608 (bk. 5), 1423 (bk. 5); p. 114 (bk. 4), p. 115 (6 vols.).
Antonius Musa, *1143.
Antonius (de Prato Veteri), *1289.
Antonius (de Rampegollis), 37 (?), *672, 702.
Appianus (Alexandrinus) interprete Petro Candido, *1075, *1199.
Apuleius, 1070.
Aquinas, *see* Thomas de Aquino.
Archidiaconus, *see* Guido de Baysio.
Aretius Felinus (i.e. Martinus Bucer), *677.

GENERAL INDEX

Books in Lists I–XXVIII (*cont.*):
A. Before they came to All Souls College
(*cont.*):
Owned by other than donors to All
Souls[1]:
Aluredus, mag., no. 182.
Apharrius, J., nos. 753, 802–3.
Barlow, A., no. 864.
Brade, P., no. 873 or 874.
Buildwas, Cistercian abbey, no.
1077.
Bulkeley, J., no. 853.
Burton-on-Trent, Benedictine
abbey, no. 932.
Bury St. Edmunds, Benedictine
abbey, no. 1251.
Bynde, S. (so long as in college),
p. 160.
Byrd, T., nos. 761, 844–5.
†Byrkhed, J. (for life), p. 160.
Chersey, mag., no. 840.
Cirencester, Augustinian abbey,
no. 182.
Corren, R., no. 824.
Cox, J. (for life), p. 126.
Edys, W., nos. 810, (811), 846,
866, 881, 883, 906, 932, 964.
Elcocke, R., no. 790.
Elkin, J., no. 857.
Fodyngton, J., no. 142.
†Gaunt, R. (for life), p. 160.
Glyn, no. 901.
Holy[. . . .], P., no. 706.
†Lacy, E., no. 12 (?).
†Lloyd, O. (for life), pp. 106, 161.
Middilton, J. de, no. 537.
†Mottisfont, J., no. 208.
Nithingall, mag., p. 164.
Northew, S., no. 308.
Pole, Margaret, no. 841.
Pole, R., no. 715.
Powell, T., no. 840.
†Racour, J., p. 163.
Ramrige, J., nos. 821, 927.
Rochester, Benedictine abbey,
monk of, no. 840.
Rogers, J., no. 841.
†Romsey, W., p. 165.
†Salter, R., no. 1323.
Sorton, R., nos. 831–2.
'Stanleia' (Cistercian abbey of
Stanley, Wiltshire, or Stone-
leigh, Warwickshire), no. 35.
†Stoke, E., no. 142.
Tennand, no. 1198.
†Wells, T., no. 635.
†Wilton, W., nos. 844–5.
Winchester, Benedictine abbey,
monk of, no. 840.

Wright, W., p. 164.
Pledged in loan chests, nos. 140, 266,
537, 1016; cf. p. 161.
Written by: Albertus 'nacione Bra-
bancie', no. 124; J. Alexander,
p. 159; J. Elveden, no. 1277;
S. Sandyr, no. 1015.
B. At the time or after they came to All
Souls College:
Alienated and subsequently owned
by: J. Fairhurst, no. 538; T.
Hearne, no. 860; Messrs.
Maggs, p. 159; N. Luttrell,
no. 535; J. Mower, no. 1149a;
O. Polwheele, no. 535; T.
Powell, no. 860; J. West, no.
860; J. Woolton, no. 145; L.
Wynne, no. 535; *see also*
pp. 176–7, 180, for present
owners, other than All Souls
College.
Bought, pp. 22, 55, 103 (3 entries);
see also Books, Payments for
buying.
Bound or rebound, pp. 171–2.
in s. xv², p. 171; no. 182.
in s. xv/xvi, p. 171, footnote 1.
in s. xvi¹ (?), no. 1057 'resarcitus
per Gressup'.
in the 1540s by Gerbrand Herks's
binder, nos. 1135–6, 1138c–j,
1144–5, 1147–8, 1149a, 1150–
5, 1165–7, 1398–1400, 1400c,
1407, 1409; pp. 165, 167,
172.
in s. xvi² by Dominick Pinart,
p. 171, footnote 3; *see also*
Books, Payments for binding.
s. xvi² by R. Garbrand's binder,
p. 172.
in 1591/2 by Thomas Middleton,
p. 171 (cf. pp. 119, 158).
in 1614/15 by Dominick Pinart,
nos. 1007, 1473, 1475, 1485,
1491; pp. 161–2, 172.
in s. xvii in., no. 1406.
in s. xviii (?), p. 172.
in s. xix, pp. 1228–65 *passim*.
in 1929 by Maltby, p. 130.
Broken up and used in binding, nos.
43, 74, 128; p. 165.
Chained, pp. viii, 105, 173–4; *see also*
Books, Payments for chaining.
Chaining asked for in wills or inscriptions, nos. 59, 245, 594, 1016,
1042; pp. 123 (Goldwyn), 126
(Cockys), 160 (Betts, Bisshope), 162 (Goldwell: cathenetur in choro).

---

[1] Names marked with a dagger are of persons listed by Emden, *BRUO*.

ADDENDA

pp. xi, xiii, xiv. There are now fifty-five leaves in the Vellum Inventory. The two new leaves have been given the numbers 55 and 56 (54 is a blank leaf of modern paper). They were found by Mr. Malcolm Underwood in December 1970 tucked inside a seventeenth-century volume of Abstracta Chartarum, one of the muniments of All Souls College now deposited in the Bodleian Library (MS. DD All Souls b. 129). They are a bifolium containing three further items in continuation of my list on p. xiii: 40. ff. 55–6. A list of books 'in theologia', s. xv; 41. f. 56ᵛ. A list of books given by John Norfolk; 42. f. 56ᵛ. A list of books given by Thomas Wyche. No. 40, additions apart, and no. 41 belong to my chronological group (*a*). No. 42 belongs to my group (*b*). No. 40 is the companion list to no. 5 (List XVIII) and is written in the same hand: I have called it List XIIA. Nos. 41 and 42 are the source of the Norfolk and Wyche lists in Ben. Reg. referred to in footnote 3 on p. xiv.[1]

p. 18. The list of John Norfolk's gift in the Vellum Inventory, f. 56ᵛ, gives ten more book titles than Ben. Reg. and records secundo folios which allow us to identify two, but, I think, only two, of Norfolk's books in later lists: cf. the footnotes to **476** and **493c.**

Tempore M' Iohannis Stokes Custodis quinti etc.[2]

libri subscripti ex dono Magistri Iohannis Northfolke primi vicecustodis.

472	1	Thomas de aquilino super tercium sentenciarum 2 fo quia materia se habet in ordine
473	2	Landulphus super primum et iiiiᵗᵘᵐ sentenciarum 2 fo tamen hoc intelligitur
474	3	Pastoralis beati gregorii pape 2 fo Ne aut humilitas
476	4	Doctor subtilis super iiiiᵗᵘᵐ sentenciarum 2 fo probacio maioris[3]
477	5	Cowton super quatuor libros sentenciarum 2 fo subiectum componens
478	6	Scriptum Egidii sui super primum sentenciarum 2 fo esset subiectum in sciencia
479	7	Augustinus de verbis domini et apostoli 2 fo perhibet. Respexit

[1] Probably Harlow's gift followed Wyche's on the now missing part of f. 55ᵛ.

[2] The added heading and the list of Wyche's gifts are in the same handsome hand as ff. 20–2 of the Vellum Inventory (above, p. xii).

[3] Cf. **1484.**

480	8	Quodlibeta doctoris henrici de gandauo a 7º libro vsque ad vltimum 2 fo hoc quod sicut numerus
481	9	Questiones super tres libros metheororum secundum M' Ioh' dons 2 fo prouocacionem (?) sciencia est
482	10	Questiones super librum de animalibus 2 fo eo quod quid dicitur anologice
483	11	Magister sentenciarum 2 fo vtrisque ea
483a	12	Scriptum fratris Roberti Cowton super primum sentenciarum 2 fo persone corumpitur (?) racione
484	13	Apparatus super Raymundum 2 fo gi discipulos qui cum
484a	14	Summa Magistri Henrici de Gandauo cum aliis libris in illo vollumine contentis 2 fo in infinitate essemus
485	15	Postillator super Genesim Exodum et Leuiticum 2 fo libus virtutibus
485a	16	Flores super libris de trinitate de doctrina et de c' 2 fo quinta veritas quod
486	17	Holkot super libris xii prophetarum 2 fo vnde in ap' l. 7 c 24
487	18	Tractatus sancti Thome de Aquilino de potestate papali 2 fo Interdum contingit
488	19	Rethorica M T de Capua Cardinalis 2 fo adiuncto describuntur illud
489	20	Omelie beati Iohannis Crisostomi 2 fo quiescat ira fratris tui
490	21	Questiones scoti super methaphisicam 2 fo habere effectus [. . .[1]
490a	22	Sanctum (*sic*) Thomas expositiue super 3 libros de anima 2 fo primo querimus
491	23	Franciscus de virtutibus moralibus 2 fo agibilia
492	24	Sermones per annum 2 fo [. .]m m[. . .
492a	25	Item alium librum 2 fo particularum corporis
493	26	Questiones theologice 2 fo queritur vt[rum]
493a	27	Tabula scripta secundum ordinem alphabeti 2 fo Mᵗ xxº
493b	28	Librum de concordia theologie et astronomie 2 fo alia occurrunt
493c	29	Communis glosa super Matheum 2 fo non negaret[2]
494	30	Librum Medicine 2 fo t[. .]ri
494a	31	Diuerse questiones in papiro 2 fo quia quando
495	32	Liber logicalis cum multis aliis contentis 2 fo vniuersales [. . .
475	33	Doctor subtilis super primum sentenciarum 2 fo [*blank?*]
	34	Item tria instrumenta (?) scilicet astrolab' triangulum et vnum (?) nauem (?)
496	35	Item burleum super libros ethicorum expositiue
496a	36	Item dedicus super li Ethicorum 2 fo [. . . .] vltimus qui quidem liber est in custodia [.] Ioh' hawkyns et cum eodem permanebit quamdiu moratur Collegio per voluntatem M' Northfolke donatoris eiusdem.[3]

[1] The first hand ends here.   [2] Cf. **1482**.
[3] Hawkins vacated his fellowship in 1484 (*BRUO*).

p. 20. List IVA from the Vellum Inventory, f. 56ᵛ. Only two damaged titles remain, but the second of them adds to what is recorded in Ben. Reg. They are in the hand of List VI.

Ex dono Magistri Thome Wyche

| 1090 | 1 | Prima pars summe Henrici de Gandauo 2 fo [. . . |
| 1089 | 2 | [. . . . . .] francisci de Me[. . . |

. . . . .

p. 34. List XIIA from the Vellum Inventory, ff. 55–6, one column to a page in the same hand as List XVIII, which I have dated *c.* 1460. The newly found list is more precisely datable than List XVIII. The wording of no. 102, one of the last entries in the main hand, suggests that Robert Cowper's death on 8 June 1452 was a very recent event. A few lines lower down an added entry records a gift on 17 April 1458. One hundred and four titles in the main hand can still be read or read in part. Thirteen of them are not identifiable in List II and may be additions to the chained library. Only one, no. 83, is not identifiable in any other list. Originally the divisions between the desks were not shown at all and the only indications of divisions now legible are written inconspicuously in the margins, '4ᵗⁱ d' ', '2ᵃ pars quarti', '1 pars 5ᵗⁱ', and 'in altera parte' about opposite nos. 39, 48, 54, 95 respectively. At a guess the divisions were: (desk 1) nos. 1–8; (2) 9–26; (3) 27–38 (incomplete); (4) 39–53; (5) 54–65; (6) 66–75 (incomplete); (7) 76–82; (8, 9) 83–104. As List XIIA was probably the current desk list from the 1450s until List XIII was made it was often improved by later hands. Some of the changes are changes of order, either by re-entering a title in another place or by adding words like 'est in 4° desco': the new arrangements are what we find in List XIII.

The additions are numerous and by several hands. Many of them are the books recorded in the same order in List VI. Some additions were entered on f. 56 below the point where the main hand ends: what little remains here is hard to read and fragmentary (nos. 154–8). The rest are in the ample blank spaces on the right-hand side of each of the three pages, more or less in their desk order, no doubt. A definite position can be assigned to eighteen of these additions; 105–6 after 1; 111 after 8; 112 after 9; 117 after 20; 123 after 43; 124 after 52; 125 after 55; 128–30 after 62; 131 after 68; 135 after 71; 136 after 73; 137 after 74; 138 after 76; 139 after 78; 140 after 80.

The evidence from List XIIA shows or suggests that the

following should be equated: **64** and **999**; **65** and **1012**; **87** and **1091**; **127** and **1022**; **169** and **1060**; **573** and **1061**; **586** and **1265**.

(f. 55)
Libri in theologia in primo dextu

28	1	Biblia 2 fo ba dei
988	2	Doctor de lira in septem voluminibus 2 fo primi numero sub
31	3	2 fo secundi quia lumin(i)s (*altered to* liber et) 'deest'
989	4	2 fo tercii dati cum
32	5	2 fo quarti pronunciata
34	6	2 fo quinti non est in
991	7	2 fo sexti secundum carnem
990	8	2 fo septimi ficaciter
994	9	Gorram super Euuangelia 2 fo cristi silicet
12	10	Vna glosa super leuiticum 'al' exod" 'edmundi lacy'[1] 2 fo hebreis
26	11	Casterton super Apoc' 2 fo vero quod accidit 'ex dono Henrici sexti fundatoris nostri'
42	12	Aliam exposicionem super Apoc' 2 fo in prima eciam et est hugo de vienna (*entry cancelled and replaced by* Item aliam exposicionem super apo' 2 fo in prima etiam *in another hand*)[1]
39	13	Boneuenturam super lucam 'et Iohannem' 2 fo non aliorum laudem
*14	14	Communem glosam super iob 2 fo omni generi 'ex dono henrici sexti fundatoris nostri' 'in 4° desc"
40	15	Communem glosam 'super 12 prophetas' 2 fo annis xvi 'in 4° d'
41	16	Communem glosam super spalterium (*altered to* ysayam) 2 fo ergo prudens 'est in 4° desco'
23	17	Communem glosam super genesim 2 fo que nostra est 'ex dono Henrici vi[ti] etc"
44	18	Spalterium glosatum 2 fo tulus non apponitur 'et est in 4° desco'
49	19	Augustinum in milleloquio 2 fo de trinit[ate]
48	20	Augustinum super [2[am]] partem spalterii 2 fo si vix[it]
25	21	Augustinum [. . . . .] encherideon 'al' manualis' 2 fo vnius colendum 'ex dono fundatoris nostri Henrici vi[ti]'
50	22	Augustinum de ciuitate dei 2 fo 'in tabula' de pudore
21 (?)	23	Augustinum de octoginta tribus questionibus 2 fo domini leuite
51	24	Augustinum de verbis domini et apostoli 2 fo sim[. . . .] (*cancelled*) sermo eiusdem

[1] A third entry of this book is a cancelled addition after no. 2: Hugo de Vienna super apocalipis' 2 fo in prima eciam.

52 (?)	25	Augustinum de quantitate 2 fo textus vniuerse intellectibilis
1049	26	Augustinum de trinitate 2 fo 'in tabula' simpliciter (*cancelled*) disputacio
56	27	Epistolas Ieronimi 2 fo vincit pudor 'ex dono doctoris Gascoigne'
999	28	Moralia gregorii 2 fo in tabula nam si illatas
62	29	Moralia gregorii 2 fo in textu mescit qui
57	30	Alium librum Iero' 'contra rufinum' 2 fo impietati
58	31	Ieronimum super marcum 2 fo Iacobus alter
*59	32	Gregorium in suis [epistolis] 2 fo patimur longius
60	33	Gregorium super cantica 2 fo vocat
1002(?)	34	Flores super spalterium [. . .

. . . .

(f. 55ᵛ)

(*) 80	35	Catonem glosatum 2 fo insuper vero
465	36	Holcot super sapiens 2 fo consciencia mala 'in tabula' 'et est in 2° desco'
*35	37	Ysiderum 'super penteteucon' 2 fo videt hic ergo
*43	38	Radulphum 2 fo loquente docetur
22	39	Stephanum Cant' 2 fo hebrei enim
18	40	Anselmum 2 fo cum igitur constet
45	41	Spalterium glosatum 2 fo itaque veterem
380	42	Spalterium glosatum 2 fo ad litteram
*75	43	Omelia Eusebii 2 fo et amicus[1]
37	44	Librum de figuris biblie 2 fo et finaliter (*entry cancelled and replaced by* Item figure biblie moralizate 2 fo et finaliter *in another hand on the recto of f. 55 and marked for insertion after no. 18*).
*19	45	Isiderum de ecclesiasticis officiis 2 fo carmine
93	46	Bradwardin 2 fo sit racione similitudinis
92	47	Bradwardin 2 fo bonum
76	48	Rabanum 2 fo in textu arcium
69	49	Primam partem Waldensis 2 fo nostre patrone
70	50	Alia pars Waldensis 2 fo textus per aduentum domini
13	51	Boneuenturam super primum et 4ᵐ sentenciarum 2 fo enim est precipuus
88	52	Thomam de cristo 2 fo necessarii siue '3ᵃ pars summe'
87	53	Thomam 2ᵃ 2ᵉ (*cancelled*) 'parte secunde partis summe' 2 fo signorum vel
*86	54	Thomas super primam partem '2ᵉ partis' 2 fo matematice
11	55	Prima pars summe eiusdem 2 fo musicus accipit
91	56	Petrum de candia 2 fo causabunt aliquem
84	57	Magister sentenciarum 2 fo in tabula an possit gingnere

[1] A second entry of this book is a cancelled addition after no. 48: Item eusebium de pascha 2 fo et amicus carni.

*20	58	Eusebium 'in ecclesiastica historia' 2 fo de cruciatibus
*73	59	Bedam de gestis anglorum 2 fo quibusdam in locis
(*) 74	60	Malmesbury 2 fo solent [. . .
79	61	Petrum in aurora 2 fo nam quasi
71	62	Reuelaciones birgitte 2 fo o vere stupenda
81	63	Librum florum 2 fo quid (cancelled) 'quia' tres
*77	64	Cronica [. . .]dam militis 2 fo quasi habra'hei'
78	65	Floretum theologie 2 fo sionis culpe
90	66	Thomam de ueritatibus 2 fo greg' omnia
66	67	Distincciones holcot 2 fo sapiens non m[. . .
65	68	Parisiensem super epistolas 2 fo [. . . . .] caritas significatur
16	69	Dicta lincolniensis 2 fo liberius et melius 'est in eleccione sociorum et alius cathenatur eiusdem materie 2 fo 'in textu' cuteret nullum'
83	70	[. . . .]s de opere quadragesim[ali] 3 fo debemus plangere
	70a	. . . . 'et est in 4° disco'
		. . . . . .

(f. 56)

120	71	Textum moralis philosophie 2 fo igitur eruditus
*1013	72	Egidium de regimine principum 2 fo cum omnis
470	73	Bartholomeum de proprietatibus rerum 2 fo nes quia
*124	74	Sharpe super libros phisicorum 2 fo sine illis
*121	75	Burley super libros phisicorum 2 fo philosophus tercio
1020	76	Petrum de crescenciis 2 fo in tabula de lenticula
1021	77	Albertum super libros phisicorum 2 fo et nigram et albam
123	78	Albertum de generacione 2 fo carnem et os
169	79	Questionem super libros phisicorum 2 fo tradit scienciam
171	80	Egidium de celo et mundo 2 fo seu dimencio
1058	81	Textum philosophie naturalis 2 fo nec leuia
187	82	Textum logice 2 fo proprium ut risibile
	83	Librum astronamie 3 fo signorum in quo est
133	84	Astronomiam abraham 2 fo et si ad eundem
127	85	Librum astronamie domini iohannis 2 fo et tunc nichil fieret
379	86	Alesen in perspectiuis 2 fo libus et quod taces
139	87	Almagest' tholomei 2 fo me'diata habetur' corda
132	88	Quadripartita tholomei 2 fo et potest homo
*135	89	Tholomeum in almagest' 2 fo tatur genus
*128	90	Librum iudicum 2 fo mutacionem
134	91	Summam iudicialis 2 fo iungatur aliquibus
131	92	Librum commendacionum antiquorum 2 fo et sci[entes] artes
129	93	Librum hermetis 2 fo les ut ostenderet '[. . .] inicio primi quaterni'
130	94	Tractatum spere 2 fo in textu et duo numeri
141	95	Medicina libri alm[az]orii 2 fo receptacula

94	96	Librum Catholicon 2 fo numquam in preterito
*142	97	Tractatum 2 fo ciam et 'accensionem'
*145	98	Rosam medicine 2 fo [. .] 'illo' sanguine
143	99	Auicen' in medic' 2 fo capitulum 25
*140	100	Antitodarium Nicholai 2 fo q. s. detur
*146	101	Item alium librum medicinarum 2 fo recedit exterius 'de-est'
1262	102	Item alium librum 'lilium' medicinarum 2 fo rat nisi per vnum ex dono Magistri Co[w]per [qui] obiit [v]iii° die Iunii anno domini Mcccc[. . .¹
1263	103	Item librum amphorismorum Iohannis Damasceni 2 fo in textu aut sanguine ex dono e[. . . . .
*147	104	Item alium librum medicine ex dono eiusdem 2 fo nisi discrecio

Additions to List XIIA

553	105	Item bibliam in anglico 2 fo Cayn and to his wief (*altered in another hand to* 3iftys).
554	106	Item aliam bibliam 2 fo Iez'r'ael ex dono Magistri Thome Bloxam
560	107	Item destructorium viciorum 2 fo in tabula arrogantia (*entry probably cancelled: cf. 118*)
*555	108	Biblia magna 2 fo prime partis scientie dei
*556	109	2 fo 2ᵉ partis vir ille
*557	110	Hugo de Vienna super lucam et Iohannem 2 fo ad eam
994	111	Item liram super euuangelia 2 fo autem inuenitur
992	112	Gorram super epistolas Pauli 2 fo usque ad extremum 'ex dono Magistri Roberti Cowper'
997	113	Prosper de Vita Contemplativa 2 fo inde tacere ⎫ 'in 2°
*996	114	Hugo de sancto Victore 2 fo rum admonet ⎭ desc[o]'
558	115	Rippington super dominicalia 2 fo est colligatio impietatis
1051	116	Item Augustinum super primam partem psalterii 2 fo nobis prophetica
559	117	Item Bacounthorp super libros Augustini de ciuitate dei 2 fo time ut dicit
560	118	Item destructorium viciorum 2 fo arrogantia
561	119	Augustinus de caritate 2 fo pergebat
562	120	Augustinus de Spiritu et anima 2 fo quibus omnia
563	121	Augustinus de Correpcione et gracia 2 fo dicere qu[. . .
565	122	Lectura Lathbury super trenos 2 fo sign[. . .
67	123	Dietam salutis 2 fo in textu tamquam infideles
566	124	Thomas de aquino super 4ᵐ sentenciarum 2 fo oris curationis
567	125	Duns super 4ᵐ impressionis parisius 2 fo et spes
1056	126	Scotus alias doctor subtilis super 4ᵐ sentenciarum 2 fo vel altera

¹ Robert Cowper died on 8 June 1452 (*BRUO*).

1009	127	Hugo de Vienna super M' sentenciarum 2 fo est de se necesse
*1010	128	Iulius Solinus 2 fo vrbe roma ex dono [. . .
110	129	Horologium sapiencie 2 fo libus preditus
1055	130	Item alium librum paruum ex dono M' Wych cum diuersis contentis 2 fo Item secundum eundem
568	131	Haymo super epistolas pauli 2 fo esse humanitatis
1011	132	*See above, after no. 69*
569	133	Item librum Sermonum 2 fo In operando et est parisiensis
570	134	Item librum tabularum diuersorum operum 2 fo ascensus
*572	135	Expositorem super musicam Boicii 2 fo Vt in Epistola
573	136	Item Iohannem Canonicum 2 fo communia (?) tenet
*574	137	Item questionista super libros ethicorum 2 fo tristiciam cum includit
575	138	Item Comment' Aueroys super libros phisicorum 2 fo diffinicio vero eius
576	139	Item albertus de origine anime 2 fo tatem eo
577	140	Item Egidius '2 fo' illam rursus
578	141	Item Comentum Boecii super porphirium 2 fo res subiectas
579	142	Topica Boecii 2 fo esse volubile
1089	143	Item franciscum in conflato 2 fo quia inessencialiter (*altered to* inequaliter)
1008	144	Item fyschacre super 4° sentenciarum 2 fo quia ista
580	145	Item quodlibeta henrici 2 fo cum falso
183	146	Liber arsmetrice Boecii 2 fo que quia
581	147	Almagest' Tholomei 2 fo signorum
582	148	Duns super predicamenta ex dono Magistri Badecok 2 fo rationis
583	149	Item Cardinalis camerac' 2 fo vero numero
584	150	Ysagoge iohanicii 2 fo hii vel quia
*585	151	Versus egidii 2 fo subpallidus
586	152	Liber gerardi cremonensis 2 fo in tabula capitulum 13[2]
587	153	Tractatus aureus de conseruanda sanitate corporum 2 fo vsus
	154	Item librum alberti 2 fo [. . . .] ex dono M Iohannis Norfolke
	155	[. . . . .] cum doctor [. . . . . . .] 2 fo [. . .
	156	[. . . . .] et dat' xvii° die Aprilis anno domini mcccclviii[3]
1064	157	[. . . . . . .] de consolacione philosophie 2 fo [. . .
418	158	Item lactancius de [. . .

Items 143–145 are bracketed together: in 5° desco

Items 150–151 are bracketed together: ex dono M' [. . .[1]

p. 110. Add to List XXVIB: *4a. Johannes Canonicus, Quaestiones in Physica Aristotelis; etc.

p. 121. The list of 'Reparations and prouisions of our Colledge . . . from the yeare 1593' made in the 1620s (Warden of All Souls

---

[1] The donor was John Racour.
[2] **586** is the same book as **1265**.
[3] Cf. p. 133, the note on ***572**.

College, MS. 3) has at 1598 the entry 'Our Librarye newly vaulted with plaister of Paris and furnished with new Deskes'.

pp. 122–3. From Lists IVA, XIIA and the newly found text of List III it appears that **582** was given by Robert Badcock († by August 1479), **554** by Thomas Bloxham, **992**, **1262**, and probably **147** and **1263** by Robert Cowper, **56** by Thomas Gascoigne, **1482**, **1484**, and one chained book by John Norfolk, and **1055**, **1089**, **1090**, and, no doubt, **1008** by Thomas Wyche.

p. 128. Add to the note on **12**: List XIIA reveals that this book was a biblical 'glosa'. Probably the 'book' on the fourfold sense of scripture was a brief piece in front of it (by Edmund Lacy?).

p. 133. Add to the note on **553**: The Chapel inventory of 1553 in Vellum Inventory, f. 9, contains the entry, 'Item biblia anglice conscripta'. This may be **553**, which is absent from List XVI.

p. 160. The occurrence of **989–92** in List XIIA strengthens the probability that these are Byconyll 3–6.

p. 165. Add to the notes on List XXVIA: *4a. MS. 87. Paper. A.D. 1473 and s. xv². 'Liber Collegii animarum omnium fidelium defunctorum', s. xvi. Contemporary binding. No chainmark. Secundo folio *Ans' probatur*. Probably given early in s. xvi. p. 226 contains a list of thirty-one fellows of All Souls in the academic year 1500–1. 'Ego sum puer quem deus amat Quod Roswell' is scribbled on f. 241ᵛ: one Thomas Rowsewell or Roswell was admitted fellow of All Souls in 1504 (*BRUO*, p. 1602).

p. 171. The front cover of MS. 82 is reproduced as pl. IV by Graham Pollard, 'The Names of some English Fifteenth-century Binders', *The Library*, fifth series, xxv (1970), 193–218: 'perhaps by John More, 1465/72'.

p. 181. Lists printed in the Addenda are not taken account of in the Concordance of Running Numbers and List Numbers.

p. 209. Names for the Dragon, Floral, Fruit and Flower, and 'Rood and Hunt' binders are suggested by Mr. Pollard, loc. cit. 210–13.

PRINTED IN GREAT BRITAIN
AT THE UNIVERSITY PRESS, OXFORD
BY VIVIAN RIDLER
PRINTER TO THE UNIVERSITY